ALSO BY MARK KINGWELL

UNRULY
VOICES

UNRULY VOICES

ESSAYS ON

DEMOCRACY,

CIVILITY,

AND THE

HUMAN

IMAGINATION   MARK

KINGWELL

BIBLIOASIS

FIRST EDITION

Library and Archives Canada Cataloguing in Publication

Kingwell, Mark, 1963-
       Unruly voices : essays on democracy, civility and the human imagination / Mark Kingwell.

ISBN 978-1-926845-84-5

   1. Democracy. 2. Courtesy. 3. Imagination--Social aspects. 4. Political culture. I. Title.

JC423.K55 2012   306.2   C2012-901710-8

 Canada Council   Conseil des Arts
for the Arts   du Canada

 ONTARIO ARTS COUNCIL
CONSEIL DES ARTS DE L'ONTARIO

 Canadian   Patrimoine
Heritage   canadien

Biblioasis acknowledges the ongoing financial support of the Government of Canada through the Canada Council for the Arts, Canadian Heritage, the Canada Book Fund; and the Government of Ontario through the Ontario Arts Council.

PRINTED AND BOUND IN CANADA

 **MIX**
Paper from
responsible sources
FSC   **FSC® C107923**
www.fsc.org

Sir, more than kisses, letters mingle souls ... (Donne to Wotton, 1598)

for Molly, with much love and kisses many

CONTENTS

Introduction:
Incivility, Zombies, and Democracy's End

When we are all guilty, that will be democracy.
—Albert Camus, *The Fall*

I SPENT MY CHILDHOOD as a pint-sized political junkie, the kind of dork who collected those matched sets of gas-station coins with the prime ministers' heads on them. When, in the summer of 1974, my father was transferred from the air force base outside of Summerside, PEI, to the flight training school in Winnipeg, I lobbied hard for us to visit Ottawa on the way, to see the Parliament Buildings. My two brothers were hostile and indifferent, respectively, but I won the day. We reeled in the long ribbon of the eastern Trans-Canada and headed to the capital so that I could experience the little thrill of walking up that small incline to the front steps, of taking in the elegant lineaments of the most beautiful neo-Gothic building in the world. Inside, I imagined the soaring rhetoric and penetrating ideas, the rhetoric and reality of democracy in action. I thought great men and women did great work there, representing our interests in keen, brilliant debate.

I know, I know. But I still get a little bat-squeak echo of that first naive take whenever I walk up those steps. The last time, in the spring of 2009, was for something called "Breakfast on the Hill," a morning lecture series for academics held in the Parliamentary Dining Room, itself a nerd-linger's dream, with its separate panelled alcoves for each province. My talk was about leadership and the political virtue of civility. Among other things, I echoed the Great Liberal Leader's call for more civil exchange to make our country (and maybe even him) great.

Here's what Joanne Chianello of the *Ottawa Citizen* wrote about it later: "Ignatieff writes that 'if our politics are good, we can keep our disagreements civil.' And indeed, the theme of civil dissent ran through Kingwell's early-morning talk Thursday as well. 'Incivility,' he told the audience, 'doesn't just threaten the etiquette of interchange, it threatens democracy.' But while Kingwell was taking comments following his speech, two Liberal parliamentarians began their own conversation at their table—clearly audible to all those around, the speaker, and certainly the woman asking the question. They seemed oblivious to the irony of their incivility."

Not just audible, actually. They practically shut down one whole side of the room. "That's why we don't take our students to visit the Commons anymore," a high school teacher told me afterwards. "They're too shocked by the bad behaviour of the MPs."

Yup. That air of bozo entitlement, coupled with a routine disregard of anybody else's views or right to speak: pretty much your basic definition of incivility. If these two, washed up by chance on the silver beach of late-capitalist power and wealth, are even partly indicative of what our elected representatives are like—and they are—then we're all in a mess of trouble, though not for the reasons you may think.

Only a child could find surprise in the idea that MPs are rude. I mean, really. "Have you ever been in the House of Commons and taken a look at the inmates?" a P. G. Wodehouse character wonders of the Mother of All Parliaments, the exalted model for the one in Ottawa. "As weird a gaggle of freaks and sub-humans as was ever collected in one spot. I wouldn't mix with them for any money you could offer me." Some would say that in this context rudeness is, if not quite a job requirement, then at least an understandable occupational hazard. And there may even be a simpler explanation of the MPs' behaviour. "If people were talking over Kingwell, then that's not so uncivil," ran one online comment on Chianello's story. "They've probably heard the speech before and got bored. I've heard it, and it's frigging boring."

To which the only rational response is *fuck you*.

Just kidding. But it is difficult to make the argument for the value of civility when the immediate response to the argument is don't frigging bore me, you longwinded dork. (I added the longwinded dork part, but it feels right.) I've been defending the political virtue of civility in spaces both academic and popular, public and private, for almost fifteen years. Lots of other people were at it long before that. I don't think it's boring; but then, I don't think I'm a pompous jackass either. Pleas for civility are commonplace even as current discursive practice places a growing premium on rudeness and incivility in everything from opinion-dominated newspapers and unbridled blog posts to groomed television hatchetmen and politicians whose idea of a good riposte is escalating the insult. This is one of those instances, like the NHL playoffs and prime-time television, where things really have become worse in recent years. Underneath the road-rage politics and bratty teenage campaign rhetoric there is actually a creeping nihilism here, a disregard for the very idea of reason.

Well, who cares? You should, even if you never watch those shouting matches that pass for Sunday-morning political commentary or pay a lick of attention to the dueling reductionists of the op-ed page. Parliamentary democracy is nothing more or less than a conversation among citizens, both directly and by way of their elected leaders. Here, and only here, can our interests and desires be made into law. A good conversation is a delicate thing to sustain, as anybody knows who has attended a dinner party where there was wine. We all have a direct personal stake in seeing it thrive, because every time a good citizen checks out, the tactical forces of incivility lower democracy's value one more notch.

———

An argument, in politics or anything else, can be approached at least two different ways. If we agree with the position, we will be inclined to *identify* with the argument, tucking it away for future use. This is what fancy theorists call a hermeneutics of belief. If, by contrast, we disagree with the position, then—if we don't simply reject it outright—we tend to *investigate* the argument, looking for where it went wrong. Call this a hermeneutics of suspicion. The irony is that the latter stretches the mind far more than the former, but most people do not turn the tables and investigate their own ideas even as they identify with them. Only by doing that can we ever come to see the weaknesses, as well as the strengths, of what we already believe.

It is sometimes said that literacy is the "software of democracy." I will make various versions of that argument in the essays that follow, but for now let's be more accurate, and more demanding. The real software of democracy is not bare literacy, which permits and even enjoys all manner of rhetorical nonsense and short-sighted demagoguery. It is *political* literacy, the ability to engage in critical dialogue with ideas both agreeable and disagreeable, interests that align with ours and those that do not. We need to learn this skill, run it, and revise it constantly by repeated engagements. We must be prepared to sacrifice something we value, for the sake of larger goods. That is the only thing I, or anyone, could mean by civility.

If we do not repair our political conversation, if we do not demand that elected leaders speak rationally if they want to go on claiming the privilege of representing our interest, then we all lose. And when that happens, when insult-swapping and bogus claims have filled the conversational air to such a degree that we can no longer hear, let alone appreciate, a sane voice with a good idea, a *just* idea—when that happens, we will have no one to blame but ourselves.

The arguments I make about democracy are all offered, here, in print: pages between covers, the poor benighted book. The gesture of offering this book enacts an old paradox. Moveable type is a democratic medium because it works to dismantle the elite capture of knowledge; but books are an anti-democratic medium because they claim singular, non-dialogic authority. As Plato noticed more than two millennia ago, in the *Phaedrus*, the trouble with books is that they say the same thing over and over, won't answer questions, and can fall into the hands of people who either can't understand them or who will misunderstand them in dangerous ways.

Despite these Platonic drawbacks—which are only further entangled in paradox by being delivered via the printed version of a dialogue—moveable type has been more creative than almost anything in history besides war. Marshall McLuhan could thus make the following claim in his famous 1969 *Playboy* interview, apparently not kidding: "As an extension of man, it … was directly responsible for the rise of such disparate phenomena as nationalism, the Reformation, the assembly line and its offspring, the Industrial Revolution, the whole concept of causality, Cartesian and Newtonian concepts of the universe, perspective in art, narrative chronology in literature and a psychological mode of introspection or inner direction that greatly intensified the tendencies toward individualism and specialization."[1] What, no designated hitter rule? No molecular gastronomy?

Even assuming some viable future for Captain Codex and his minions, one can't avoid the fact that the subject of democracy is both over- and underdetermined. Overdetermined in the sense that there are every publishing season, every news cycle, more and more thousands, hundreds of thousands, of words thrown in its general direction. But underdetermined because the central one of those words used in political discourse—'democracy' itself—quickly becomes an opaque signifier. It belongs on Orwell's list of ideologically suspect locutions, noted in "Politics and the English Language" (1946): "When one watches some tired hack on the platform mechanically repeating the familiar phrases—*bestial atrocities, iron heel, bloodstained tyranny, free peoples of the world, stand shoulder to shoulder*," Orwell says, "one often has a curious feeling that one is not watching a live human being but some kind of dummy: a feeling which suddenly becomes stronger when the light catches the speaker's spectacles and turns them into blank discs which seem to have no eyes behind them."

Perhaps, even worse than this, 'democracy' has become a mere shell of itself, not so much misleading as empty, drained of all content. And if so, is it even possible to write about democracy without contributing, possibly simultaneously, to a sort of escalating linguistic pathology: piling words on top of words, the most important of them meaningless all the while. We are demented wolves howling at a reflection of the moon! Surely silence is the only sane option left.

Jennifer Egan sounded a haunting note about language, technology, and democracy in her 2010 novel, *A Visit from the Goon Squad*.[2] The novel's long final section, "Pure Language," is set in 2021. A postwar baby boom has created a biofascist regime of happy, amoral consumer-children—"pointers"—who drive their parents' actions, and money, and prefer texting to talking, even when standing face to face. Helicopters buzz over Manhattan, whose west side is now flanked by a bunker security wall that attracts strolling families looking to enjoy the sunset over Hoboken. The pointers' parents, meanwhile, are bewildered by the changes, and find their old-school moral reactions, especially anything concerning authenticity or selling out, routinely mocked. The one bit of good news, as far as one can see, is that strollers are banned from all public gatherings because they make emergency evacuations too difficult. The breeders have to carry their kids around in slings or titanium packs.

The shifts in value and language have left open pits in the quarry of language. Rebecca, wife of the aging protagonist of the section, "was an academic star. Her new book was on the phenomenon of word casings, a term she'd invented for words that no longer had meaning outside quotation marks. English was full of these empty words— 'friend' and 'real' and 'story' and 'change'—words that had been shucked of their meanings and reduced to husks. Some, like 'identity', 'search', and 'cloud', had clearly been drained of life by their Web usage. With others, the reasons were more complex; how had 'American' become an ironic term? How had 'democracy' come to be used in such an arch, mocking way?"[3]

What if the word casings are just the beginning? What if the natural consequence of the shifts in language is, like the shifts of moveable type, an alteration of human consciousness? If McLuhan is right that technological changes can create the notion of the individual—the basis, however fictional and slight, of the equality claims embedded in the very idea of democracy—then it is surely possible that further changes will distort, or even dissolve, that notion. *Technology*, after all, is not this or that tool, or even the sum total of tools; it is, rather, a world view. In particular, it is that view of the world that frames the world as disposable, as clusters of resources awaiting processing and consumption. But this includes, crucially, ourselves. Suppose the current version of our immersion in the technological world view has the ironic consequence that we hollow out our own sense of worth by way of consumption: of our preferences, our 'likes', our 'friends', our 'stories'.

Then we would have become *person casings*, to match the scree of word casings scattered about us like so many peanut shells. Our zombie-selves might continue on, perhaps indefinitely, breeding and reproducing the blind biofascist army of children, what Egan's narrator calls "the incarnation of faith in those who weren't aware of having any left."[4]

But the faith remains empty when its breeders are shells of themselves, disindividuated and eviscerated not by having desires denied, but precisely by an endless, and so finally meaningless, satisfaction of desire. If the paradox of the book was that it is at once democratic and authoritarian, the paradox of democracy is that it is at once in the service of individuals and the self-defeat of those individuals. When everybody's somebody, nobody's anybody. This used to be a rap against democratic levelling; now it just sounds like the metaphysical consequence of politics in a seven-billion-human world.

I suppose one could count this ironic endgame of modernity a democracy of sorts, taking away the scare quotes of the word casing, but only to reveal the even scarier truth. This democracy would be the pallid reversal, or maybe negation, of Camus's moral egalitarianism. Instead of the democracy of equal guilt, it would be the democracy of equal innocence: there would be no one left to feel guilt or responsibility for anything.

Isaiah Berlin offers a helpful reminder here, in his celebration of Johann Gottfried Herder, the great German romantic.[5] The key to this tension is Herder's notion of *einfühlung*, or empathy, which underwrites all political systems that aspire to the liberal condition. There is, Berlin argued, a "hermeneutic of empathy" that operates between free individuals when they attempt to coordinate their actions and live together fruitfully. That is, I must approach the other with the presumption that this is someone capable of suffering, someone vulnerable. Unless and until I do that, there can be nothing between us, and no amount of law or regulation will overcome a lack of empathy.

There is a similar argument to be found in Adam Smith's *Theory of Moral Sentiments* (1759), his first and greatest work, though Smith would use the more common eighteenth-century term *sympathy*.[6] His book opens this way: "How selfish soever man may be supposed, there are evidently some principles in his nature, which interest him in the fortunes of others, and render their happiness necessary to him, though he derives nothing from it, except the pleasure of seeing it. Of this kind is pity or compassion, the emotion we feel for the misery of others, when we either see it, or are made to conceive it in a very lively manner." Smith defined sympathy as the capacity to "derive sorrow from the sorrows of others" and suggested "[t]he greatest ruffian, the most hardened violator of the laws of society, is not altogether without it."

This last claim is surely optimistic: a capacity to feel pain at the pain of others is just that, a capacity, not a lived reality. To make fellow-feeling operative requires another, and even greater capacity of mind: imagination. "Though our brother is on the rack, as long as we ourselves are at our ease, our senses will never inform us of what he suffers. They never did, and never can, carry us beyond our own person, and it is by the imagination only that we can form any conception of what are his sensations," Smith tells us. "By the imagination, we place ourselves in his situation."

Smith, like Kant, was a product of the Enlightenment's faith in humanity, and there was no doubt in his mind, or in Herder's, where that imagination should best be cultivated. It was philosophy, and poetry, and art that would serve to expand our ethical imaginations. Also commerce in the widest sense, that is, the exchange of ideas with other people, moving among different cultures and contexts to smooth down the sharp edges of our natural self-regard. In short, what is called for is the kind of expansion of mind and soul that used to be called a liberal education, formal or otherwise.

The reasons for writing books are the same now as they ever were, and this despite everything I have so far acknowledged about the coming zombie tide of disindividuation. A book is the only vehicle we have so far devised for creating the special space of sustained engagement between one mind and another. Perhaps we are moving towards a world in which people don't want that engagement, where word casings are the only things left and texting replaces discourse, but I doubt it. And even if we are, who cares? I'm here now, so are you, and we have this moveable type to play with, to make dance in strings of letters along lines, making all kinds of sense as we go.

Maybe the deep truth is that there can be no self unless there is an other to recognize in empathy. If so, then the end of democracy we need to confront is not its cessation, the collapse of language and individualism, but its end understood as its point or purpose, its *telos*—what an Aristotelian would call its *final cause*. Empathy is not an enabling condition of democracy; no, empathy is democracy's outcome, its product, the condition towards which democracy aims. *Until* everybody's somebody, nobody's anybody.[7] And all books instruct us in this core lesson because they show, in the words of a successful novelist, "naked minds complicating themselves by extended submission to a machine of words that some other human threw together."[8] That 'extended submission' is why we write; and why we read, too.

———

How, then, to go on? Despite everyone's best efforts—the cynic would insist, *because* of them— the word 'democracy' remains among the most confused in the language. Etymology tells us it is merely rule by the people. But which people? What kind of rule? Despots and invest-ment bankers aside, everyone says they want democracy but no one can ever say exactly what it means, or whether we have it. The Arab Spring and Occupy movements of 2011, and the Quebec student tuition pro-tests of 2012, gave apparent new life to populist protest but the regimes they opposed—authoritarian, capitalist—remain largely unchanged. In most countries of the world, democracy still means the best govern-ment money can buy.

Meanwhile, the very technology that made these movements possible, in the new era of so-called social media, was generating other, less hopeful effects. Studies now show an 'empathy deficit' among heavy users of elec-tronic rather than face-to-face contact, such that their ability to identify with, and feel concern for, unknown others is diminishing. This is, in effect, a failure of moral imagination brought to us by the very devices—the tablets and pads and phones—we imagined would set us free.

It may be that every generation imagines its political challenges are uniquely difficult. I see four factors that, if not unique, make for the spe-cial set of challenges we now face in democratic politics. They are:

1. Wealth inequality. This is now at levels unprecedented in modern his-tory, the greatest gap between rich and poor since the Great Depression. The Occupy movement's "one-percent" rhetoric is easy to deride, and their lack of concrete policy easy to dismiss, but there is no arguing with the numbers. Taking the extreme but leading example of the United States, one finds that the richest fifth of the population controls 85% of the country's wealth, while the poorest fifth controls an amount so much lower than one percent that it registers statistically as zero. Despite these facts, people remain confused about the realities of wealth distribution: in surveys a majority of Americans regularly report their belief that the top quintile controls only 60%, and further reported that the fair figure would be closer to 35%—that is, fully 50 points below the actual dis-tribution, and against a background of commitment to free enterprise, individual effort, and success.

Whenever such numbers are mentioned, of course, especially in North American politics, there is an immediate hue and cry from politi-cians about "class warfare" and "the politics of envy." Here's the news: class warfare was declared two decades ago, by the rich upon the poor, with the Bush tax cuts. And yet, analysis shows that this kind of out-of-whack distribution is actually bad for the economy: not only do the very rich not produce the many jobs they claim as their instead-of-tax contribution to the economy, like the very poor they tend not to spend money, thus failing to stimulate growth. And here's another bit of news: everyone, rich and poor, claims they want a fairer distribution. "[P]eople think things should be fairer in some sense than they are [and] there's wide agreement about that," Harvard business professor Michael Norton has noted of his data on the subject. "So if we look at very rich people and very poor people, or if we look at Republicans and Democrats, all of these groups think that wealth should be more equally distributed." Americans say they want their wealth distribution to look, Norton said, like that found in "countries that are amusingly dissimilar to us, such as Sweden."[9] You can decide for yourself how amusing that is.

2. *Asymmetrical polarization.* To take the most prominent and harmful example, American politics has become measurably more divided over the past four decades, such that the most liberal Republican is much farther to the right of even the most conservative Democrat, hollowing out the very idea of middle ground. But the polarization has been skewed to the right. According to political scientist Jacob S. Hacker, author of a study of the trend, since 1975 "Senate Republicans moved roughly twice as far to the right as Senate Democrats moved to the left" even as "House Republicans moved roughly six times as far to the right as House Democrats moved to the left."[10] This alone explains the failures of the Obama Administration to effect middle-of-the-road compromises; but the effects extend well beyond the Beltway or even the United States. Political gridlock at the centre of Washington carries toxic global influence, especially in economic issues but likewise in international affairs, where the country maintains its bizarre combination of exceptionalism and unmitigated foreign interventions, especially wherever there is oil.

3. *Distrust of government.* Skepticism toward elected leaders and their policies has been an accepted virtue of democratic citizens at least since de Tocqueville. But distrust is more than skepticism: it is the presupposition that government *will not*, more than merely in a given

instance *does not*, work for the common good. Such distrust is currently at its highest levels since the era of the Watergate scandal and the Vietnam War. What is arguably worse is that the current widespread distrust is (a) generalized and virulent, not based on specific betrayals or failures; and (b) warranted, insofar as ample evidence suggests that so-called democratic governments, especially in the most advanced countries, are in effect bought by elements of the moneyed interest to protect their investments and incomes.

Consider just the United States for a moment. The U.S. tax code all by itself, with its low capital gains rates and 'carried interest' exceptions, would be enough to establish the point. But the rise of Super PACs since the Citizens United decision of the Supreme Court, wherein campaign contributions are construed as 'speech' and therefore must be unlimited, has skewed the system even more in the direction of dollars. During the 2010 mid-term elections, for example, 72% of the money spent on political ads, most of them in the currently favoured form of character assassination, would have been prohibited before the court's decision. Add the highly selective stimulus packages and tax 'reforms' of the past decade and there can be no doubt: this is government of the few, by the few, for the few.

The majority are right to distrust a system so consistently gamed against them. But government itself is not the enemy, despite the toe-curling anti-state refrain offered by every tired Washington insider campaigning as a limited-government outsider. The enemy is undemocratic moneyed interest, which pervades far more of life than government ever could. Sadly, people are subject to aspirational delusions, and so mistake their interests even as they target the wrong villains. The reason there is widespread support for lower capital gains taxes is not that most people declare capital gains and so have selfish interests to protect—they don't. The reason is that most people wish they were the sort of people who declared capital gains. Thus does legitimate skepticism decline, first, into distrust, and then into misdirected cynicism. So it goes.

4. Empathy deficit. Researchers at the University of Michigan, in a 2010 study, found that American college students are 40% less empathetic than they were in 1979, with the sharpest dip—of 48%—marked in the past decade.[11] "Generally speaking," said one author of the study, "there's a lack of empathy as narcissism increases." Commentators have noted that the two are in turn, and ironically, linked to the rise of online connectiveness. "You don't really have an emotional connection with someone on Facebook," in the words of Jean Twenge.[12] Or, to use my kind of words, the self we seek so desperately in the endless funhouse-mirror labyrinth of social media is always already an uncanny doppelgänger, a pad-poking zombie-self.

Is the empathy deficit a real finding, marking a real trend, or is it a statistical blip? Even if the trend is real, what does it mean? And how secure is the connection to attendant factors such as growing narcissism, use of social media, and increasing time spent in front of screens rather than people? There are no accepted answers to any of these questions—so far. But the implications are plenty alarming even as speculation. What does it say about the endless hunger for 'contact', even where there are flesh-and-blood friends sitting right in front of us, that there is a restaurant game wherein the first person to reach for one of the cellphones placed on the table is stuck with the entire dinner tab?[13] (I will always win this game, but only because I may be the last North American adult alive who has never owned a cellphone.)

—

Against this background of crisis and possibility, this collection of essays focuses on the question of how democracy and imagination are related. Written in the years of the global economic and political crisis that began in 2008, they explore the deep roots of democratic thinking that are too often ignored in daily flurries of punditry and media noise. The collection moves from the familiar to the uncanny, from the optimistic to the (arguably) nihilistic, seeking along the way to resuscitate what we might call the *poetics of the democratic imagination*: the leap of faith required to view the other as a person, as someone worth caring about. Beginning with the basics of democratic thought, including demands for justice and respect for the individual, the essays branch into the neglected political question of how literature affects the way we see others.

The idea of the individual, the main pillar of democratic thought for nearly four centuries, is undergoing shifts both subtle and profound.

Only by returning to the question of selfhood—how is it that we are what we are?—can any light be shed on the deepest regions of the demand for democracy. The narrative assumptions of selfhood, the structure of reflection on past actions and future possibilities, is so much taken for granted in our lived experience that we most often fail to remark both the political implications of that narrative and, more deeply, the fragility of its construction. The very idea of consequence—I mean the notional shift from a childish sequence of *and then, and then* to an adult sequence of *and thus, and thus*—is a contingent and uncanny work of political art. More so now than ever before it must be interrogated, not assumed, precisely because it is evidently (we might say literally) coming apart in our hands.[14] That is, the more we try to mirror the self in devices and desires, replacing ethical reflection with multiple reflected images of our 'likes' and 'friends', the more we consume the modern conception of the individual, in effect eating its brains.

Thus there are discussions here of Hobbes and Machiavelli, but also of Melville, Flaubert and Glenn Gould. Poets, monsters, idlers, and clowns share space with intellectuals, presidents, and philosophers. Formally, the pieces range from traditional essays and reviews to dialogues, interior monologues, and deliberately dreamy, open-ended meditations. Taken together, this collection documents a period of thought and critical engagement even as it plots the trajectory of a new democratic politics—a politics of sympathy and strangeness—that might be equal to the world that we are busy fashioning. That may sound grandiose. More modestly and probably more accurately, these articles sketch one person's attempt to negotiate the idea of personhood in relation to the political, even as that personhood is shifting and morphing more swiftly by the week—the fast zombie of democracy, circa the end of the new millennium's first decade.

Notes:

1 Quoted in Alec Scott, "Marshall's Laws," *U of T Magazine* (Autumn 2011), p. 30.

2 Jennifer Egan, "Pure Language," in *A Visit from the Goon Squad* (Anchor, 2010), pp. 323-24. Novelist Russell Smith addressed the problem of the so-called 'systems novel' in a *Globe and Mail* column (14 September 2011), citing Egan and Franzen alongside William

Gaddis, Don DeLillo, Thomas Pynchon, and David Foster Wallace, as well as science fiction authors William Gibson and Neal Stephenson. The systems novel, Smith wrote, is "a certain kind of ambitious American novel that attempts to portray how the entire society works, with particular attention to economic systems or powerful ideologies that provide a regulating framework for the characters' actions." This ambition leads to a rather obvious criticism, namely that the systems in question only concern a small, overprivileged, probably American minority of the global population. "Freedom for an Oxford don," as Isaiah Berlin admitted in "Two Concepts of Liberty" (1958), "is a very different thing from freedom for an Egyptian peasant." (How much more true when it is *Freedom* rather than freedom.) But Berlin goes on to note that there is both truth and claptrap in the standard objection. "The Egyptian peasant needs clothes or medicine before, and more than, personal liberty, but the minimum freedom that he needs today, and the greater degree of freedom that he may need tomorrow, is not some species of freedom peculiar to him, but identical with that of professors, artists and millionaires."

3   Egan, *A Visit from the Goon Squad*, pp. 323-24.

4   *Ibid.*, p. 330.

5   Berlin, *Vico and Herder: Two Studies in the History of Ideas* (Chatto & Windus, 1980).

6   They are not the same, and when I use Smith's vocabulary in public talks, people often "correct" me on the point. But the current cult of automatic empathy—*I feel your pain!*—is confused. As Smith points out, nobody feels anybody else's pain; it's not possible. The only value in preferring empathy over sympathy is that, through long usage, 'sympathy', like 'pity' and 'charity', has acquired a slightly condescending connotation.

7   Margaret Atwood makes a version of this point with reference to the biologist Frans de Waal and his book *The Age of Empathy: Nature's Lesson for a Kinder Society* (Random House, 2009). The capacity for empathy is, like consciousness, an emergent property of brain complexity; but it is not obvious which comes first, potentially reversing the usual assumption, held by everyone from Descartes, Hobbes and Hegel to most contemporary politicians and economists, that Self is prior to Other. See Atwood, "Flying Rabbits," in *In Other Worlds: SF and the Human Imagination* (Signal/M&S, 2011), p. 21. Atwood also quotes, on. p. 61, the Gibson line about the future being here already, using the 'unevenly distributed' variant.

8   Jonathan Lethem, "Radisson Confidential," *Harper's Magazine* (October 2011), pp. 20-21, on the audience he had as a young writer of science fiction; the text is drawn from various pieces included in Lethem's collection of essays, *The Ecstasy of Influence* (Doubleday, 2011). Atwood, too, begins her discussion of SF (*ibid.*) with a rather tortured, if funny, discussion of where her work might, or should, fit within the tangled genre lines of science fiction, speculative fiction, fantasy, wonder tale, and fable.

9   Quoted in Jonathan Kay, "Barack Obama is right: wealth inequality is a threat to capitalism," *National Post* (25 January 2012).

10 Quoted in Ryan Lizza, "The Obama Memos," *The New Yorker* (30 January 2012). Hacker's book is *Off Center: The Republican Revolution and the Erosion of American Democracy* (Yale, 2006); it in turn uses data gathered by political scientists Keith T. Poole and Howard Rosenthal.

11 The study was performed at Michigan's Institute for Social Research and widely reported; see, for example, Keith O'Brien, "The Empathy Deficit," *Boston Globe* (17 October 2010).

12 See Jean M. Twenge and W. Keith Campbell, *The Narcissism Epidemic: Living in the Age of Entitlement* (Free Press, 2009).

13 My favourite discussion of the game was Scott Feschuk, "I see you think I'm not very interesting," *Maclean's* (23 January 2012). He suggests that there are three categories of people of sufficient importance to justify constant checking of emails and text: "1. Brain surgeons who abruptly left in the middle of brain surgery and are checking in to see if maybe they ought to go back and finish the brain surgery. 2. Current presidents of the United States of America. (Basketball scores only.) 3. Cuba Gooding, Jr. (When so few job offers come your way, you simply can't be tardy in replying.)"

14 This would normally be the place to cite some heavy-lifting theory books on narratology and selfhood. Instead I will offer this quotation from a genius of narrative contingency: "The way old Freddie told me the story it was as limpid as dammit. And what he thinks— and what I think, too—is that it just shows what toys we are in the hands of Fate, if you know what I mean. I mean to say, it's no good worrying and trying to look ahead and plan and scheme and weigh your every action, if you follow me, because you never can tell when doing such-and-such won't make so-and-so happen—while, on the other hand, if you do so-and-so it may just as easily lead to such-and-such." (P. G. Wodehouse, *Young Men in Spats* (McClelland & Stewart, 1936), pp. 10-11.) At this point in the story, which is related in the smoking room of a London club, a pale-faced young man with a hangover excuses himself in order to seek a headache cure. Exactly!

1

All Show:
Justice and the City

W<small>E ALWAYS ENTERED</small> the *Globe* building on Front Street by the back door, through the elevated parking lot, walking up the car ramp from Wellington Street. Using the back ramp was a sign of belonging; the front doors, with their heavy festooning of Art Deco ornament, were for official visitors and other outsiders. Richard Needham, the legendary columnist who looked like a street person or proto-grunge street person with his baggy dungarees and woodsman's shirts, descended the ramp every noontime, smoking greedily, having filed his day's quota of diary entries and caustic replies to reader letters. "There goes a living legend," the city editor said to me one day, returning from lunch. Barely living, I thought. Inside the chaotic newsroom, not yet colonized by cubicles but instead a press of second-hand desks, we shared the boxy computer terminals because there weren't enough of them and took rewrite by cradling the rotary phone's heavy-spined handset on the shoulder. We would loiter outside in the parking lot, or on the ramp itself, to smoke or swap gossip. One writer told me there that he had just received a six-figure advance for a book about a retail chain, something in those days I found hard to credit, almost mythological.

The ramp was the portal to a parallel universe, or at least to the underbelly of the one I usually occupied. Each morning I walked into a city of injustice, crime, death, and optimism. I worked at the *Globe* for five years during the 1980s, alternating with terms at graduate school in Britain and the U.S., and had the raw experiences every general-assignment city desk reporter does. It was always a shock to take up the job again after months of just sitting around and reading. I saw my first dead body, a woman incinerated by a gas explosion. I walked up to male prostitutes on Church Street, fence-jumping Jamaican cricketers on the UCC grounds, gypsy fortune tellers on the streets of Yorkville, and illegal drag racers on the long deserted lanes of industrial-park Markham, and asked them to tell me their stories. I called a grumpy staff sergeant at 52 Division every night for two weeks, trying to get him to tell me something I could print. I was threatened, in person and over the phone. I got kicked out of a corrupt landlord's office in Regent Park. I did title searches in City Hall to find out who owned what. I sat in the harbourmaster's office when it still had a view of the harbour and no steakhouse on the ground floor and admired his Italian suit and bland charm.

I listened to a lot of politicians and lawyers lie. I talked to athletes, actors, cops, firefighters, burglars, junkies, and a guy who walked into the newsroom one day and claimed to have built the bridge on the River Kwai. I missed the key line at a coroner's inquest, when a young girl, describing the accident that claimed her sister's life, said "I felt myself drowning," because I was distracted by a pretty reporter from another paper. I sat in the small bedroom of a man in Mississauga with my shoes off and my notepad out. His wife, mother, and two daughters had all just died in the Air India explosion. I had knocked on his door and been admitted like an honoured guest instead of the intruder I was. His handed me photos of the women. "My whole world goes dark," he said.

City desk reporting, at least in its ideal romantic form, is a kind of *flânerie*. Unlike their investigative colleagues, city reporters aspire to the status of purposeless walker and connoisseur of the city's sights, smells, tastes, and textures. In the newspaper business this is still called newsgathering but, given the chance, it more often feels like loitering with intent. The great forebears of the city-man are Addison and Johnson, even Hemingway, not Woodward and Bernstein. This idealized city-man floats through the streets with nothing but a notepad and his curiosity, taking down dialogue, overhearing gossip, noticing details. Like the *flâneur*, he makes his aimless desire a project, that very aimlessness providing the only necessary aim. A better scene, a bigger story, lies ever around the next corner, and the next. I was twenty-two years old and I had a business card and a laminated police ID that both said I was a newspaperman. I walked around my city with a new freedom and keenness, seeing it as grittier, uglier, and tougher than before, when I was confined mostly to that misleadingly porous enclave of self-absorption we call the university.

In truth, I was on specific assignments most of the time, and we drove more often than we walked. *Flânerie's* devotion to the 'totalizing male gaze', meanwhile, to say nothing of its apparent insouciance and connoisseur's detachment from reality, was already unpopular in the politically correct 1980s. The notion of *flânerie* nevertheless retains an important truth: we are all *flâneurs*. Each one of us must negotiate the streets of our city, mean or otherwise, every day. And what is revealed by this is that the hard-bitten corners of the city are no more real than the clean and civil ones—but also no less. Toronto, like all cities, exists in more than one way at a time; it is many places at once. Its architecture and plan make this obvious over and over.

Consider the mundane gift, rare in many North American cities, of having its major university right in the middle of town, traffic and commerce flowing around and through some of its best buildings. Even at the time of city-man adventures, switching off bouts of study with days of bylines and interviews, I could not decide which site felt more natural. I was studying theories of justice for half the year, wading through the muddy shallows of a great but unjust city the other half, and one side always called back to the other, making claims of greater reality. The passing years have found me returned to what people consider a cloister, but which is better seen as an incubator of ideas. The value of the urban university is undiminished because, among many other things, it keeps asking us to define and refine what we mean by a just city.

The hucksters and tourism shills tell us that Toronto is an intellectual city, a city of ideas. Even as I write, its expansive creative class is busy racking up the social capital we're told is essential to postmodern civic success. In one sense this is hardly news. The year I arrived at the University of Toronto, 1980, Marshall McLuhan died. His influence was so pervasive that his physical existence had been rendered almost superfluous, a development he would have appreciated. Harold Innis, less well-known but arguably more brilliant, had tracked the change, already well under way, of Canada from a resource basket into a linked series of communications nodes, held together by thought. Northrop Frye was still lecturing and would last another decade. Allan Bloom was testing out his Straussian esotericism at Sidney Smith Hall. All of them had long since put Toronto on any map of ideas worth consulting, long before news-magazine polls and website ratings. None of us who studied here, living in big shared houses in Kensington or the then mostly ungentrified Annex, had any doubt about that.

That fact has not changed. But the economic and social conditions of ideas have changed, here as much as elsewhere, putting the city on the brink of a certain kind of identity, and a certain kind of success: a creative-class boomtown. My suggestion is that we are thinking about this possibility in exactly the wrong way. The question for Toronto now is not whether ideas can flourish in this place, because demonstrably they do, but what consequences in justice that flourishing will entail. On the edge of new identities and possibilities, what is our idea of justice?

Most recent discussion of "idea cities" has betrayed a strange lack of political awareness. The talk has largely revolved around first the fact and then the consequences of what Richard Florida breathlessly called "the Big Morph." In *The Rise of the Creative Class* (2002), his oddly hucksterish work of bestselling urban geography, Florida noted not just that a city's economic success could be accurately correlated with its "Bohemian Index": the number of "writers, designers, musicians, actors and directors, painters and sculptors, photographers and dancers" to be found in the urban population. He also argued that this group was increasingly indistinguishable from the business leaders and entrepreneurs that a pre-postmodern picture would have seen as the creatives' natural opponents. Instead of opposing, they were blending. "Highbrow and lowbrow, alternative and mainstream, work and play, CEO and hipster are all morphing together today," he wrote. "At the heart of the Big Morph is a new resolution of the centuries-old tension between two value systems: the Protestant work ethic and the bohemian ethic."

The point had already been illustrated at length by the journalist David Brooks in his sometimes wry work of amateur social theory (Brooks called it "comic sociology") *Bobos in Paradise* (2000). The fusion of bourgeois and bohemian—hence the unfortunate bobo, deliberately reminiscent of clowns and monkeys—resulted as a natural consequence of the information age, creating a new upper class, to quote the book's subtitle. The postmodern information economy, which McLuhan (and Innis before him) had so deftly analyzed, created, for the first time in history, a situation where ideas were as "vital to economic success as natural resources or finance capital." Bobos are the natural aristocrats of an idea-based world. If twenty-first century Toronto, perhaps Canada *tout court*, was trending away from material resources and towards non-material ones—a think nation, a concept incubator—this was all very good news indeed.

"These Bobos define our age," Brooks claimed. "They are the new establishment. Their hybrid culture is the atmosphere we all breathe. Their status codes now govern social life." The images of bobo work and play are now stock-in-trade, if not mere cliché, of cultural description: SUV-driving, NPR-listening, Adorno-quoting upper middles who live for expensive fair trade coffee and organic baby arugula, and hang a "Free Tibet" flag over the three-car garage of the house in Berkeley with a three-bridge view. (In Toronto, a lake view, proximity to Starbucks, the CBC, and access to Cumbrae Farms organic beef.) Such images—I will return to them in subsequent essays—naturally generate absurdity, especially since cultural habits are always also ethical ones. "The visitor to Fresh Fields is confronted with a big sign that says 'Organic Items today: 130'," Brooks wrote. "This is like a barometer of virtue. If you came in on a day when only 60 items were organic, you'd feel cheated. But when the number hits the three figures, you can walk through the aisles with moral confidence."

Nevertheless, Brooks was even more enthusiastic than Florida about the possibilities of the new reality. The bobos, he suggested, are an "elite based on brainpower" rather than family ties. In an especially hilarious riff, he dismantles the presuppositions of the *New York Times* wedding announcement page, then argues that intelligence has replaced pedigree as the basic sign of social distinction. "On the *Times* weddings page, you can almost feel the force of the mingling SAT scores," he says. "It's Dartmouth marries Berkeley, MBA weds Ph.D., and summa cum laude embraces summa cum laude (you rarely see a summa settling for a magna—the tension in such a marriage would be too great)." And so "[d]umb good-looking people with great parents have been displaced by smart, ambitious, educated, and anti-establishment people with scuffed shoes." The resulting smugness and apparent cultural contradictions are, he suggests, like a five-dollar latte, actually worth the price. "Today the culture war is over, at least in the realm of the affluent," the book concluded. "The centuries-old conflict has been reconciled."

Despite the upbeat, almost triumphalist tone of these claims, and the swift popularity of the Big Morph thesis, the reality was, as usual, a lot more complex and depressing. Brooks and Florida both wrote before the events of September 11th, 2001, changed the political and cultural landscape of the United States. The red and blue zones of the stolen 2004 election—comically rendered by a Swiss cartoonist as "Jesusland" and "the United States of Canada"—revealed a nation just as riven as ever, if no longer along the yuppie/hippie lines that had been reliably firm since the time when the yuppies were captains of industry and the hippies were poets and philosophers of the Concord school. There was no Big Morph, just a redrawing of lines and a shifting of cultural weight: multiple minimorphs.

Structural injustices, meanwhile, remained as devastating as ever, disparities in wealth growing even more obscene under cover of this cultural-critical sophistication. One critic called Brooks "the idiot savant of social analysis"—great at discerning the telling detail, but wholly unable to see the political meaning of anything. Brooks had it both ways, mocking the bobos even as he celebrated them, laying down pseudo-intellectual covering fire for the cheerful complacency at their heart. The happy claims for bobo meritocracy, meanwhile, are, over and over, revealed as just a new version of the old lie called the American Dream, which functions *mutatis mutandis* among the privileged on both sides of the border. Ivy League universities—surely an essential bobo gateway—still support legacy admissions, alumni giving, and private investment: all facts guaranteed to continue success by lineage rather than talent.

Even in the places where a bobo fusion is arguably real, such as turn-of-the-millennium Toronto, with its Queen Street mix of money and art, its Spoke-Club social porousness of media, finance, and the arts, the development was, as many critics pointed out, actually very bad news for the creative types. The bobo fusion, such as it was, deprived them of their natural enemies, not to mention the source of much of their self-image: that sacrificing worldly success for creative fulfillment demonstrated moral superiority. Erase that shift in value— project all value on a single scale that morphs creativity and wealth— and many formerly successful bohemians are revealed as mere losers. Perhaps less seriously, the single value scale eliminates the possibility of satire, something already noted as a casualty of a celebrity culture in which no outrage or indignity is more imaginable than the nightly reality.

The Toronto-based critic Ryan Bigge noted that the idea of the artist or writer as an entrepreneur used to be a joke, an essential piece of the healthy overall opposition between bourgeois and bohemian. In the novel *Babbitt* (1922), Sinclair Lewis uses the eponymous character, a witless champion of civic boosterism, to make the point. Speaking at the Annual Get-Together Fest of the Zenith Real Estate Board, quintessential zippy go-getter G. F. Babbitt notes one of the great prizes of America's dedication to progress. "In other countries," he says, "art and literature are left to a lot of shabby bums living in attics and feeding on booze and spaghetti, but in America the successful writer or picture-painter is indistinguishable from any other decent business man." At the time, this was funny because Babbitt's claim was so preposterous; nowadays, it is merely the sad, mundane truth.

The natural but unfortunate reaction to the collapse of a value distinction is a rearguard action. As fauxhemians move in to gentrify an area, generating Starbucks franchises and Pottery Barn outlets, driving property values up and grotty art galleries down, the 'real' bohemians, about to lose their studios, lofts, and self-image, arise in protest. Claims of authenticity are made, ever more emphatically and frantically, in an attempt to ward off the threat by force of magic. Justin Davidson, writing on the blog of *New Yorker* music critic Alex Ross, noted with some dismay the new concert hall planned for Hamburg, Germany, designed by the Swiss firm Herzog & De Meuron, which adds a complex of billowing glass sails to an existing harbourfront warehouse. This latest example of the repurposing of industrial buildings as cultural venues joins Tate Modern reconstruction in London (also by Herzog & De Meuron) to the creepy extermination-camp vibe of Toronto's own Distillery project. Davidson summed up the central point this way: "I have to admit to some queasiness about the current enthusiasm for fitting out power plants, factories and warehouses as postindustrial pleasure domes. Isn't there something inherently decadent about taking the means of production and transforming [it] into the means of consumption for the bourgeoisie?" These repurposed downtown workhorses, while clearly a good idea in an age of unbridled sprawl, rubbed the authenticity types the wrong way, stirring a vague unease.

This reaction is of course foredoomed to incoherence, a fact indicated not least by Davidson's use of that telltale nostalgic adjective 'decadent'. Decadent! In an age that celebrates decadence as its baseline assumption, this always-already-sold-out culture of ours, this is a charge without purchase, a holdover from a distant age of political belief. Consumption is what is produced by a postindustrial economy. In fact, we could go further. We no longer merely produce consumption; in an experiential economy—a post-postindustrial age—the main product is ourselves *as consumers*, under the sign of consumption. And we consume that spectral product even as we produce it, cannibalizing our identities and desires with every entertainment choice or shopping-district purchase. The process may be given a name, a label that philosopher Paul Virilio applied to the process by which a sick nation feeds off its own citizens rather than distant peoples: *endocolonization*.

The simplest reason the boho reaction cannot succeed, however, is that bohemian authenticity, like coolness more generally, is part of a spectral economy. In Thorstein Veblen's terms, which influence many of the arguments in this book, it is a *positional good*; that is, it depends for its value on the ability to differentiate one person from another. Like all positional goods, absent the relevant other person—otherwise known as social context—and the good loses value. It is no longer a good. In the case of boho authenticity, as with cool, the good itself is not even a thing, so when the context shifts you have nothing at all left except a disgruntled memory. Music that, once cool, is rendered uncool by mainstream success—the ever familiar cycle—is still music. You can still listen to it, maybe even enjoy it 'ironically', possibly phase it back into cool somewhere down the fashion line. But authenticity is nothing without the inauthentic comparator.

In short, when aesthetically inclined people *with money* choose to look and act, live and talk, just like poor artists, the poor artists cannot win because the rules of the game have changed. Indeed, the game is over; there is no game. And authenticity, together with its identity-defining properties, disappears in a puff of self-referential smoke. A respondent to Davidson, musicologist Phil Ford, noted that he used to think of the Weisman Art Museum in Minneapolis—another converted brick warehouse—as "a rec center for bobos." He counselled a sort of uneasy, or maybe defeated, acceptance of the value collapse. "The unpalatable truth of the arts world in America is that you have to learn to love bobos," Ford said. "Or at least not long to see them hanging from the lampposts of some post-revolutionary Artsylvania. Because, let's face it, if you're working in the arts, you're not too different from the clientele. Hate on the bobos and you're just hating on yourself. And middle-class self-loathing is so cliché."

———

Well, who cares? What impact, if any, does all this have on a city's life, let alone its level of justice?

For many people, none at all. This is a tempest in an artsy teapot. The rearguard actions will run their futile course, creating lots of unhappy bohemians, but the rest of the town has no stake, hence no interest, in the endgame. To them, this is indeed two kinds of privileged types having a pointless struggle over their narcissistic identities. Fair enough. But the larger Florida/Brooks idea—in fact also the more humane Jane Jacobs idea that precedes both—is that creative-class success has a trickle-down effect on a city's prosperity, not just its appeal. Mixed-use neighbourhoods and human-scale buildings create street life, lower crime rates, and encourage civility. The more art galleries, restaurants, jazz clubs, theatre companies, and great architecture a city can boast, the thicker its tax base and the livelier its economic growth. Given the background presupposition that a rising tide floats all boats, or merely that tax wealth translates into redistributed benefits, the bottom-line claim is that we're all better off living in a Big Fusion city. But are we?

This question is never easy to answer. Jacobs's own optimism about neighbourhoods, so influential around the globe, is actually predicated on a specific normative position, derived negatively as an objection to what she mocks as the "Radiant Garden City Beautiful" school of suburban growth. The inner-city alternative she proposes is just as top-down as the arrogant planners she opposed—a fact that makes her argument against 'prescriptive' urban planning *prima facie* contradictory. For Jacobites, prescriptive planning is fine as long as they get to do the prescribing: thou shalt not build tall; thou shall not make condos available to shallow wealthy people. At the same time, through no fault of her own, the neighbourhoods Jacobs celebrates as exemplary in her classic *The Death and*

Life of Great American Cities—the West Village in New York, the North End in Boston—have been annexed by 'inauthentic' moneyed types as surely as our own King Street West or, indeed, Bloor Street Annex, where Jacobs spent the last years of her life. This is probably inevitable. The very things that make these good places to live make them targeted places for the super-rich to live. The West Village, for all its charm, might as well be a gated community when it comes to housing costs. Success breeds success, and then failure.

Behind these charges lurk some bigger questions. Is a vibrant city even available to all those who live there? Who benefits from, for example, Daniel Libeskind's vaunted renovation of the Royal Ontario Museum? Who gets value from the art-world makeovers of the Drake and Gladstone hotels? In one obvious sense, merely the few thousand (or even hundred) people who regularly visit and enjoy those amenities. In a subtler assessment of urban value, though, we do all derive some benefit from these changes in our urban fabric. The museum is a monument as well as a house of artifacts, there to feast the eyes. The culture centre is a destination we need not visit in order to like the fact that it is there in case we want to. Toronto has, in the two decades since I was on the *Globe* city beat, finally become a city where, as E. B. White said of New York, one has the freedom not to attend.

In addition to these subtleties, which only partly mitigate objections to creative-class prosperity, the notion of an idea city is afflicted by a peculiar conceptual blindspot. Suppose we are an idea city. Suppose being so means everyone is, somehow, better off. We could go on chasing our own tails as a leading creative city, but where would that get us? Where, in all the so-called creativity, is our idea of the idea that matters most in an idea economy? Again I ask, where is our idea of justice?

Surprisingly, given otherwise good intentions, we don't talk about this. We talk about growth, about wealth, about real estate. We talk about sprawl, that great destroyer of common civic feeling, that antiglue. From a combination of policy and economics, five million of us are now flung, barely coherent, across nearly 6,000 square kilometres of territory. We talk about cultural diversity and its challenges, whipsawing from self-congratulation to recrimination. We talk, sometimes, about beauty, or the sore lack of it on almost every corner of this vast, disorganized place. We talk about activism now and then, our utopian ideals aired out in jaunty collections of optimistic DIY culture (and Jacobs herself, to be fair, tried to broach the subject in her later, inconclusive works—significantly phrased as quasi-platonic dialogues). We even talk about a subject in fact very close to justice, namely civility. This is, we might say, the symptomatic presentation of a deeper disease. We note how, despite a reputation for politeness, we are getting ruder and rougher by the day. How we never look at each other on the street—assuming we're on the street in the first place. How we are all wrapped up in ourselves, five million small packages shunting along and back in the vast spiderweb of highways, subway lines, streetcar routes, and sidewalks. Symptom noticed. But what then?

Toronto is not a city in the modern sense of a unified whole. I suspect it never will be, and probably need not try. Toronto is, instead, a linked series of towns held loosely together by the gravitational force of its downtown core and the pinned-in-place effect of the surveillance rod we call the CN Tower. Like Canada in general, that triumph of communications technology in defiance of all nationalist sense, Toronto is postmodern in both its geography and its psychogeography. There is a physical centre, in the sense of a summing of vectors like a centre of gravity, but there is no normative or mythic one, no single agora or narrative. This much is obvious, and often said. But we continue to fail in grasping its political significance. The modern justice idea is, to paraphrase liberal eminence John Rawls, that in a given population everyone should enjoy as much liberty as possible, consistent with the least well off being as well off as possible. You are free to exploit your talents and advantages to your benefit, as long as doing so generates no deficit, and ideally a benefit, for those less talented or advantaged. (Rawls says we would all favour this idea, if we did not know which talents or advantages we might have: the so-called 'veil of ignorance'.) Thus, for example, your increases in wealth may be taxed, and the resulting revenue channeled back to those who share the social space with you, your fellow citizens.

The crippling fiction of modern justice is not so much that of the veil of ignorance, which is a mere device of representation, a thought-experiment, as it is the background assumption of a coherent population. Nations may offer such stable populations, at least to a greater degree than cities; that is one reason why important tax bases are typically national, not civic. But cities are characterized by movement, not only internal—the essential hustle of the city's life, its coursing blood, moving at every speed from languorous *flânerie* to harried commute—but also over its thresholds. Even if we attempted a sort of rationalist solution to the problem, such as a general justice rule that all those affected by a decision must be party to it, we are still left with a fistful of prior unsolved questions. Who is part of a city's population? Who are my fellow citizens? What do I owe them—not in distribution of goods and services, but in distributions of care and, especially, power?

For a threshold city, on the brink of something that might be greatness, here is my appropriately liminal suggestion. Justice in the city means a radical openness to the other. Not just an appreciation of the other as a fellow-traveller, or, worse, a competitor for scarce goods and prizes; but a sense of the other as capable of prompting your own estrangement, a loosening of the stable ropes of selfhood. Modern distributive models of justice rightly place emphasis on the fate of the least well off; in a non-distributive idea of justice, we can update and expand this idea: a city, like a people, shall be judged by how it treats its most vulnerable, its weakest members. These may not necessarily be the poorest: consider the systematic disadvantage, in an idea economy, of truncated education, learning disability, and low access to the technologies of success. Torontonians talk about the value of otherness, celebrating cultural diversity in word, but they do not walk that walk. The smug inwardness of our *de facto* stealth neighbourhoods, the vertical gated communities of condo developments, the lifetime preoccupation with the averted gaze—all this shows a city not confident enough to engage with itself. The gravity of downtown is reduced, as so often, to the cash nexus of retail transactions, democracy soured into a form of narcissistic pathology and sense of entitlement for a few, invisibility for the many. Race and class, poverty and hatred, cannot find a point of intervention when the discursive space of the city is limited to surfaces.

The desires of the city's existing life are worthy. We all want a chance at identity, at joy even. But those desires are too often deflected, or perverted. We have spectacle without engagement, growth without hope. Busy trying to convince ourselves we are trending in the right direction, we don't stop to ask of ourselves, *what is a city for?* The oldest answer we know is also the best one: a city is an opportunity for justice, for realizing something greater than the sum of its individuals' desires. Because justice is neither a static condition nor a discursive space, but instead an ongoing experiment in living, it concerns not just the present and proximate but also the distant and future. Cities, like persons, are neither entirely material nor entirely spectral; they are reducible neither to their built forms nor their inhabitants at any given time. They are self-replicating entities, layered systems of movement and intercourse that never settle, even for a moment. It has been said that architecture exists not in space but in time. Likewise with cities more generally, what Hannah Arendt identified as the "space of appearances," which both predate and outlast you or me. In the built environment of a city, inhabited by citizens, space becomes time, and vice versa. The justice of a city can never be confined to the interests of, to quote G. K. Chesterton, the "small and arrogant oligarchy of those who merely happen to be walking about." It is always guided by the oppressions of the past as well as the interests of the future.

Justice is thus the constant pursuit of the possible, the idea of what is to come. It is not a steady state, nor a fixed outcome; still less an institutionalized plan or centrally directed program. The last point merits special emphasis, because the idea of a just city is often misunderstood as the vision of a Just City, a City on the Hill. Here, for example, is Kingsley Amis weighing in on the point with typical bullying pseudo-logic. Defending his opposition to communism and decline into conservative complacency, Amis noted that he had "seen how many of the evils of life—failure, loneliness, fear, boredom, inability to communicate—are ineradicable by political means, and that attempts so to eradicate them are disastrous." He continued: "The ideal of the brotherhood of man, the building of the Just City, is one that cannot be discarded without lifelong feelings of disappointment and loss. But if we are to live in the real world, discard it we must." The telltale false dichotomy of 'real world' and something else—the world of theory, perhaps, or Theory—gives away the fallacy in play. Failure, loneliness, boredom and the rest may well be ineradicable, simply because they are part of the human condition, but political means must be among the ways we address them. I don't say politics is the only way, and we can agree that *some* attempts at authoritarian eradication have proven dangerous. But what is equally true, in the one and only world there is, is that all those conditions are, among other things, political. We don't seek a Just City where they are absent, only a just city where we might, to take one relevant example, cope with boredom by talking about what ails us rather than by shopping.

Contrary to the standard Machiavellian objection, justice of this humane and provisional sort is not antithetical to civic glory. Though a city in pursuit of glory may neglect justice, the opposite does not hold: a truly just city is always a glorious one, because it allows greatness even as it looks to the conditions of strangeness posed by the other. It does not oppose development, including grandiose development, for the sake of some cramped sense of its own modesty; but it does demand, over and over, that all development be, at some level, in the service of everyone. Such a city starts with you, on the street, lifting your gaze and looking, for once, into the face of that person passing. This urban gaze is not male, or female; it is not casual or demeaning; it is not totalizing, it is liberating. It is the gaze that recognizes, in the other, a fellow citizen, which is to say one who has vulnerabilities, desires, and ideas just as you do.

These thoughts have been themselves a deliberate exercise in conceptual *flânerie*. Sometimes you have to walk before you can run. Sometimes, too, walking, not getting there, is the real point. We have a choice before us. We can continue to congratulate ourselves on how interesting and vibrant and creative we—some of us—are. Or we can bend some of that intellectual energy to the hard task of asking what we—all of us—could be. Justice in the city, like consciousness in the self, is an emergent property of complexity. As with the elusive object of the *flâneur*'s desire, it is always slipping around the next corner. Toronto, like any potentially great city, is always on the verge of it. That's why we keep walking, looking, glancing, noticing—and talking, to each other, about what matters to us.

2

The American Gigantic

[I]t was announced my old flame Bethany Applebaum is making a mint help-
ing the doltish progeny of the rich gain admittance to our nation's leading uni-
versities. Bravo, Bethany! Tuck those little one percenters in all safe and cozy.
Keep that ruling-class razor wire sharp and shiny!
—Sam Lipsyte, *Home Land* (2004)

AMERICAN SOCIETY'S GREATEST piece of sleight of hand, the persistent belief that it is classless, suffers periodic epistemic cataclysms.
Sometimes, as in the dislocated Third-World images of Katrina-chased
black refugees begging for water or clambering onto buses, they are
unignorable. Other times, we conspire to make them almost invisible—if more telling. Scant weeks before the hurricane devastation that
preoccupied the national airspace, an event of the sort that only makes
its way to National Public Radio or the back pages of the Focus section caught my attention. The annual meeting of the AFL-CIO, the
country's largest labour body—a conjunction of two mighty umbrella
unions gathering a dozen others—was splitting in half. Led by Service
Employees International Union honcho Andy Stern, a significant por-
tion of the body, including Teamsters, United Food and Commercial
Workers, and the coalition group Change to Win, were boycotting the
meeting and heading out on their own.

The wedge issue? The final divide? Lobbying versus organizing. Yes,
that's right. The defectors still believed in actual union drives and what
Stern did not hesitate to call "the American dream for workers"—not
just one lobby group among countless others crowding the buttonhole
concourses of the Capitol, but a force for social justice. The same people
who brought you the eight-hour day, minimum wage, and the weekend.
The moment was pregnant for its futility as well as nobility. Organized
labour in the United States now represents between 8 and 12% of the

total workforce, a sharp decline from the 35% who were unionized during big labor's heyday. With soft union-busting tactics of the Wal-Mart variety now the norm—excluding labour reps from stores, straw-polling underpaid workers with fear-soaked questions—the prospect of greater organization is dim. Offshore labour is too cheap, Chinese imports too numerous, and domestic politics too distracted by religious hooey like 'intelligent design'. The idea of a general strike, or a food riot, or a violent May Day demonstration is these days unimaginable, even laughable—an image from another story altogether.

Of course, the idea of American citizens drowning and starving to death while their government dithered about how to help them was likewise unimaginable—until it happened.

Stern's invocation of the American dream is a useful reminder of the instability that lies at the centre of the United States. A tension persists between two versions of the dream, a difference frequently elided for reasons both innocent and sly. One dream—the older one, as it happens—is about a society that takes justice seriously and offers a structure of mobility, what John Locke called "the career open to talents," combined with care or compensation for the least well off. The other dream is a vision of acquisition pure and simple, though often romanticized in terms belonging to an American television comedy of the 1950s—where the median income of depicted households was, in today's dollars, less than a third of what is seen in television's current ten most popular shows. Even idealization is subject to the laws of inflation, apparently, and dreams get priced out of their own market when material success overpowers all other values. At that point, they are naturally subject to the massive debt financing characteristic of the current domestic economy. After all, the idea that one might have to wait to realize the dream is unthinkable. The dream is, in a familiar paradox of human desire, both demanded immediately and deferred constantly.

The two dreams are in fact contradictory, but substituting the latter for the former—along the way making the enjoyment of material goods a governing virtue of American life—has, in effect, created a third, hybrid American dream: the hallucination that a country where poverty is more widespread by the year, and where the gap between rich and poor is growing with the aid of tax cuts and low-cost estate transfer, is actually both (a) wealthy and (b) just. Between 1979 and 2001, the after-tax income of the top one percent of American households rose 139%, to more than $700,000; the income of the middle fifth enjoyed just a 17% lift, to $43,700, and the income of poorest fifth struggled with a 9% rise. Despite its vast GDP, or maybe as a perverse function of it, poverty is growing in America, not declining: the Census Bureau reported last year that 12.7% of the population lived in poverty in 2004, up from 12.4% in 2003. The U.S. now ranks 24th among industrialized nations in income disparity; only Mexico and Russia rank lower.

Everybody's getting richer, after a fashion, but the super-rich are doing so way faster and way more, pulling ahead even as the majority fall behind. This can be hard to see: sleek durables, complex leisure activities and, above all, cheap credit are easy to come by, fueling the bubble of equity. This is comfort without reflection on comfort's conditions of possibility: the diminishing marginal urgency of leisure goods generates a diminishing marginal urgency of the questions leisure is supposed to allow.

The quintessential expression of the dream today can be heard in almost any sports broadcast, courtesy Ameriquest Mortgage, one of the country's largest home financing concerns, who have several camera blimps and a massive advertising budget. The company took out a service mark on this slogan: "Proud Sponsor of the American Dream." For those who, like me, had not heard the phrase "service mark" before, it is defined by Webster's as "any word, name, symbol, device, or any combination, used, or intended to be used, in commerce, to identify and distinguish the services of one provider from services provided by others, and to indicate the source of the services." Not only is the American dream brought to you by Ameriquest Mortgage, in other words, but nobody else is doing it quite like them.

The idea of an American dream is so firmly planted in the loam of national consciousness as to appear chthonic, primeval, originary—a natural property of the whole democratic experiment. But like most ideologies, the dream is a construct with human, not divine, provenance. Nobody can claim utter certainty when it comes to the proverbial, indeed mythic, language of a nation; nevertheless, most historians credit popular chronicler James Truslow Adams with coining the phrase 'American dream' in his 1931 volume of dewy optimism, *The Epic of America*. Adams was no apologist for the current arrangements. The

American vision, he wrote, is "that dream of a land in which life should be better and richer and fuller for everyone, with opportunity for each according to ability or achievement. It is a difficult dream for the European upper classes to interpret adequately, and too many of us ourselves have grown weary and mistrustful of it. It is not a dream of motor cars and high wages merely, but a dream of social order in which each man and each woman shall be able to attain to the fullest stature of which they are innately capable, and be recognized by others for what they are, regardless of the fortuitous circumstances of birth or position."

Do you hear that, dear friends and neighbours? *Not* motor cars. Not! High wages? No, not them either. For that matter, the passage does not even mention the houses, Chevrolets, and white picket fences that feature so centrally in homespun versions of the dream circa the post-war boom—the rhapsodic appreciation of the breezeway and the bungalow so deftly skewered by Don DeLillo in *Underworld*. No things of any kind. Richer life, yes, but in the sense of fuller; a dream of order and self-actualization. Indeed, by today's protracted ideological standards, where U. S. Supreme Court Chief Justice John Roberts is considered a moderate, Adams's rhetoric is nothing short of hard-left looniness, socialism in all but name. And yet, the position is here espoused not merely as viable in America but as the essence of the American project, so epic in proportion and scope. Indeed, his talk of "opportunity for each according to ability or achievement" must help explain that enduring irony of American high schoolers consistently attributing quotations from *The Communist Manifesto* to Thomas Jefferson or the Declaration of Independence. From each according to his ability!

—

But before Adams there was Alger. For popular dissemination of the dream's siren call, nothing can match the dozens of dime novels penned by Horatio Alger, Jr. The familar Alger tales of bootstrapping youngsters clearing hurdle after hurdle to go from applecart-pusher to tycoon had already burrowed deep into the American psyche—often, to be sure, against ample Golden Age evidence to the contrary. Even that great social engineer Plato could not have desired a more able propagandist of social class than someone who sustains the illusion of mobility, especially if mobility is keyed to ability. "If from the brass fathers there are born sons with unexpected gold or silver in their composition," Socrates tells his nodding companions in the *Republic*, "we shall honour such and bid them go higher, some to the office of guardian, some to the assistantship." Which sounds pretty nice, until you recall that the entire gold, silver and brass business is an example of that lie we choose to call noble, a myth intended to keep everyone in their proper place. In short, what Marx would surely have recognized as a dominant ideology.

Just to be sure this strange tale of innate caste takes hold, Socrates suggests eliminating all the adults in his hypothetical city before deploying the myth of the metals. But he should have been more confident in its genius. Every tyrant knows that a whiff of possibility is a more effective security from revolt than any amount of force. Next time, it could be me! Or my son. Meanwhile, just say no to the capital gains tax. "Mobility is the promise that lies at the heart of the American dream," the *New York Times* rightly noted in a 2005 feature package on the dream, even while reporting that economic evidence suggests upward change in social position is limited, and may even be declining.

More than half of families earning less than $30,000 a year nevertheless report that they have achieved the dream, or soon will; 45% of respondents said they were in a higher class as adults than when they were growing up. Perhaps indicating the lengths to which citizens will go to make this true, the U.S. Bureau of Economic Analysis reported that Americans' total 2005 spending outstripped earnings by $41.6-billion— the first year spending exceeded earnings since 1933. The will to believe is stronger than ever, in short, even while access to the dream gets mortgaged inside and remains limited outside. (The official goal of 70,000 refugees admitted to the United States yearly has not been met once in the years since the security crackdowns following the September 11th terrorist attacks. Canada, with a population one-tenth the size, admits 30,000 refugees every year.) Economic mobility in the United States is actually lower than in Canada or Scandinavia, and no higher than in France or Britain. And yet, nobody says much about the Norwegian dream or French equality of opportunity—maybe because nobody feels the need to.

Alger's fictions served the same purpose as Plato's myth of the metals, not via state-sponsored tyranny but out of something much harder to identify or oppose, namely, a generalized wishfulness. In a democratic society, the privileged have as large a stake as anyone in the idea that their wealth and position have been earned, not granted by mere luck or, worse, a skewed social structure. Everyone wants to sign on to the story.

But we make a mistake if we read the American dream as a narrative, even a subtle and rich one. It is, rather, a matrix of all possible stories, an incubator of individual dreams and a tangle of meanings, where sense is distorted by layering of word and image. One measure of success for any ideology is its narrative fecundity. I mean the ability to accommodate a variety of individual paths—your story and mine—within its universe of significance. The American dream is Lacan's "master signifier," the heart of the symbolic order. Here, the modern superego of Freudian orthodoxy, which works to deny our desires, is replaced by the postmodern superego which indulges obscene enjoyment of its own desires. The dream does not specify a narrative arc; its genius is to accept your own personal tale as an expression of itself. The only effective way to interpret a dream is as a kind of rebus. A sound is transformed into a picture, phonemes are rendered as graphics. Only when we translate the logic of the dream will its folded layers of significance come clear.

Here is one ironic shard of meaning. Alger himself was not able to claim America had allowed him to live the dream and end up better off than his father. A Harvard legacy—that is, son of a graduate and granted admission because of it—he squandered a comfortable job as a Unitarian minister over charges of sexual misconduct and turned to writing in desperation. His personal narrative fecundity produced the string of make-good novels from *Ragged Dick* (1867) to *From Canal Boy to President* (1881), but without limning a success story in his own terms.

—

They say George W. Bush went to Yale and I am prepared to believe it. I wonder if he ever found his steps wandering towards the Sterling Memorial Library. Not to the labyrinthine main stacks, said to be the inspiration for the mazy bibliotower of Umberto Eco's *The Name of the Rose*, but to the sleepy drawing-room of deep leather-covered armchairs and shelves of old novels named for someone called Livonia and her Brothers. Here, on long afternoons, many a slack undergraduate has whiled away the hours with slumber and popular works of a long-gone era. The shelves are chocked with the heroic class fiction of the early 1900s, *Boltwood at Yale, Andy at Yale, Stover at Yale*—all of them making it to New Haven with hard work, steely determination, and their stiff, football-tempered spines.

In cultural terms, these books, mostly published between 1910 and 1930, are the necessary second wave after Alger. For the lucky or the smart, university plots the transition from home to working life. Truly self-made men may be admirable and worthy of emulation, but they are scarce; these books, and their wide audience, understand that collegiate jockeying for position is far more to the point in American life—especially if by 'life' we mean who makes it and who doesn't. Then as now, getting in means getting on. They are as familiar in their lessons as they are unfamiliar in their slang.

Nevertheless, it is impossible, at least for a university professor, to read these books, with anything other than astonishment. Two things stand out—neither of them to do with such obvious relics as mandatory chapel, celluloid collars, or cigar-smoking in dorm rooms. First, no one appears to do any academic work, and when characters discuss curriculum at all it seems mostly work on the order of high school Latin. Second, the students—or 'men' as they prefer to call themselves—are both highly polished, sporting smart suits, silk ties and business-like attitudes presumably modeled on their fathers, and painfully, acutely ambitious. They writhe in agonies of uncertainty over 'making the Lit' or 'cracking the first eleven'. While today's Yalies probably worry about STDs and the LSAT, a century ago all thoughts ran to whether or not one had made the right moves, from freshman orientation forward, to be tapped for Skull & Bones or Scroll & Key.

The resulting social conditions are homoerotic to a degree that sails well past the routine levels to be found in any hierarchical all-male cult—football team or frat house, regiment or priesthood. Upperclassmen are the nexus of crushes and rumor, inspiration of awe. Football captains are legendary figures, newspaper editors the shapers of world opinion. "Isn't he a king?" Dink Stover marvels of a sophomore he meets on the train to New Haven in the September of his freshman year. "He made the crew last year—probably be captain; sub-tackle on the eleven. I played against him two years ago when he was at Andover.

Isn't he a king, though!" The first third of F. Scott Fitzgerald's *This Side of Paradise* gives a striking poignancy to this collegiate comrade-love. In one scene of Fitzgerald's novel, freshman Amory Blaine and his friends rush to their rooming-house window merely to have sight of a celebrated junior-class poet as he passes by on his way to dinner.

In the Boltwood and Andy books, this hero-worship is tempered by a pervasive doctrine of moral hygiene, the suggestion that admiration and emulation are the reliable route to probity and success. Even in the racier Stover volume, the moral compass is reliable. Protagonists may, like Dink Stover, lose themselves briefly in drinking binges or ill-advised outings with "swift" townie girls; they may even, for short horrific periods, doubt the legitimacy of the rigid class system they are asked to perpetuate; but invariably they return to their right minds, the innate tight-ship virtue and upright posture characteristic of the good Yale man.

Virtue and opportunity are here conflated. The College Entrance Examination Board, adopted by the Ivies in 1905, was the principal test for admission; that's why Boltwood and Tom Regan, as much as a boarding-school hero like Dink, can aspire to Yale if they scrimp and save and work hard. But scrimping and saving are just the beginning of fitting in to the college mold, and success is about more than just brains. Yale, says Regan stoutly in the Stover book, neatly articulating the conflation, is "a college where you stand on your own feet, all square to the wind."

By the time George W. Bush attended Yale, things were far different. Open admissions had led to a post-Depression influx of unsavoury but clever homunculi—which is to say, Jews—who seemed set to outnumber the foursquare Boltwood Bootstrappers. Essays and interviews supplemented the standardized tests so that 'athletic' and 'upstanding' young men could once more gain ascendancy in New Haven and Cambridge in the golden years after the Second World War. Bush is the clear wonder boy of that era, when brains were not the issue in American success stories, despite the mythology of general Ivy League brilliance— a mythology unsustainable to anyone who has ever taught at one.

As a legacy—his father George Herbert Walker was, as we well know, captain of what Dink Stover would have called "the nine"—George W. could enter Yale without barrier and earn his gentleman's Cs without censure. He benefited from an admissions system that, following an alarming rise of Jewish students in the 1920s, cracked down on such traits as shyness and unmanliness—also, just to be certain, shortness. The popular novels of the early century imagined a meritocratic and virtuous Ivy League even as they lovingly depicted an exclusive jocky WASP heaven. They were nevertheless more honest than we are today, at least on one crucial point. Despite the board exams, they did not suggest that attending Yale or Harvard was about intellect, because they knew it was about class—and football. When intellect was briefly rewarded and reality met illusion, reality was altered to fit: if open admissions meant the Yale of old was being trampled underfoot by clever Jews from Brooklyn and Hoboken, then admissions standards had to change. Or, if Jews still managed to get in by 'passing' for normal, they must eventually, like Ben in Louis Begley's *The Man Who Was Late*, transmute pursuit of the dream into alienation and, finally, suicide.

What did not change was the idea that attending these schools correlates strongly with subsequent wealth and status. One analyst of the system recently went so far as to define preference for legacies, accurately if cynically, as a luxury-brand loyal-customer reward: if you spend so much with the same carrier, you expect an airmiles payout at some point. But these and similar 'honest' justifications for selection merely beg the obvious question—in fact, two of them. Why are athletic ability and aggressive friendliness so highly valued in American society that they are virtual guarantees of a dream position, especially if sealed with the indisputable approval of an Ivy League degree? And why, if elite universities are really social-class finishing schools rather than brain factories, do they consistently maintain the reverse?

The answer to the second question is clear enough: the legend of smart Ivy Leaguers is just part of the general dream-mythology that sustains meritocratic delusion in American life. Intelligence, unlike socioeconomic origin, is thought to be a virtuous divider, a legitimate basis for discrimination and reward. Therefore, smart people should be allowed to get into Yale or Princeton and enjoy the rewards therefrom.

But it isn't smart people who get in, it's well-groomed and well-funded people. Everyone acknowledges that an Ivy League sojourn is tantamount to a seal of social approval, yet the prevailing myth makes that emblem a merit badge rather than the family crest it most often resembles. The fiction of merit is maintained by the peculiar alchemy of elite universities, which magically transform inherited social privilege: first into brains (or the assumption thereof, just as good), and then, hey presto, into 'earned' social privilege. College education is like income: there's a lot more of it out there nowadays, but the upper percentiles are still getting more, and better, than their share. At 250 of the most selective universities in the United States, the proportion of students from upper-income families has grown, not declined, over the past three decades.

Even if elite colleges really did select purely for intelligence—say, as measured by SAT scores alone—the assumption of virtuous division according to intelligence is debatable. Certainly intelligence is distributed *differently* than is social position—there are poor smart people and dumb rich ones—but it is not obvious that that distribution is *more just* than the other. We prefer intelligence as a distributor because it is "natural." But even without raising doubts about standardized tests and the sort of "intelligence" they reward, we could wonder why we naturalize this particular human trait. After all, isn't that more or less a gold, silver and brass story? The hidden issue is that there is no point in lauding meritocracy if nobody ever examines what counts as merit, and why.

Hence the answer to the first question. Social success is predicated on many factors that are both intangible and awkward. Tall politicians generally fare better than short ones. Gregarious executives are more successful than taciturn ones. Good looks are strong predictors of both social acceptance and wealth. These are natural traits, but ones we cannot, barring exceptional honesty, bring ourselves to consider as meritorious. There are honest moments. The mother of a friend of mine confesses that she has always considered handsome men better—that is, ethically more worthy—than plain ones. Not long ago I overheard a student from a selective midwestern school being asked about his college. "I hear that's a great school," his companion said. "Oh yeah," he agreed, "everyone is really good-looking."

Brains, by contrast, together with less quantified but popular traits such as hard work and dedication—maybe, nowadays, with godliness thrown back into the mix—are qualities considered reason for legitimate reward. Life is unfair, the common story goes. But instead of working to minimize the effects of unfairness, we will construct an idea about *good* forms of fairness. We will add a side story about social mobility which, if anyone were paying attention to the main story, would be quickly revealed as incoherent. Meanwhile, the rewards of one round of success will be allowed to accumulate and pool, passed from father to son, so that social mobility, like time, becomes a unidirectional vector for the rich but not for the poor—something not even Plato's guardians imagined possible, since they were supposed to examine the soul of every newborn for metal-merit.

Then, talking fast, we will praise the whole thing as a dream—a curious but telling descriptor—and sell it far and wide in the marketplace of ideas. And the kicker is that everyone will want to believe it. The alternative, after all, would be to acknowledge that the whole game is rigged.

———

"'Americanism'," said Martin Heidegger, "is something European. It is an as-yet uncomprehended form of the gigantic."[1] Current readers can be forgiven for thinking there is a typographical error: surely the European thing is anti-Americanism? But this remark was written in 1938 and, as so often, Heidegger meant something not quite what we are inclined to expect: first, that judging anything technological or 'fast' to be American is a naive European tic; also, second, that the New World inherits an aspiration that is stalled and thwarted in the Old. There is a truth lurking in the routine charge of Americanism, already a Continental pejorative in the 1930s. What kind of truth?

Something like this, I think. Though we must take care not to be hasty in understanding it, Americanism as a world-picture—as a construction of thought, not polity—is a metaphysical reaction to modernity *organized in the form of scale*. Americanism, if it means anything, signifies that largeness is all. Supersize me! Go big or go home! Notwithstanding well-meant documentaries or op-eds, this truth cannot be seen from within American self-regard any more than it can be judged from a position of Euro-disdain. The reason is that this truth conceals itself in the form of use, effect, or purpose. "The American interpretation of Americanism by means of pragmatism," Heidegger goes on, "still lies outside the metaphysical realm." The gigantic has a deeper meaning than "blind mania for exaggerating and excelling"; it is a flight into the incalculable.

Contemporary ears may think to discern here routine condemnation, perhaps more Gallic than German, of the gigantic food portions, obese bodies, hulking SUVs, and vast wastelands of box stores and monster homes now standard to the landscape of cultural criticism. Americans, making up just 5% of the world's population, consume a third of its energy. A whopping 30% of Americans over 20 are clinically obese, up from just 14% in the 1970s. The associated medical costs of obesity were $75-billion in 2003—almost as much as tobacco. Even sexual attraction, that presumed natural baseline, might be shifting with the growth of double-wide America: in 1985, 55% of U.S. adults said they found overweight people less attractive than others; in 2005 only 24% said this. Talk about the American gigantic.

We make a mistake if we reduce the gigantic to mere symptoms, however, especially if those symptoms are understood only as expressions of greed. A better statement of the American gigantic is probably the Empire State Building, that total mobilization of technology and labour which opened its doors in 1931—the same year Adams's *Epic of America* was published. The skyscraper, with its embodied desire for transcendence through height, is an American invention, a fantasy building of the New World. Such a dream may have obsessed Le Corbusier in France or the Futurists in Italy; it may be, now, a property mostly of East Asia's surrealistic skylines; but it was born on the streets of Manhattan and Chicago, the boulevards of dreams where Depression-era economics bought exceptional skill for pennies a day.

That was the dream that exercised the imagination of Adams as well as the architects of the New Deal. Working together, high to low, not only could everyone do better, they could create great things. They could *be* better—better citizens and people, richer in spirit as well as dollars. If the American dream offers a naturalization of heaven, mundane counterpart to the transcendent visions of post-mortem bliss, the Empire State is, Depression and all, its proper symbol. Not for nothing does Deborah Kerr, in *An Affair to Remember* (1957) call it—twice—the "nearest thing to heaven we have in New York." And not for nothing would I later take this phrase as the title of a book about the culture and politics of the building.[2]

Instead of sustaining that vision, the dream becomes the unofficial ideology of liberal capitalism, whatever its nationality. Initially a work-save-achieve ethos designed to oppose, and eventually replace, pre-modern hierarchies based on bloodline or social favor, it generates instead a cancerous pathology, a runaway version of itself. The result is a mixed dialectic of the material and ideal: the presumed *telos* of family, house and car deployed to underwrite all that abstract rhetoric about freedom and opportunity. So far from being a healthy codependency, this blithe base-superstructure pairing masks a corrosive truth: the American dream is perhaps the most effective means ever devised to achieve Virilio's state of endocolonization, that feeding of a nation's population upon itself. The American dream is a zombie virus, consuming resources and citizens alike in an endless round of renewed desire and positional goods, obscuring the realities of class and race, erasing evidence of difference.

Combined with the political conditions of empire, this otherwise merely depressing narrative of desire becomes a twisted form of theoretical endgame. A war about oil, fuelled by fear, fed back through country-and-western jingoism and football-game flyovers, sustained by claims about freedom and the American way of life (including single-occupant driving), all suspended in the ether of patriotism—the world has not witnessed this rough beast before.

Speaking to *New York Times* reporter Ron Suskind on the eve of the 2004 U. S. election, a Bush Administration aide explained the new postmodern condition to the liberal intellectuals of the Eastern Seaboard (and whoever else may be presumed to read the *New York Times*). Such people belong to "what we call the reality-based community," the aide explained, where people "believe that solutions emerge from your judicious study of discernible reality." This was a view of things for which he clearly felt some pity. "That's not the way the world really works anymore. We're an empire now, and when we act, we create our own reality. And while you're studying that reality—judiciously, as you will—we'll act again, creating our new realities, which you can study too, and that's how things will sort out. We're history's actors ... and you, all of you, will be left to just study what we do."

But the American empire is not only postmodern, achieving a degree of unchallenged power undreamt-of even by the most extravagant relativist; it is also *allegedly liberal.* In contrast to previous empires, which were more straightforward in their designs on domination, or found quasi-moral justifications thereof, as in the case of Britain assuming "the white man's burden," the current example clings to a habitual position of exceptionalism. (Though, in fact, it was America's burden in the Philippines of which Kipling was writing when he coined the now reviled catchphrase.) Postmodern imperialism employs a rhetoric of liberation and human dignity, and remains unwilling to offer clear admissions of aggression. Its violence is real and undeniable but rendered always inexplicit, hidden behind claims of national security or distant oppression. It will not acknowledge any moral authority outside of itself, yet appears untroubled by internal contradictions in its own moral position, the recourse to lies and false justifications for exercising power.

This is no mere lack of honesty; it is a fundamental incoherence at the core of liberal empire, and the irony is that only the persistence of the American dream makes the paradox obvious. The dream isn't merely the latent virus of endocolonization; it is also the sign of enduring contradictions in exercising distant force in the name of freedom. Every massive SUV speeding along the interstate sports a yellow or red, white and blue ribbon—cultural contradictions of late capitalism, moving at a steady 70 miles an hour. The young airborne officers and men who watch in grim silence as President Bush attempts to justify the collapsing invasion of Iraq are doubtless weighing up the finish-the-mission message with their own desires for home and comfort: the actual white picket fences and two-car garages to be seen on armed service bases from Fort Bragg to Scottsdale. Indeed, this irony is the bitter centre of an earlier gulf-war tale, the rogue heist film *Three Kings* (2000), in which Mark Wahlberg and George Clooney spend most of their renegade tour of duty discussing which sports car or big-screen television will grace the house when Iraqi gold is theirs. Why we fight!

—

American dreams have probably always been as numerous, and as various, as the people dreaming them; and they have always been suspect properties, tales of possibility that keep the engine of the market running at a brisk clip. They were aspirational fictions long before every fashion magazine and makeover show got ahold of the concept, using it as tony justification for the facilitation of that most commercially profitable of human emotions, envy. But the core ideas of self-creation, self-respect and hard work—the essential virtues of the Protestant ideal that shaped America—have been lost in a flurry of spasmodic evangelical counter-claims that render the culture of American aspiration fundamentalist rather than political. Where once religious belief offered guidance in the pursuit of social justice, now social justice is understood as a smokescreen for tolerant forces of evil that must be swept away.

While liberals were busy trying to make equal opportunity a reality, conservatives have massed their power to oppose evolutionary science, stem-cell research, abortion, gay marriage and universal health care. Both seem to miss the crucial fact that the dream used to carry a hint of utopia without the dangerous ideas of central government and social planning. Rather, big dreams could be made real by a combination of money, invention, and confidence, the sort of collective achievement embodied in the Empire State Building, the tallest building in the world from 1931 to 1970 and the product of self-made men, populist politicians, and all that cheap multi-ethnic labour. Now that New York is a controversial property in the American psyche, part Gomorrah and part embattled theme park, it is hard to imagine that conjunction of forces moving the nation in the same way now, let alone creating something so crazily beautiful as the Manhattan skyline.

The dream goes banal, in the bland, self-aggrandizing ambition of Donald Trump or Martha Stewart, far more compelling as television spectacles than as entrepreneurs, coming alive when firing people rather than hiring them; or it gets off-loaded into the Bush Administration 'base' of rock-solid Christian belief combined with tax cuts for the rich, a hybrid of apocalyptic Rapture safeguarded by plutocracy, the ones who sustain an 80% approval rating for a leader whose wider population grants him just 37%. The rest of us are left to carve out identities from the usual array of consumer options and exposure to Paris Hilton's breasts and pet dog. No wonder, perhaps, that the dream can then fester and sicken at the margins, generating new forms of anti-heroic opportunity: violent individualism, self-destructive freedom, the internal disruptions not of terrorism but of total self-belief. High school massacres. Fertilizer truck bombs. Road rage.

It used to be that one could dream of both a better job and a better world; indeed, one could reasonably hope that the two were somehow related. Now Americans dream of holding on to some minimal sense of political belief in a society guided more by opaque communion with God and free-market declensions—not to mention election theft and lies in the service of invasion—than by a shared sense of justice. The foreign adventures continue, pumping oil in one direction and young men and women in the other. Over it all stands a version of that joke sign sometimes to be found above the bars of neighbourhood taverns: *free drinks tomorrow*.

Whitman's invitation for us all to become American, to taste the freedom of self-creation, declines into final pathology. Call it the New New Deal. It applies to all of us, regardless of passport; everyone really is American. The catch is, we don't have the dream; the dream has us.

Notes:

1   Martin Heidegger, "The Age of the World Picture," in *The Question Concerning Technology and Other Essays* (William Lovitt, trans.; Harper & Row, 1977), p. 153. Subsequent quotations are taken from the same passage, which is footnore no. 12 to Heidegger's main text.

2   Mark Kingwell, *Nearest Thing to Heaven: The Empie State Building and American Dreams* (Yale University Press, 2006).

3

Masters of Chancery:
The Gift of Public Space

PUBLIC SPACE MAY BE the age's master signifier—the material real-ization of civility's optimism and hope for discursive effective-ness. A loose and elastic notion, it is variously deployed to defend (or attack) architecture, to decry (or celebrate) civic squares, to promote (or denounce) graffiti artists, skateboarders, jaywalkers, parkour aficio-nados, pie-in-the-face guerrillas, underground capture-the-flag enthu-siasts, flash-mob surveillance-busters, and other grid-resistant everyday anarchists. It is the unit of choice when it comes to understanding pol-lution, predicting political futures, thinking about citizenship, lauding creativity, and worrying about food, water, or the environment. It is either rife with corporate creep and visual pollution, or made bleak by intrusive surveillance technology, or both. It is a site of suspicion, stimulation, and transaction all at once. For some, it is the basis of public discourse itself, the hardware on which we run reason's software. Simultaneously everywhere and nowhere, it is political air.

Given the seeming inexhaustibility of the political demand to reclaim public space, what is strange is that nobody admits they have no idea what it is. Most of us assume we know, but more often than not the assumption is a matter of piety rather than argument—and confused piety at that.[1] Consider the text of a recent open letter to the mayor of Toronto from the Toronto Public Space Committee, an activist group concerned about surveillance cameras: "The proposed police cameras will be surveying public spaces throughout the city. We feel that it is reason-able to assume that law-abiding citizens should be free to walk the streets and enjoy the public spaces without being monitored by the police. The very act of monitoring reduces the freedoms we all value within our pub-lic spaces. It puts into jeopardy our rights to privacy and anonymity, on the streets of the city ... We can choose to not frequent a private business which makes use of cameras; we cannot, however, choose to avoid traversing the streets of our city. We cannot avoid being effectively followed by these cameras in our daily lives."

The concern with cameras is a real one and indeed central to the political debates about public space, especially in cities. In Britain, there is one CCTV camera for every twelve citizens, with more coming, and no clear consensus on whether these enhance safety, intrude on privacy, encourage *1984*-style snitching, or (of course) all three. But even staunch opponents of the surveillance society may think that something has gone wrong in assuming public space is somehow rescued simply by evading the camera's gaze. What, exactly? To find out, I want to raise here two rude, basic questions that nobody seems to ask: Is public space actually a public good? And if so, exactly what kind of public good is it?

—

In classical economics, a good is public when access to it is not gated by ownership, so that its benefits—those things that distinguish it as a good, something to be desired—are available to everyone; moreover, one person's use of the good does not diminish another's ability to use it. In the jargon, such goods are non-rival and non-excludable. Arguments that certain goods are public come in different forms: they may concern tangible things (grazing land, fish in the sea, the air we breathe) or intangible ones (education, cultural identity, political participation). Because they are non-rival, public goods are theoretically unlimited, even if they often become scarce as a result of use.

How is that? Well, suppose the public good is a natural resource, such as potable water, whose supply is limited even as its value to everyone is obvious. Access to such goods is supposed to be of common interest. Unfortunately, when unmanaged, even abundant public goods are frequently subject to what the economist Garrett Hardin called "the tragedy of the commons."[2] It is rational for each one of us to take advantage of a public good, but to the extent that we all do, and increase our advantage as interest dictates, the ultimate effect is the destruction of the resource. A public good (non-rival, non-excludable) becomes a commons good (rival, non-excludable). To complete the division, we can note that private goods are rival and excludable (we compete for them and you can't have what I have); while so-called club goods—clubs themselves, but also pay-to-enter entertainments and the like—are non-rival but excludable (anyone can enjoy, but at a price).

The most significant challenges here lie on the rivalry margin between commons and public goods. Hardin's held-in-common grazing-land example makes the point vivid: each one of us has an interest in feeding as many of our livestock as we can, but as more and more people do so, the common land soon reaches, and then just as quickly passes, its limits of use. Result: everybody loses for winning.

The typical responses to this threat are regulation or privatization. Neither is without cost. Privatization of some common goods—air, for example—is economically untenable as well as offensive to the common need. (Though note that privately supplied water, sold in bottles for profit, is now widely accepted: a market intrusion on water consumption that should raise a red flag in political discourse, especially in lately popular arguments that access to water is a right that merits inclusions in the Universal Declaration of Human Rights.) Regulation of resources, like all law, is difficult to enforce at the margins. It also risks what we may call the *regulatory ratchet effect*: the more law you have, the more you will need, and you cannot go back once you have begun—a problem with regulation noted as early as Plato's *Republic*. To be sure, depletion of the resource is also subject to ratchet effects: use begets more and greater use to the point of failure.

Other problems afflict non-material public or common goods. Take education, which most people like to consider (and all politicians claim to be) a public good. In theory, there is no reason why it should not be one. My enjoyment of the benefits of education should not hamper yours; after all, there is more than enough to go around. But in practice, higher education is structured in the form of institutional influence and attendant institutional access. Not everyone can get into Harvard, and Harvard enjoys a non-material prestige effect which translates reliably into other, decidedly material goods. The competition for access therefore generates a zero-sum game—my having the good of a place at Harvard means you cannot have it, lest the prestige effect be defeated by dilution. We find higher education quickly sliding into the paradoxical category of a positional public good, something that in principle is universally available but which nevertheless falls prey to rivalry and exclusion.

Arguably there is also a distinct category of public positional goods, or those sometimes called goods of excellence. The good of youth, for example, is universally distributed at birth and declines at the same rate for everyone, yet it rapidly and inevitably establishes a positional hierarchy in terms of sexual desirability or earning power. An Olympic gold medal is a good theoretically available to everyone in that it is publicly contested, openly judged, and definitively awarded; but only one person or team can ultimately enjoy it. Neither of these goods can be purchased: one does not buy an Olympic medal except as a souvenir or collector's item, while youth can only be bought in the form of a surgical fiction. Absent the taint of cheating or corruption—alas, large caveats, especially in professional sports—such goods retain both desirability and scarcity without ever being depleted. Social status is a public positional good, in the sense that it is universally competed for but scarce by definition, hard to get yet available to everyone. It is awarded only by the esteem of others, and because status is mutable as well as intangible, it is easily tangled or confused with more obvious and calculable factors such as material wealth or parentage. As with youth, one cannot compete for the latter good—the genetic lottery is a closed gate in the system, immune from regulation—while the former good usually generates a race to the bottom.

In the classical ideal theory, positional public goods and public positional goods should be contradictions in terms: anything zero-sum is not public and anything public not subject to relative gain. In reality, the various hybrids of publicness and exclusive competition are unfortunately common. And such hybrids are much harder to regulate than ordinary goods. Environmental quality or beauty in a landscape are other positional public goods: in theory, open to all and non-rival, but in practice, they are frequently gated by access and opportunity costs. The given landscape view may be obtained only from a private house, for example, just as the privilege of attaining admission to an elite university may be preferentially available to the daughter of a wealthy graduate (this is what makes her, in that telling usage, a "legacy"). Theoretical general access is almost always unevenly distributed in fact. Here we have only to think of the alleged public goods known as equality before the law and the rightful pursuit of happiness. The latter in particular tends to generate the competitive equivalent of a commons tragedy, a race to the bottom. Ever struggling to establish position against their neighbours, individuals compete so hard that everyone ends up spending more than they have. Once more working in ratchet, they progressively price themselves out of their own happiness market, but on a wide social scale.

Because happiness is not itself subject to political regulation, at least in liberal states, and because the public good of status lies beyond their ambit, governments tend to manipulate the competition instead, using regulation, taxation, or reparation to express a common interest in the distribution of public goods. In an ideal world, the income produced by regulation would manage the first kind of public goods, such as scarce land or fresh water, so that they survive commons tragedies; or it would maintain a vigourous public interest in goods that tend toward competition, such as education, to avoid unequal use or races to the bottom. Of course, whatever economists may say or prefer, we do not live in a realm of ideal theory.

Does public space meet these conditions? Framing an answer to that question is important if we are to assess the strong claims in favour of protecting such space. By the same token, the question is difficult to answer in part because space falls somewhere between the tangible and intangible. It can mean material facts such as right-of-way easements on private fields, or the sidewalks and parks of a city. These are there for everyone's use and enjoyment and, absent vandalism or overuse, they should remain available and undiminished for both you and me.

But public space can also mean something larger and looser: the right to gather and discuss, to interact with and debate one's fellow citizens. Indeed, the first definition is too narrow for most activists because, even if material facts and built forms are crucial to public space, the merely interstitial notion of public space is too limited. This larger notion of public space brings it closer to the very idea of *the public sphere*, that place where, in the minds of philosophers at least, citizens hammer out the common interests that underlie—and maybe underwrite—their private differences and desires. Here we seek to articulate, according to an ideal theory, *the* common good, not just a bundle of specific ones. Public space enables a political conversation that favours the unforced force of the better argument, the basis of just social order.

This notion of a singular public good bears both a semantic and a justificatory affinity with Rousseau's distinction between the will of all (mere aggregation of interest) and the general will (what is actually good for everyone); also with the liberal claim that what interests the public is not identical with the public interest. The trouble here is not that rational-public-sphere versions of public space are romantic fictions, though they may well be that. Ideals and romances can be powerful political levers, after all, just as reason's normative power can be effective even amidst widespread irrationality. No, the real problem is that these ideals clash at base and in principle with the presumed authority of private appetite operating in economic reason, where goods are understood as things to be used, enjoyed, or consumed.

A different sort of tragedy of the commons obtains when the order of priority runs from private to public, or from individual to social. Indeed, the lurking problem here is that the line between private and public will be blurred so decisively by the larger reign of capital that the very idea of 'public' is reduced to an empty signifier. Now instead of having a healthy threshold function which, in the ideal democratic case, insists upon public reason-giving for any decision concerning the line between public and private, there obtains a negation of the gap between public and private, between image and reality.[3] Instead of the destruction of a public resource from overuse by individuals, we observe the conceptual obliteration of publicness itself because of presuppositions of propertarian individualism. A shopping arcade or street is a public space only in the sense that there each one of us pursues his or her own version of the production of consumption.

Note two crucial ironies of this clash. First, private individuals enter into the so-called public space as floating bubbles of private space, suspicious of intrusion by strangers and jealous of their interests. This is the 'right to privacy and anonymity' cited by the Toronto Public Space Committee. It has both a specific urban version, often cited as a gift of cities as against small towns or rural locales, stranger-status as a pleasurable respite from being known or addressed: one thinks here of the glamour and excitement Simmel, for example, attaches to urban anonymity.[4] This right also has a more general political value: think of our cherished anonymity in the voting booth as against the demand to state one's name in a criminal court. But on this common model, 'public' space is not really public at all; it is merely an open marketplace of potential transactions, monetary or otherwise, between isolated individuals. Contracts are engaged, sometimes generating negative externalities—noise, crowding, traffic—which are shouldered as opportunity costs for the general activity. Or the transaction may be a silent one of letting the other be, a positive externality of namelessness and solitude amid the hustle and bustle of other strangers' various projects and movements.

Here the ongoing concern with surveillance, which is often deployed as a concern over public space, really entails an obliteration of it. "It is fashionable to complain how, today, when one's extreme personal intimacies, including details of one's sex life, can be exposed in the media, private life is threatened, disappearing even," Slavoj Žižek notes. "[T]rue, on condition that we turn things around: what is effectively disappearing in the public display of intimate details is public life itself, the public sphere proper, in which one operates as a symbolic agent who cannot be reduced to a private individual, to a bundle of intimate properties, desires, traumas, idiosyncrasies."[5] The well-documented spectacle of former French president Nicolas Sarkozy jet-setting and canoodling with his supermodel girlfriend, Carla Bruni, may be taken as a case in point. In the past, this private matter, in remaining private, would have bolstered Sarkozy's public role as a man of both passion and discretion. "[T]his time the media is not trying to pry into the private life of a public man," David Remnick commented in *The New Yorker* magazine; "this time, a public man is trying desperately to parade his private life in front of the media."

The second irony is that, as a direct result of the first, any porousness of public and private, say from technological change, generates a confusion which is invariably resolved in favour of the private. This is what has occurred in the protest letter from the Public Space Committee, which confuses public space with individual extension of private space. Social networking websites, to take another example, are sometimes praised as a form of public space; but they are invariably defended by users as, in the breach, private. Narcissistic, competitive, and isolating, these systems leach interest and energy away from the real world even as, user by user, they work social interaction free of actual spaces. Fearsome stories of coordinated harassment and suicide are deployed to keep the confusion active. The only occasion for, or response to, the issue involves a legal presumption of individual rights; only their violation prompts regulatory interest in the 'electronic commons'—and it is doomed to failure anyway, since transnational networks supporting such websites are impossible to control with traditional mechanisms. Touted as freedom, in fact these networks are no more than unsupervised orgies of self-interest and self-surveillance, vast herds of humans indulging the evolutionary aping behaviour philosopher René Girard labels "mimetic desire"—and which some of us call lemming behaviour. Even Charles Taylor, who saw that absent any other values, individual freedom invariably gives way to vanity and relativism, could not have predicted the sad aimless anti-democratic reality of the interwebs, where friendship is a commodity.

Thus the strange case of unpublic public space. Even when nobody in particular owns a given area of a city, concrete or virtual, it hardly matters. That space is, conceptually speaking, owned by the dominant rules of the game, which are hinged to the norm of private interest—notwithstanding that they may destroy privacy at the very same time. As Kristine Miller notes in her analysis of selected 'public' spaces in New York, among them Federal Plaza and Times Square: "The story of each location reveals that public space is not a concrete or fixed reality, but rather a constantly changing situation open to the forces of law, corporations, bureaucracy, and government. The qualities of public spaces we consider essential, including accessibility, public ownership, and ties to democratic life, are, at best, temporary conditions and often completely absent."[6] Of course they are! Conceiving ourselves as individuals, the great legacy of modern political thought, reveals itself as a kind of booby prize, because the presumption of clashing private interests everywhere suffuses the spaces, all spaces, of life. Typical arguments for safeguarding public space, inevitably phrased against this background and so in its terms, are always already lost.

For illustration of this point, consider one haunting narrative of that dominance, from a century and a half ago.

Herman Melville's "Bartleby the Scrivener"—significantly subtitled "A Story of Wall-Street"—has for generations offered readers the unsettling spectacle of a man who appears to refuse to live. Bartleby, the mysterious copyist who appears one day in the "snug" chambers of a smug, well-to-do Manhattan lawyer, at first takes hungrily to the dispiriting job of hand-copying legal documents: "As if long famishing for something to copy, he seemed to gorge himself on my documents. There was not pause for digestion." Bartleby's craving is all for work, and he takes to the task of copying with an aura of perfect mechanical efficiency, a *pre-facto* Xerox machine in—albeit somewhat cadaverous—human form.[7] "I should have been quite delighted with his application, had he been cheerfully industrious," the lawyer admits. "But he wrote on silently, palely, mechanically."

The lawyer who narrates the tale "of that strange class of men," the copyists, writes as one recalling a surreal turn of events. He does not lack for self-knowledge, noting how he liked to follow the dictum that "the easiest way of life is the best" and repeating his association with John Jacob Astor, whose name "hath a rounded and orbicular sound to it, and rings unto bullion." The plaster bust of Cicero on his desk is an ironic tribute to eloquence from a man whose entire legal practice is without litigation or courtroom appearance. The narrator is a Master of Chancery, an office that provides him a comfortable and untroubled livelihood. Readers will not need to be reminded that chancery is the court of law concerned with wills and estates. The lawyer is a man who makes his living at the transactional margin between life and death— especially in dispute. (Dickens's tragic and interminable *Jarndyce v. Jarndyce* in *Bleak House* is a chancery case.)

Bartleby, that paragon of biddable labour, soon reveals new depths. First he refuses to check over his work. Then to fetch a document for the lawyer. Then to join an office conference with the other copyists, Nippers and Turkey—the latter a man of uneven temperament and the former a man who "knew not what he wanted," forever adjusting his work table in search of optimum height. Then to speak, move, or eat. By the story's midpoint, Bartleby, once a fearsome and seemingly unstoppable engine of mechanical reproduction, has by stages attained a condition of near stasis. In the world of movement that mid-nineteenth-century Wall Street represents, the shifting transactions and circulating paper of the legal and financial capital, he is motionless and unresponsive. His is not the rejection of work-time imperatives enacted by the aimless wandering of the *flâneur*, that hero of nineteenth-century culture and twentieth-century theory, celebrated especially in Benjamin's sprawling *Arcades Project* (and in the earlier essay of this volume, "All Show: Justice and the City"). Bartleby does not amble or loaf, tasting experiences and indulging the stimulating, various leisure options of the urban environment, walking slowly nowhere in particular as a kinetic critique of the rushing, straight-line trajectories of the working world. He does not walk at all; he does not even venture outside if he can help it. The street is not his friend or his scene. In his speeding up to a standstill, he is already a much more disturbing and baffling figure than the *flâneur*, whose strolling leisure can all too easily be assimilated and commodified in the form of the mall-bound shopper.[8] In his refusal of all motion, Bartleby is, instead, a new figure altogether, a singular instance of the *anti-flâneur*. He rejects the demands of the world of work, Wall Street's logic, but not in favour of the world of leisure; both realms are, for him, impossible.

And yet, *refuse* and *reject* are not quite right here, because Bartleby's notorious expression of non-cooperation, the phrase that irks the narrator even as his other underlings begin subconsciously to echo it, is "I would prefer not to." This is not refusal, then, in the sense of active objection, but neither is it the expression of an active desire, the way we might speak of a voting preference or preference among offered goods. Bartleby's progression is one of staged nullification, as he moves from not-working to not-answering to not-moving to, finally, not-living. He dies in prison, removed there from the lawyer's former offices when, in a panic of frustration, the lawyer has uprooted his practice rather than continue to confront immovable Bartleby and his "dead-wall reveries," so different from daydreaming or wool-gathering. Cajoling him with promises of comfort and food even in prison, the lawyer receives the story's most affecting line: "I know where I am," Bartleby says to him, and turns his face to the final wall.

Bartleby's is a story of walled streets, and walls, as well as of Wall Street, the "cistern" of the lawyer's office and the blank wall of emergent skyscraper blotting the sky from Bartleby's window view. But it is also the story of a wall of peculiar resistance to the logic of capitalist presupposition, expressed in the norms of work and pleasure, office and home. Lest that claim sound too flat-footed, we note that it is likewise a story of a peculiar tension that is lodged in the heart of the modern liberal project, and its presumptions concerning identity, privacy, and publicity. Bartleby insists on himself as an exception (again, if 'insist' is even the right word to use), with such claims of exception understood as being the prerogative of all under the conditions of individual right. And yet, his exceptionality is too extreme to be accommodated by those conditions, highlighting instead the actually exception-hostile liberal state, the state of individualist conformity. Difference is what makes us individuals, it is what we all have—but not too much![9]

Elizabeth Hardwick, in her perceptive essay on Melville's story, "Bartleby in Manhattan" (1981), notes that the existential generality of the story is in tension with the specificity of its historical setting, which is less the gloried Manna-Hatta of Whitman's ecstatic songs than it is the violent near-slums of Five Points, main site of *Gangs of New York*. ("Bartleby the Scrivener" was published in 1853, ten years before the New York Draft Riots that feature in the climax of Martin Scorsese's 2002 film.) From this perspective, Bartleby's not leaving the office at the end of the work day highlights, if only negatively, that which he prefers not to do. "[I]t is very easy to imagine from history where the clerks, Nippers and Turkey, are of an evening," she writes. "They are living in boarding houses, where half of New York's population lived as late as 1841: newlyweds, families, single persons. Whitman did a lot of 'boarding around,' as he called it, and observed, without rebuke, or mostly without rebuke, that the boarding house led the unfamilied men to rush out after dinner to the saloon or the brothel, away from the unprivate private, to the streets which are the spirit of the city, which are the lively blackmail that makes city citizens abide."[10]

Lively blackmail and the *unprivate private* are the two poles of the commercialized social order. Inside, space is private in name but subject to crowding, density, stacking, and endless subdivision. Outside, rescue from the 'third place'—not home or office—is at best double-edged. "Bartleby is not a true creature of Manhattan," Hardwick goes on, "because he shuns the streets and is unmoved by the moral, religious, acute, obsessive, beautiful ideal of Consumption. Consumption is what one leaves one's 'divided space' to honour." This phrase *divided space* is central for Hardwick. It means the way space is divided between public and private, to be sure, but also how private space itself is always divided, between apartments or houses, the thin, contested thresholds of private property and privacy. It recurs in two subsequent Hardwick essays, those on Edith Wharton and Henry James, whose New York characters typically had less first-hand experience of it.[11] (Though spare a thought for poor Lily Bart in Wharton's *The House of Mirth*, reduced to labour by conflicted nature, sitting chilled in Bryant Park and dying alone in a sad rooming-house chamber, whether from suicide or accidental overdose we will never know.) Bartleby will not play the game of capital by the rules of general economy—which rules demand, first, the production of consumption and then, as a consequence, the production of excess, paroxysms of luxury.[12] Bartleby's course is itself excessive, however, a luxury of not-doing. He prefers not to work. He prefers not to eat. He prefers not to leave work for the sake of either an unprivate private or an unpublic public. And though his preference ultimately means death, he lives on as a challenge to the accepted order of things— what Althusser calls 'the problematic', that realm where problems and solutions alike are delineated under the rubric of the possible.[13]

This is not an overtly political act—there is no call to arms—but it is one with political significance. Just note how the otherwise comfortable lawyer cannot shake off his sense of responsibility and confusion in the encounter, which begins to resemble a capitalist reprise of Hegel's master/slave dialectic. The lawyer is beholden because Bartleby is infinitely withdrawing from care and sense, without actively resisting anything and certainly without being infinitely demanding. His is not a utopian gesture, rather it is a gesture of refusal to engage. His "resistance to amelioration," to use Hardwick's phrase, together with his refusal to enter the accepted lists of consumption—in all senses—make of Bartleby the endgame example of critique. With this "gesture of subtraction at its purest" (Žižek), where "body and statement are one" (Hardwick), Bartleby challenges the very idea of making sense according to the terms of sense that are presumptively accepted. "This is how we pass," Žižek argues, "from the politics of 'resistance' or 'protestation', which parasitizes upon what it negates, to a politics which opens up a new space outside the hegemonic position *and* its negation." In other words, his withdrawal is not an *objection*, which might be taken over and nullified by power's dominant play. As Jean Baudrillard has crisply put it, critique is "complicit with what it denounces" because "critique always precedes what it criticizes." Bartleby's gesture is not critique; it is, rather, a refusal to play the game at all as it is currently ruled—thus creating the possibility of a new game altogether, albeit one with a grim end under present conditions.[14]

"At present I would prefer not to be a little reasonable," Bartleby tells the lawyer in response to one especially desperate charitable offer. With this, he gently rejects—note that oddly formal mitigation of *at present*—the basic tenet of all private-to-private exchange, the very foundations of a liberal public sphere and public goods: the norm of reasonableness and civility. In this rejection he articulates what the homeless denizens of our contemporary urban public spaces can only embody, a helpless exemption to the rules of the social game. Bartleby's own kind of homelessness, his peculiar lack of accommodation, differs in both tenor and location. He lies—rather, stands—somewhere between the poor unaccommodated man of Lear wandering the heath and the shabby tramp who has no place to sleep because a city bylaw has decreed that all public benches must be designed to roll you off them or with barriers that allow sitting but not lying. Bartleby is not only the *anti-flâneur*; he is also the ultimate loiterer. In this he calls attention, among other things, to the real opportunity costs associated with taking up even the bare roles of social personhood, that smooth negotiation of private and public.[15] Like both the homeless and the uncrowned Lear, Bartleby loiters because he has nowhere else to go. Once situated, he prefers not to submit to the ironies of public space structured by consumption. He prefers not to move on. He prefers not to be reasonable. His preferences, so far from being moves or claims in a larger game of justification and negotiation, stand as insults, undigested remainders. Result: confinement, starvation, death.

Bartleby is not Kafka's hunger artist, not quite comprehending his own refusals and withdrawals, seeking an approval and acclaim that has deserted him; Bartleby knows, to the end, where he is—and how he got there. With this knowledge, his action becomes a figure of purity, a violent gesture free of determinant content. His "perfect act of writing" becomes a "pure act" of ever potentially not-writing. Giorgio Agamben, drawing inspiration from Walter Benjamin's critique of determinate violence, notes with approval the suspended potentiality of this preference not to. In the Arab tradition, Agamben writes, Aristotle's notion of agent intellect—thought without determination—"has the form of an angel whose name is *Qalam*, Pen, and its place is an unfathomable potentiality. Bartleby, a scribe who does not simply cease writing but 'prefers not to', is the extreme image of this angel that writes nothing but its potentiality to not-write."[16]

But note for the record that this mystical-anarchist Bartleby is distinct from the ruthless-authoritarian Bartleby posited by Žižek, as indeed both are distinct from Hardwick's exhausted-anti-consumer Bartleby. The commonality in all three decodings of the preference gesture is, however, obvious. Bartleby's mildly expressed preference is experienced *as violence*.[17] Whatever meaning the refusal has—or none—it remains a disruptive and dissociative fact, an indigestible ethical and political remainder marking the contested threshold between potential and act, self and other, private and public, insanity and reason.

———

I will not attempt to adjudicate the multiple-Bartleby dispute here. Regardless of the specific interpretive frame used to parse his gesture, we can say this for certain: Bartleby enacts a refusal to act, and in this manner he exceeds all standard grids of sense-making. Without bias, we may then say that the truest account of Bartleby is that he is an *epokhé*, or bracketing of meaning, such as might be found in the phenomenological tradition, the setting aside of a framing natural attitude in order to examine it as what it is. 'Account' is then immediately wrong, however, since he (and his story) will not submit to the calculating narrative desire of the master of chancery, that keeper of accounts. And though his act (or non-act!) is thus outside of meaning, it is never without meaning since it queries meaning's own conditions of possibility. Exceeding the logic of contract and exchange, it is a gift—albeit a very peculiar one—whose value cannot be calculated and whose debt can never be repaid. Bartleby's condition is, finally, an ethical one insofar as it reveals at the end its epistemological basis: he knows where he is. Can we say the same?

In addition to the realm of wills and estates, chancery law was historically concerned with matters of bankruptcy and confession. Let us confess, as Melville does in his story, the bankruptcy of our current notions of public space. We are all masters of chancery in the sense that we profit to varying degrees from the current arrangement, but in the end, like Melville's lawyer, the inequalities and contradictions of that arrangement will not be resolved by more pious gestures in the direction of revitalized or reclaimed public space. What is needed is a more radical reorientation—and inheritance. The estate we inherit is nothing less than democracy itself, for democracy is a—perhaps *the*—chancery case.[18]

On the unfortunate prevailing view, public space is at worst a positional good, where enjoyment is a competition, and at best a quasi-private good, available for everyone's selfish use. Nowhere does it manage to evade or transcend the presuppositions of the property model. In the collective unconscious public space is leftover space, the margins that remain between private holdings and commercial premises, the laneways and parks in which we negotiate not our collective meanings but our outstanding transactional interests, the ones not covered by production and consumption. Even nominally public institutions, such as the large cultural temples of museum or art gallery—artifact-holding artifacts of a democratization of aesthetic experience—do not outpace this unconscious diminution of meaning. They are beholden to private donors, their architecture decided by opaque competition, their curation a matter of esoteric intimidation.

None of which is to say that there is not much enjoyment to be had in these spaces, even as there surely was in the saloons and brothels of Melville's New York. But arguments that remain engaged with the enjoyment question leave the larger presuppositions unquestioned. The suspicion of surveillance, though similarly mired, contains a kernel of awareness. The non-private streets and parks are still under the eye of the state, which monitors the presence of individuals via its monopoly on 'legitimate' use of force. Each one of us is made forcibly aware of the traces we leave whenever we traverse these spaces, the swirl of bodily fluids and DNA as well as sheer visibility that is the stock-in-trade of forensic evidence. It is not a coincidence that cultural glamour currently attaches to the details of the forensic mechanism, technologies of visual spectacle celebrating the technologies of criminal localization as in the inescapable *C.S.I.* franchise. David Caruso snatches off his sunglasses, falls backwards out of the frame intoning, just before the repurposed Who song clangs in, "And that, my friend, is ... murder." The lesson carried by this televised mythologeme is that you are always present in the trace of potential guilt, the collar you cannot remove. In English sporting slang, a boxer or wrestler is *in chancery* when he is pummeled repeatedly while his head is locked in the opponent's crooked arm.

Such pre-controlled public spaces are precisely what Althusser predicted as the final victory of ideology under conditions of individual interest, since not even the countermove of looking back with personal recording technology—what the cyborg innovator Steve Mann has dubbed *sousveillance*—changes the background order of things.[19] Both being seen and seeing oneself are forms of being called to account: the "Hey, you there!" summons of the state that Althusser labelled *interpellation*, carried within each one of us as the expectation of singularity. Insistence on individual position and individual right—individual sight, individual claim—masks the fact that, in public and private alike, we are always already in the grip of the state. Even if we try to turn cameras back to bear on the state's functionaries—no bad tactic for specific battles of charge and counter-charge—it is the state which controls the exception as well as the force of executing that exception.[20]

The deeper reason for this tangling is that contemporary western societies remain an uneasy hybrid of associational and authoritarian social forms; and their citizens more socially conditioned than (as they imagine) autonomous. Democracy is a confusion of claims for individual liberty made among state-controlled structures of order and security which may, at any moment, revert to violence. Calling for more *sousveillance*, though apparently liberating, is a move that merely returns us to the incoherent objections of the Toronto Public Space Committee.

The salvation of this state is, theoretically, that *we the people* are the sovereign power, and that its mechanisms are thus always subject to our public decision and consent. And yet, the structural irony remains. The mechanisms for exerting this mechanism-control are themselves subject both to the state's regulation and the de facto trivialization and commercialization characteristic of the private-public order. Consider the vast 'war chest' needed to contest an election, or the distorting feedback effects of exit polling and media saturation. The rational public sphere remains a chimera, albeit an essential one for the politico-cultural surround to gesture towards, as long as the actual public spaces of our polity are merely public goods in the use-value sense, and the public interest reducible at any instant to the sum of what interests the public.

—

There is one further resonance to be recalled about the chancery court, the unspoken centre of Bartleby's demise. In English common law, chancery court accepted claims made in excess of the strict text of the law. That is, equity or fairness arguments could be levelled there, against black-letter application of statute—a nuance that saves common law from the tyranny of bureaucratic heartlessness. Chancery recognizes that justice is not achieved simply by mechanism, however efficient.

As with the court, so with a just society. There can be no useful recourse to public space unless and until we reverse the polarity of our conception of publicness itself. It is sometimes said that the threshold between public and private must be a public decision. True, but go farther: the public is not a summing of private preferences or interests, nor even a wide non-rival availability of resources to those preferences or interests. It is, instead, their precondition: for meaning, for work, for identity itself. We imagine that we enter public space with our identities intact, jealous of interest and suspicious of challenge, looking for stimulus and response. But in fact the reverse is true. We cannot enter the public because we have never left the public; it pervades everything, and our identities are never fixed or prefigured because they are themselves achievements of the public dimension in human life.

This is unsettling, and sometimes unwelcome. The right to anonymity is a fragile negotiation, and sometimes we will be seen and recognized for who we are. Sometimes we may experience the even less welcome instability of finding ourselves the spectators, the lookers, the judgers. James Stewart's character L. B. 'Jeff' Jeffries, in Alfred Hitchcock's *Rear Window* (1954), does not think he is a voyeur, only a photographer bored with his injury-forced immobility and loneliness. But his eye draws him into the various worlds of his Manhattan courtyard neighbourhood: romance, despair, salvation, ambition, success, and of course, murder. In an agony of indecision about what he is seeing and what to do about it, he wonders whether he has any right to look. His equally unnerved socialite girlfriend, Lisa Fremont (Grace Kelly), cannot engage the issue. "I'm not much on rear window ethics," she says. But it is the rear window, Hitchcock suggests, that is really the one before us, even if we pretend not to look. The point, which suffuses the film, is raised explicitly in an earlier exchange, this time semi-mocking. Stella, the massage therapist helping Jeff with his recovery, offers a comment:

> *Stella:* "We've become a race of Peeping Toms. What people ought to do is get outside their own house and look in for a change. Yes, sir. How's that for a bit of homespun philosophy?"
> *Jeff:* "*Readers Digest*, April 1939."
> *Stella:* "Well, I only quote from the best."

Which seems to dismiss the point as a matter of pop-sociology guff. And yet it is Jeff's police detective friend, Lieutenant Doyle—the state embodied in the form of a person—who makes the decisive judgment (even if he is wrong about the murder Jeff believes he's seen). "People do a lot of things in private they couldn't possibly explain in public," Doyle says. Indeed they do; and sometimes they have to try and explain even if they don't want to, and can't. Urban life is public life, the courtyard is the city, and proximity inevitably creates the complicated shared gazes of the unprivate private—which is to say, the always already public.[21]

We cannot escape these facts, and we can only control them to some small degree—a degree small enough that we ought to pause and wonder why control is even the issue, why we imagine that our selfhood is so stable or so inviolate. In fact it is neither, and the city forever reminds us of this. The city evolved even as we did, and it now pushes us relentlessly toward new self-conceptions, developing notions of personhood beyond the horizon of stability—which was never stable in any event. Reconsidered under terms such as these, public space is never interstitial, marginal, or left over. It is contested, always and everywhere, because identity is ever a matter of finding out who we are in the crucible of perspective-reciprocity. Public space is not a public good so much as an existential one—one without which democratic politics is impossible, since without a viable *res publica* there is no *demos*, and vice versa. Upon this conceptual reversal, or what we should rather call the constantly renewed twinning of self and other, of public and private, of gift and thanks, the feared call of the state transforms into the unsettling but necessary call of the stranger, my fellow citizen, without whom I am nothing.

Hey, you there.

Notes:

1 I plead guilty: my defence of public space in *The World We Want: Virtue, Vice, and the Good Citizen* (Viking, 1999) was certainly optative and perhaps a little sentimental; I attempt a more rigourous examination in *Concrete Reveries: Consciousness and the City* (Viking, 2008), especially ch. 8.

2 For the canonical statement of the problem, see Garrett Hardin, "The Tragedy of the Commons," *Science* 162 (1968), pp. 1243-48.

3 Guy Debord, perhaps typically for him, calls this negation the final triumph of capitalism. See *The Society of the Spectacle* (Donald Nicholson-Smith, trans.; Zone Books, 1995). For more on threshold functions and their importance for urban life, see *Concrete Reveries*, especially chs. 7 and 8.

4 Georg Simmel, "The Metropolis and Mental Life" (1903), reprinted in Kurt Wolff, ed., *The Sociology of Georg Simmel* (Free Press, 1964), at pp. 409-24.

5 Slavoj Žižek, "Notes towards a politics of Bartleby: The ignorance of chickens," *Comparative American Studies* 4 (2006): 375-94, at p. 381; reprinted in Žižek, *The Parallax View* (MIT Press, 2006), ch. 6. Remnick, lamenting the loss of "organized hypocrisy" in politics, chalks the issue up to Sarkozy's insecure male vanity: "what is particularly pathetic is his delusion that Bruni is a notch on his belt, when he is so obviously a notch on hers" (*The New Yorker*, 28 January 2008).

6 Kristine F. Miller, *Designs on the Public: The Private Lives of New York's Public Spaces* (University of Minnesota Press, 2008).

7 Scriveners were not always mere copyists. Jonathan Rosen notes that John Milton's father was employed as a scrivener at the beginning of the seventeenth century and acted as an moneylender as well as a drafter of legal documents—an employment so regular and lucrative that the poet, born in 1608, never had to work for a living. See Rosen, "Return to Paradise," *The New Yorker* (2 June 2008).

8 For more on this process of assimilation, see "Idling Toward Heaven: The Last Defence You Will Ever Need," introduction to Joshua Glenn and Mark Kingwell, *The Idler's Glossary* (Biblioasis, 2008).

9 The fact that this critique of liberalism can be lodged by both the left and the right creates an interesting political tangle; Carl Schmitt's version of the position has lately become a familiar touchstone for leftist thinkers such as Chantal Mouffe, in, for example, *The Challenge of Carl Schmitt* (Verso, 1999) and *The Return of the Political* (Verso, 1993).

10 Elizabeth Hardwick, "Bartleby in Manhattan," in *American Fictions* (Modern Library, 1999), p. 8; the essay was first published in 1981. There are of course multiple Bartlebys, even speaking only politically; Armin Beverungen and Stephen Dunne, in "'I'd Prefer Not To': Bartleby and the Excesses of Interpretation," *Culture and Organization* 13:2 (June

2007): 171-183, suggest that this interpretive fecundity is itself a site of *textual* surplus or excess. The story generates an ungraspable and always unresolved remainder not exhausted by Negri, Hardt, and Žižek's 'political' Bartleby, Deleuze's 'originary' Bartleby, or Agamben's 'whatever' Bartleby. "On the basis of these interpretations we derive a concept of excess as the residual surplus of any categorical interpretation, the yet to be accounted for, the not yet explained, the un-interpretable, the indeterminate, the always yet to arrive, precisely that which cannot be captured, held onto or put in place" (p. 171). The character Bartleby refuses to be assimilated within the story; the philosopheme 'Bartleby' likewise refuses to submit completely to any single interpretive assignment or form of consumption!

11 Hardwick, "Mrs. Wharton in New York" (1988) and "Henry James: On Washington Square" (1990), both reprinted in *American Fictions*.

12 Georges Bataille puts it best, in *The Accursed Share, Vol. 1* (Robert Hurley, trans.; Zone Books, 1991): from the particular perspective, the problem of economy is one of *scarcity*; from the general perspective it is one of *surplus*, ever renewed growth and spending, leading finally to a luxury-dominated public world. Written a century after Melville's story, the following could easily be a characterization of Bartleby's challenge to that world: "A genuine luxury requires the complete contempt for riches, the somber indifference of the individual who refuses work and makes his life on the one hand an infinitely ruined splendor, and on the other, a silent insult to the laborious life of the rich" (*The Accursed Share*, pp. 76-77).

13 Louis Althusser, "On Ideology and Ideological State Apparatuses: Notes Towards An Investigation," *La Pensée* (1970); reprinted in Althusser, *Lenin and Philosophy and Other Essays* (Monthly Review Press, 1971 and 2001).

14 Žižek, "Notes," p. 393.

15 Ann Levey, discussing a proposed bylaw in the city of Calgary, noted the irony of statutes that associate the norm of civility with such routine forbearances as not urinating in public or sleeping in public. Because the homeless have no private retreat and must attempt to reside in public, their very existence is uncivil ("Privatization of Public Space: The Politics of Exclusion," symposium on urban philosophy, Canadian Philosophical Association, University of British Columbia, 2 June 2008).

16 Giorgio Agamben, *The Coming Community* (Michael Hardt, trans., University of Minnesota Press, 1993; orig. *La communità che viene*, 1990), p. 37.

17 It is entirely likely that these different Bartlebys—and there are still others possible— would, assuming a confrontation arranged in the imagination, regard each other with suspicion and perhaps even violence. The genius of Melville's character is that the significations of Bartleby outstrip the denotations of his figure. I thank Devlin Russell for this insight.

18 Jacques Derrida dilates on length on the notion of "inheritance" while discussing his anti-realist conception of *democracy to come*; see both *Rogues: Two Essays on Reason* (Stanford University Press, 2004) and *The Politics of Friendship* (Verso, 2005). The latter book includes important critiques of Carl Schmitt (see below). Democracy is a promise, or a gift, we inherit; but it is also a legacy that we (may) continue. Bartleby's private/public 'unassimilation' is a complex property within this already complex gift economy.

19 The term is introduced and the practice defended in Steve Mann, "Oversight without undersight is an oversight" (unpublished paper, 2008); it plays on the *sur* = over / *sous* = under replacement just as his title plays on the doubleness of meaning in 'oversight'. Mann's idea of prophylactic self-recording as a form of freedom jibes with the recent interest in such "looking-back" events as recording police brutality or deception with cellphone cameras. The minor flurry resulting from these reversals shows how minimal their effect really is: looking back is still a form of looking, and while important in calling functionaries to account, it implicitly affirms that the main technology of *veillance* remains in the hands of the state.

20 "Sovereign is he who decides on the exception," Carl Schmitt writes as the first, flatly declarative line of his *Political Theology: Four Chapters on the Concept of Sovereignty* (George Schwab, trans., MIT Press, 1985 and University of Chicago Press, 2005), p. 5. The original text was published in 1922, revised in 1934. Schmitt, "the Hobbes of the twentieth century," is a political arch-realist and anti-liberal who argues that all sovereign states define themselves by means of a friend/enemy distinction, the essence of the political as such. From this vantage, liberal procedural democracy—where legitimacy flows from the people to the state, via public debate and decision—is a dangerous myth. A divergent assessment of political exception, inflected by 9/11 and the Bush Administration's response, is offered by Giorgio Agamben in *State of Exception* (orig. pub. 2003; Kevin Attell, trans., University of Chicago Press, 2005).

21 One feels the need to curb this insight, but with no clear argument for how. Except to note that the line connecting *Rear Window*'s Jeffries to sleazy porn-star voyeur Jake Scully in Brian de Palma's Hitchcock homage *Body Double* (1984), then to serial-killer voyeur Patrick Bateman in Bret Easton Ellis's 1991 novel *American Psycho* (also a 2000 film with Christian Bale)—who claims to have seen the de Palma movie 37 times—is one that is, at least, unnecessary!

4

Retouching the Void

Discussed in this essay:
9/11 Memorial Plaza (2011); Michael Arad, architect

IN HIS 2003 MEDITATION on (among other things) the tortured, and torturing, state of democracy after the September 11th terrorists attacks, Jacques Derrida wondered what had happened to irony. "[I]s it not also democracy that gives the right to irony in the public space?" asked the endlessly rhetorical author's voice. "Yes, for democracy opens public space, the publicity of public space, by granting the right to a change of tone [*Wechsel der Töne*], to irony as well as to fiction, the simulacrum, the secret, literature, and so on." Let us recall that it was just such changes in tone, irony in particular, that had been culturally outlawed in the immediate wake of the attacks, the End of Irony proclaimed in complacent pundit-speak even as David Letterman and Jon Stewart, once and future boyish servants of the imp within, wept on television.

In the intervening years there has been a pretty constant renegotiation of the terms of reference—irony was back, or irony about irony was the new sincerity, somehow embodied by the suicide of David Foster Wallace—but the conditions of possibility in public space have only grown murkier. Public space has been declared 'over' by leftist critics—a favourite move in the larger game—even as cities around the world struggle to accommodate demands for more available places to play, entertain, transact, meet, flirt, and enjoy life. 2011's Occupy Wall Street protest sketched a depressingly familiar narrative arc, with its initial optimism soon mired in local NIMBYism, police crackdowns, and the binning of books into dumpsters belonging to the Department of Sanitation. (This casual discarding is somehow more insidious than burning them: why symbolically destroy something that nobody takes seriously anyway? Easier to turn them into garbage.)

What looks like public space is still to be found in our towns and cities, but it is best not to push your claim to collective ownership very far: that's when the real owners, or the police, show up. The usual incidental costs of entering such spaces, enduring the visual pollution of advert and the presence of crowds, have now been joined by uncertainty and ubiquitous state security. Meanwhile, the rational public discourse that philosophers from Socrates to Kant believed would thrive in public space is nowhere to be seen, replaced, zombie-fashion, by a ravenous hive-mind simulacrum of tweeted rage, mendacity, narrow partisanship, and casual character assassination. Irony may be back on the cultural menu, but real changes of tone are as rare as ever and radical departure from the structured expectations of public space is all too likely to result in rapid expulsion. We are free to be you and me—but within fairly rigid constraints of acceptable comportment. Spaces that allow, or even demand, strange and outlandish gestures, high-percentile moves on the crazy scale, are almost never created. The police do not have to be present for their namesake—the *polis*—to exert its control over the individual.

I know, I know: not news. But note, in this regard, that Derrida deliberately interpolates the German phrase *Wechsel der Töne* in his text, alluding to Hölderlin's essay of that title as well as to the musical term of art. For Hölderlin, aesthetic experience is predicated on serial changes—really interchanges—in the tonal and metric registers, such that real beauty is possible only when elements combine in proper measure. Ironic changes of tone in public space aren't just about a different manner of speaking or acting; they ought to create, instead, a sort of strangeness that is the enabling condition of all public beauty; and democracy has—again, at least in theory—granted us the right to this beauty. But how beautiful is this democracy?

The 9/11 Memorial in Lower Manhattan, which opened in September, 2011, on the tenth anniversary of the attacks, is as charged a location as any place on the planet. Rarely does a 16-acre plot bear so much symbolic weight: at a minimum it is the site of a murderous evil that claimed nearly 3,000 human lives, the first battlefield in our latest clash of civilizations, and the simplistic symbolic justification for the worst political error in recent memory, the invasion of Iraq. Everyone is by now aware of the long delays in the rebuilding project and the conflicts among the many interested parties—city, port authority, owners, families, architects. The site has never been exactly pedestrian-friendly, closed off from surrounding streets during the WTC's existence and, despite observation decks up top, clearly devoted to the business of business. When the towers fell, there were heartfelt impromptu trib utes scattered around the perimeter, but confusion and anxiety reigned. As the clean-up labored on, design after design came and went, each one scuttled by this or that objection, until it began to seem that the terrorists really were winning. The ongoing failure to rebuild showed America's softness, its lack of will. The enduring scar in the ground became a psychic wound as well as a physical one. The master plan for the destroyed blocks around what was the World Trade Center has become an object lesson in how not to get things done, even as the decade-long post-9/11 security clampdown has generated its own weird logic of what can be done, and how fast. For a decade, the stymied construction and blasted hole at Ground Zero has offered spectral reflection of the dark state of the union.

—

"It somehow suddenly went from 'too soon!' to 'what's taking so long?'," Michael Arad says of the temporal haze that enveloped the project during the middle of the last decade. Arad is the architect whose design was chosen for the memorial plaza on the WTC site, an eight-acre interior expanse that will eventually be surrounded by five mid- to high-rise buildings and flanked on one side by a decorative passageway by the Spanish sculptor-architect Santiago Calatrava. The first of the buildings, an undistinguished and much-maligned tower by David Childs of Skidmore, Owings & Merrill, is almost complete. It bluntly shuts off the northern side of Arad's plaza with a prosaic volume of angled glass surfaces. Two other buildings, on the east side, are partially completed. The fourth and fifth, including a design by Britain's Norman Foster, are several years away from realization.

Arad, a tall and handsome man, is an Israeli citizen who was born in London in 1969. His father was a diplomat. His neat haircut and tortoiseshell horn-rimmed glasses give him an academic appearance, and somehow conspire to make him seem absurdly young. Newspaper profiles of him, especially in Israel, like to mention that he did his three years' military service in a commando brigade of the Israeli Defense Forces, but these days he looks more like the company clerk with a taste for symbolist poetry than some special-ops heavy. Evident enthusiasm for his design is balanced by awareness of the many aesthetic and political compromises it has been forced to suffer. His original design, one of more than 5,000 that were submitted in the competition for the memorial, remains alive in his sense of the realized space, known as *Reflecting Absence.* "The first vision was actually in the Hudson River," he tells me. "I imagined the river torn open. I had an idea of two voids, forever cascading into themselves, creating an absence, a lack." This was before he even considered entering the competition for the design commission. To visualize the idea he created a tabletop model of a sort of anti-fountain, using materials acquired from Bed, Bath & Beyond and the skills of a modelmaker friend. He shows me an image of this black block of fluid, with its infinite interior flow of water, set atop the roof ledge of his East Village apartment building. In the image the skyline of Manhattan is doubled, visible in the near distance but also reflected in the slick blackness of the model. The effect is surprisingly eerie, even with the project's somewhat homely origins.

We are sitting in the security office of the 9/11 memorial, talking the design through before going out to the plaza itself. It is before opening time on a rainy weekday, and we will later be able to wander the spaces of the memorial without the prearranged passes, long line-ups within concrete and hurricane-fence barriers, and labyrinthine security checks that are currently a major feature of any visit. For a time, we will be alone in the memorial except for two servicemen and a small group of nuns. This herding security-consciousness, in part a consequence of the construction going on around the plaza, is just one of the wrinkles that complicate the experience of *Reflecting Absence.* Arad's conception is of an open and public space, a place that is at once a destination for mourning and remembrance and an urban square in which people work and play.

"That last word was important to me," he says, showing me the text that accompanied his design submission where 'play' is indeed the last word. "I wanted to be sure that people saw this not as a grim site, but as a place to enjoy." Not everyone is likely to accept the idea, given the overdetermination of 9/11 and its consequences. Just a week after my visit to the memorial, the Dutch architecture firm MVRDV was excoriated for creating a luxury high-rise design for Seoul, South Korea, that included twin towers with a blooming middle section vaguely reminiscent of images showing the two stanchions of the World Trade Center belching mingled smoke and fire. (You can apparently fold a U.S. twenty dollar bill such that the White House can be made to look like a tower engulfed in flames, but that is maybe taking play too far.)

"I remember going to Washington Square Park a few days after 9/11," Arad tells me. "There were some people gathered there, not many, maybe a dozen, and there was this sense of community that felt very powerful. No ceremony, just being together in a place. As an architect of course I knew about the importance of public space, but that was the first time I felt it, felt how it could both reflect and foster community." His idea for the memorial, once the cascading pools had been shifted in imagination eastward from the river and into the plaza, was of a clearing, a space of reflection in the midst of the city's bustle. The initial effect of the flat plaza is muted, spare, like the public square of a sleepy European town. Standing on the southwest corner of the space, he gestures farther south and east. "You have old New York there, on a street plan laid out by the Dutch. And when the five towers are done, you'll have a surround of new buildings. In the middle, with Greenwich and Fulton streets opened up, will be this space."

The two voids sit within the footprint of the fallen towers and are surrounded by a growing pattern of young oaks planted on what Arad, working with landscape architect Peter Walker, has called an "abacus-like" pattern, like beads on wire. When they are more fully grown, the trees will create a canopy of blooming leaves within the space, which currently feels sparse and rather austere. There are sections of turf in the deployment of the plaza that likewise suggest a city park or square. When—or if—the plaza is fully opened up to the city around it, it is not clear how much it will still feel like a memorial, or even a destination. It will never achieve the ensorcelling stillness of Maya Lin's Vietnam Veterans Memorial in Washington, D.C., or—to take a controversial example of non-memorial public art—the bold gestural genius of Richard Serra's *Tilted Arc*, which graced (some would say obstructed) New York's Federal Plaza, not many blocks north and east of here, between 1981 and 1989. But the bronze walls of the two downshafts, whose still unseen depths act like sinkholes in the bare expanse, draw you close.

Embeddedness in ordinary city life could be a good thing, even a provocative one, especially if one imagines this park as allowing the shifting tones of democratic irony, the multiple uses and subject positions of freedom. How wonderful, really, if a place of remembrance could accommodate moods and actions both solemn and joyful, a sameness-meets-difference version of the heterotopia, like a cemetery where one is comfortable jogging or walking a dog or a jingoistic equestrian war monument that doubles as an impromptu jungle gym.

At the moment, ironies of a different register dominate the square. Maybe predictably, the memorial has become a tourist site on the same list, judging by the carriage of people entering as the official hours began, as visits to FAO Schwarz and the Abercrombie & Fitch flagship store. There is some respectful gazing about, but also a good deal of cellphone-camera flashing and even some smiling group shots. The confusion is simultaneously human and creepy, as if people in public spaces cannot muster any other form of behaviour than answering the camera's demand for an idiot grin. In this instant, the constraints of public space generate jarring tones that do not interplay: the conformity of self-commemoration, the ceaseless pixelization of experience, Facebook fascism. This, combined with the discomfiting reminder of airport security procedures, threatens to unbalance the whole idea of memorial. The architect Bruce Kuwabara pointed out to me a subtler destabilizing feature: at night, the reflected lights at the bottom of the two voids creates a strange 'dark runway' effect on either side, as if one were in a landing aircraft.

———

Arad had originally planned the memorial part of the design to be underground, with the names of the fallen—the flights, the towers, the first responders—rendered in a kind of wall, or veil, between the viewer and the watery space beyond. Unidentified remains from the north tower were to be buried within. But security concerns and objections from some of the families forced a revision, so that now the mourning space is in the plaza itself, and the names rendered in laser-cut bronze plates that edge the voids, the corners neatly chamfered in a way that quotes Minoru Yamasaki's original WTC design and incidentally allows those of smaller stature or in wheelchairs to view the spaces below.

Placement of the names was a problem that occupied Arad and his colleagues for over two years, as they tried to balance the aesthetics of spacing and alignment against the various partisan forces calling for arrangement by name, or firm, or station number. He eventually adopted a modified version of what he calls "meaningful adjacency," such that requests to have associated names placed near each other could be accommodated. During the day, the cut-out names generate shadows; at night, they are lit from within the 10-foot bronze sections. Today, the rain is beading in wet archipelagos scattered along the bronze surface. "Look at that," Arad says. "That's really beautiful."

If you approach from the current entrance, the south tower's footprint lies ahead and to the right, and walking slowly towards it you can see only the four feet or so of the surrounding wall, or ledge, where the names are displayed. The sound of falling water grows gradually louder. At just about the point where a name comes into legible focus, your eye will clear the angled edge of the wall and fall into the open space of the 30-foot drop, water cascading from all sides, running from a clearly raked line of white fingers into an undifferentiated flow at the bottom. Another step and your eye will tumble into the second drop that lies centred within the first, a dark square emptiness, a void within a void.

The effect is powerful enough to raise goosebumps, a combination of the minute fear that accompanies all sudden views into open space below us together with a sublime sense of nothingness, an awareness of loss. The distracting runway reflection aside, at night the smaller voids are so dark they obscure any sense of their edges, erasing visual distinction—in Arad's words, "all verticality is visually gone." Our media imprinting being what it is, and the event being what it was, one cannot help but feel in that moment the weight of the collapsing towers, their interior steel skeletons melted in the explosion's heat, falling into themselves, creating a mass grave at the foot of Manhattan. The presence of absence has rarely been aesthetically rendered with such restraint and power. "I wanted to show that this is not an abstraction, it's not a political calculus," Arad tells me. "It's something that tore people's lives apart."

Any aesthetic rendering is of course open to objection, and there are problems both within and surrounding the design. While the flow of water on the horizontal surface, a dense black granite known as jet mist, is particularly beautiful as it sluices into the lower space, creating a sort of infinite downward cascade, the waterfalls themselves, ingeniously designed by Canadian water-effect specialist Dan Euser to form four clean corners in each space, court a judgment of banality. Of all the canonical features of landscape design, waterfalls run perhaps the greatest risk of declining into kitsch, even when nicely realized and rhetorically associated, as these have been, with 'cleansing' and 'healing'.

Constrained by the original vision of a pool for each fallen tower, there is unavoidable duplication in one's experience of the plaza as a whole. Worse, the heating and cooling infrastructure has been accommodated in eyesore housings on the west edge of the site, and the triangular above-surface structure of the future museum, designed by Mark Wagner of Davis Brody Bond Aedas, closes down the space on the east side of the plaza between the two pools. It is also designed in a style that might be called Space-Age Garden Shed. Though the museum itself will retain the exposed slurry wall of the excavated site—a favourite feature of master planner Daniel Libeskind and something Arad praises as one of "the remaining traces that speak so eloquently of absence"—the building on the plaza itself seems weirdly out of joint with its site.

There are thornier issues still. Composer Karlheinz Stockhausen's rash remark, just days afterward, that the 9/11 attacks were "the greatest work of art ever" were widely reviled, and quickly retracted, but nobody can deny that one lasting effect of the attacks was a shift in visual consciousness. The hijackers turned terror into spectacle, one with global distribution, and did so using two iconic machines of the age, the skyscraper and the passenger jet. The sober consideration that the 'aesthetic' realm concerns feeling and sensation is enough to see that this publicly enacted mass murder possesses a dimension of arousal that stays vivid in the memory. No one who witnessed it, especially mediated by television, can forget the sick, riveting horror excited by the second plane's impact into the South Tower. To counter this memory aesthetically, in a memorial, entails a confrontation with the negative sublime: experience of the unspeakable. Here, the standard imperative that 'we must always remember' butts up against a reality whose details are so awful that we would prefer to forget.

The choice of Libeskind as the master planner of the reconstruction was inspired, in part, by his sole undisputed architectural success, the Jewish Museum in Berlin. Its combination of disquieting silhouette and suggestive interior spaces manages at once to recollect and to refuse the Holocaust. His influence has proven minimal in New York, despite a flurry of sometimes embarrassing publicity when he was first brought on board in 2003. Conflicts with Childs, who entered the project at the insistence of Larry Silverstein, the real-estate developer who holds a long-term lease on the property from the Port Authority, made headlines. Libeskind had no experience with high-rise design, while Childs and SOM are experts at going high. (The world's current tallest building, Dubai's Burj Khalifa, is one of theirs.)

So Libeskind's proposed design for a 'Freedom Tower', rising 1,776 symbolic feet high and saluting the Statue of Liberty across the harbour, was simplified and reduced to Childs's current dull exterior. Demoted, or kicked upstairs, from the position of architect to that of master planner, Libeskind can now claim, according to some estimates, just 4% of the overall square footage as his own design. Ego battles aside, one serious consequence of all this design-by-committee is that, in the coming flurry of construction by a roster of name-brand architects, Arad's plaza must shoulder the weight of remembrance. It is how people will experience the site at large, and where they will confront the issues of shared calamity, including the erosions of freedom made in the name of freedom. Arad's subtle, almost anti-monumental aesthetic sensibility has, in effect, become the nation's lens on a traumatic memory. No figures, no narrative, no assigned meanings.

———

As Arad and I are walking between the pools, a security guard approaches. He is thickly built, about sixty, in a blue uniform. He has a walrus moustache that makes him look liked a slim-line version of former Bears head coach Mike Ditka. "Are you the architect?" he asks Arad.

"Yes." There is instant wariness, but also pride—a common reaction to this miniature time bomb of a question.

"People keep asking me about this," he says, pointing to the museum. "What's this supposed to mean?"

"Um, I didn't design that," Arad says. He does not offer to say who did. "It's not mine."

"Oh, okay," the guard says, undeterred. "But so tell me. What's with the pools, the two pools?"

Arad has been talking to me in metaphors and theoretical terms for over an hour. He has explained material choices and the "dozens of iterations" his firm went through before they got the name placement issues more or less settled. He has spoken with eloquence of his concerns with "individual and collective loss," his desire to create "a place of communion" that embodies the "secular spiritual" but also retains a feeling that is "stoic and compassionate even as it is also defiant." He pauses a second to frame a suitable answer.

"Well, I wanted to create a void," he says. "Two cascading voids."

"I see," the guard says. "Thank you." He seems to mean it: he now has something he can pass on to punters in the plaza, straight from the designer's lips, when they stop him to ask.

"Classic architect moment," I say to Arad. He nods, smiling slightly.

"It's hard to explain, and it would take too long," he says. "And I can't really say that I first imagined it in the river! But I'm glad that it doesn't have a simple or singular explanation. Some people may hate it. But others will love it."

Yes. But that cannot solve the fundamental problem which the plaza illustrates, a heightened version of the affliction of all public art, namely that it is a tragedy of the commons waiting to happen. As individuals experience and judge the aesthetic element, enjoyment and disappointment jostle together and overwhelm that very experience. The art is submerged under the volume of its availability, and success generates failure.

A Steven Millhauser story from 2006 offers a poignant account of what I mean. In the story people begin building transparent domes over their homes and property; soon towns and cities follow suit, until eventually a massive dome is successfully erected over the entire country—an architectural triumph on an order almost beyond imagination! But now, inside the dome, once moving and sublime sights appear diminished. "Events themselves, under such conditions, have receded in importance, have become aestheticized," the narrator notes. "Experience is beginning to feel like a collection of ingeniously constructed arcade games."[1] (I'm not quite sure what to make of the fact that the audio version of this story is read by Alec Baldwin, a man who was thrown off a plane for playing an arcade game on his cellphone.)

The 9/11 memorial—this commons of the tragedy, threatened by its own status as a place to visit, an ingeniously constructed destination—cannot escape these tangles. But perhaps it can offer a partial respite, a silent declivity. For many of us who were living in New York in the months after the WTC attacks the most moving tribute will always be those square beacons of light, silent, fragile and temporary by design, that were sent high into the Manhattan night in March, 2002, and every September 11th since. Arad's design constructs no such height, but it nevertheless conjures the particularity of that memory and so achieves some of that weightlessness, that freedom from expectation. The rest is silence.

Notes:

1 Steven Millhauser, "The Dome," in Dangerous Laughter: Thirteen Stories (Knopf, 2008).

5

The Tomist:
Francis Fukuyama's Infinite Regression

Discussed in this essay: Francis Fukuyama, *The Origins of Political Order: From Prehuman Times to the French Revolution* (FS&G, 2011)

IT STANDS TO REASON that 500 pages of an author's company should offer the reader some insight into a writer. So I can tell you that Francis Fukuyama does not favour exclamation points (I counted just one in the half-millennium of prose), that he has a voracious, some would say vacuum cleaner's, interest in the details of bureaucracy, and that, despite an early reputation as a neo-con point man, especially circa the publication of his 1992 Hegel-inflected debut, *The End of History and the Last Man*, he is when it comes to political theory judicious to the point of opacity. Never have so many pages about what Hegel called "the slaughter-bench of history" been rendered with such wearying evenness.

On the other hand, to say that is not to say much. Fukuyama does not reveal himself here, and whether that is because there is little to reveal or because Fukuyama has become gun-shy is a mystery which this book quite sensibly refuses to solve. Fukuyama's stolid insistence on not taking sides, and of delivering judgments of strictly local range— particular articles by specific scholars are desultorily challenged, big ideas mostly get a pass—renders *The Origins of Political Order* one of those quietly punishing *omnium gatherum* tomes that will offer rebukes from the shelves of private libraries and reading rooms across the continent for not being read.

Fukuyama is no Casaubon: the work stands completed, and in its early pages a second volume is threatened. His fault is not failed ambition but banal delivery. One senses trouble early when the author notes a story, attributed here to Stephen Hawking, concerning causal explanation. A scientist is challenged by an old woman indignant at his big-bang cosmology. Can he prove that the earth does not, in fact, as she believes, sit atop the back of a turtle. He replies by wondering, con-descendingly, what the turtle is standing on. Another turtle of course, she tells him. And that turtle, what supports it? At which point the aged questioner holds up a hand and says, "I can stop you right there, young man. It's turtles all the way down."

Fukuyama likes this tale so much he returns to it a half-dozen times, such that it becomes the dominant metaphor of a book other-wise mercilessly free of them. For him the multiple turtles stand in, as far as I can tell, for the idea of multivalent causality: that is, there is no single master key that unlocks the puzzle of political order, and theories that suppose otherwise are guilty of theoretical arrogance, reduction-ism, Whiggish assumptions about progressive history, or ideological spe-cial pleading. "Most purportedly general theories of development fail because they don't take into account the multiple independent dimen-sions of development," Fukuyama somberly warns us. Instead he sets out to offer many causes, many factors, many routes to stability and its opposite: that's how politics works.

Fine, except this is actually quite peculiar, and for several reasons. It does not really matter that the turtle story, at least when I first heard it as an undergraduate, was linked to Bertrand Russell, not Stephen Hawking; I'm told there are older versions that feature William James, Hindu mystics, and even perhaps (one would not be surprised to find) Michel de Montaigne or Heraclitus. The point is that the story illus-trates nearly the opposite warning to the one that interests Fukuyama. It is not a parable in favour of expansive causal accounts, it's a warning against the irrationality of infinite regress. Thomas Aquinas, applauding Aristotle's adoption of the concept of an Uncaused Cause, noted that any explanation that relies on a numerically indefinite series of prior causes is "offensive to reason." To put it crudely, an infinite regress—turtles all the way down—is not an alternative causal account to one that posits a fixed point; it is no account at all.

Fukuyama does provide a fixed cause, or cluster of them, concern-ing the origins of political order. He is rather blithe about them, in fact, employing the phrase "human nature" without much explana-tion beyond a gesture to Darwinian biology. Like almost anyone who reaches beyond the details of this regime or that, he comes up against the usual suspects of baseline evolutionary fact. Humans are primates: they like stability, they like status, and they like to gang up on other humans when that serves the first two interests. They also mistake their interests, however, especially when individually rational decisions— seeking return on investment, winning competitions of consumption, my getting sum when you get zero—generate general dysfunctions. On Fukuyama's own account, political order is largely a matter of push and pull between personal desire and collective action problems. Politics might be defined on this view not as the art of the possible, as Bismarck had it, but as one big tragedy of the commons.

Famously, such a tragedy can be avoided either by strict private property laws or by aggressive regulation of public goods. Political regimes have over the centuries evolved mechanisms to accomplish both, with varied degrees of success, but the record shows that the most persistent systems are those that fold status-seeking into the equation. Positional goods are the key to understanding political order because they create zero-sum games: my corner office, state-fair blue ribbon, or A-plus grade retain value only so long as I have it and you don't. By definition, such goods cannot be more equally distributed. We can press Fukuyama's explanatory point to a sharper edge than he would favour. Just as film critic Raymond Bellour would claim that Hollywood was a machine dedicated to the manufacture of the heterosexual couple, let us say that the state is a machine dedicated to the manufacture of preferments and rents.

—

The conclusion seeps only gradually through the solid wall of Fukuyama's prose, an emergent property of his hands-off attitude to theory. The reader cannot but see this as something of an intrapersonal rebuke from the seasoned author of *The Origins of Political Order* to the still-callow scholar who penned *The End of History and the Last Man*. The latter writer, like the youthful Wittgenstein, claimed a master key to sense-making that his older iteration would abandon. In Fukuyama's case, it was Hegelian dialectics filtered through Alexandre Kojève and then put out to conservative pastures not a hundred miles from Michael Oakeshott's cricket pitch, where stability shall be the byword of social order and all demands for social improvement the devil's work. Young Fukuyama thought that liberal democracy was the last word on politics, the final tectonic shift, and that the rest was not silence, exactly, but tinkering and tweaking at the margins.

That this weighty volume made Fukuyama an unlikely intellectual celebrity is one of those facts about the recent past that get harder to recall with every passing year. Fukuyama was not as flamboyant as Allan Bloom, whose high-toned culture-wars screed, *The Closing of the American Mind*, complete with deliberate abuses of Nietzsche and gleeful contempt for his own undergraduates, achieved an even greater notoriety (and larger sales record). The two shared an impressive success whose conditions of possibility are dwindling, namely to produce fairly serious works of ideas that were bought, read, and debated with sincere vigour and in large numbers.

In Bloom's case especially this was remarkable, since his message was precisely the opposite of the easily digested primers turned out by *New Yorker* staffers and television hosts. Bloom attacked the shallowness of American culture and scored on both its terms and his. Saul Bellow's last novel, *Ravelstein*, was a thinly veiled paean to his friend Bloom, post-success, complete with pretty boyfriend, louche tastes in clothes and accessories (Armani, Vuitton, Dunhill, Jensen, Spode and Quimper are mentioned in the space of one paragraph), and the half-serious arrogance of intellectual victory. "He had every right to look as he looked now, while the waiter set up our breakfast," the narrator says from Ravelstein's suite at the Crillon in Paris. "His intellect had made a millionaire of him. It's no small matter to become rich and famous by saying exactly what you think—to say it in your own words, without compromise."

Fukuyama was, by contrast, shy and retiring. He never seemed comfortable in his suddenly prominent role as alpha attack dog in the neo-conservative's intellectual kennel. And in truth, the match was bad from the start, as subsequent events proved. Yes, *The End of History and the Last Man* could be annexed to general American triumphalism about capitalist democracy, if one were so inclined; this was especially true given the momentary alignment of Ronald Reagan's "Mr. Gorbachev, tear down that wall!" pronunciamento with Fukuyama's more nuanced claim that Soviet ideology could not resist market influence after 1989. But the emergence of capitalist Russia was inevitable not so much as the result of intellectual failure as because *nothing on earth* could get lost in the general commodification of everything that has been going on since the 1990s. As Fukuyama grew restive with the reductionism of public intellectual life, he also moved away from the ideology-endgame arguments outlined in *The End of History and the Last Man*. His books since have exhibited a searching quality: looking for the origins of trust (1995's *Trust*) and social norms (1999's *The Great Disruption*) or even noting that gaps in economic development lead to social upheaval (2008's *Falling Behind*).

Still, no one as sensitive to history as Fukuyama can fail to realize that the past is hard to live down. And like many intellectuals, he was caught up in historical events that made the theoretical sides harder to discern: he supported anti-Saddam Hussein insurgencies in Iraq and joined in calling for Osama bin Laden's death or capture after the terrorist attacks of September 11th, 2001. But he distanced himself from the invasion of Iraq because of its basis in "narrow and cynical [political] realism" and, in a statement explaining his endorsement of Barack Obama for president in 2008, Fukuyama labelled the George W. Bush presidency "disastrous"—perhaps a predictable lament from a scholar viewing his ideas distorted by real-world exigencies.

In his first Bush term, Fukuyama said, the president had "launched an unnecessary war" that "undermined the standing of the United States throughout the world." In the second, he "presid[ed] over the collapse of the American financial system and broader economy." One might quibble on the last point, especially given President Obama's craven bailout scheme after 2008's market collapse, but you get the point. On this evidence, Fukuyama may be considered the only real neo-conservative, a *sui generis* movement of one, the way Heidegger might have been the only true Nazi. And now, of course, scant weeks before the tenth anniversary of 9/11, he can congratulate President Obama on finishing the delayed business of that extralegal Osama bin Laden assassination. Global capital punishment without trial: revenge is a dish better served late than never.

"I do not confront the general reader with a big theoretical framework at the outset," Fukuyama assures us, noting that his "middle-range" approach will avoid "the pitfalls of excessive abstraction (the vice of economists) and excessive particularism (the problem of many historians and anthropologists)." This retreat from Big Theory can be seen as a reaction to the thick swath of political history we have all witnessed since 1989. Most significant is the glaringly obvious point that Hegel's prediction about the end of history does not tally with the facts, something Fukuyama is no longer prepared to ignore. If anything, there's been too damn much history in the past two decades. And if the motive force of that has been religious fundamentalism trying to destroy modernity, or hybrid forms of authoritarian order such as China or Saudi Arabia that deploy both pre-modern and postmodern realities, these facts only heighten the need for better theoretical frameworks. Fukuyama has abandoned his dialectical spectacles, long after most people did the same (if they ever wore them). The question is, what comes in their place?

Hegel suggested that all one-sided manifestations of Spirit in the material world of history were unstable; temporary synthesis of opposing energies would always tip into instability and, eventually, open conflict. The only exception, and hence stopping rule, is the Absolute, when the force of reason and the material conditions of human life have achieved a complete and coextensive working-out. The real is the rational, and the rational is the real—it sounds so simple! The trouble, as Fukuyama demonstrates over and over, is that there are plenty of political orders that are both persistent and bad for society as a whole: they create what game theorists call a stable equilibrium that is nevertheless dysfunctional. Given the perfidy and at best very local, short-term rationality of humans, it can be no surprise that we often contrive to create systems that fail everybody and yet remain in place for many decades, if not centuries, until war, invasion, or a Malthusian population crisis consigns them from the history books. Or, to use Fukuyama's own economic jargon, "entrenched interest groups tend to accumulate in any society over time, which aggregate into rent-seeking coalitions in order to defend their narrow privileges."

Seeing how, and how often, this happens is the chief pleasure of this history book, and that pleasure redeems the author's general promise:

"The purpose of this book is to fill in some of the gaps of this historical amnesia, by giving an account of where basic political institutions came from in societies that now take them for granted." Those institutions—the state, rule of law, accountable government—are indeed the cornerstones of political order, and there is no doubt that Fukuyama's account illuminates their origins. At the same time, however, the book displays a series of strange blind spots that, taken together, seem more than coincidental; they might even call for a 'hidden writing' interpretation of the sort favoured by Allan Bloom and the rest of those scheming charismatics influenced by Leo Strauss. Is it possible that the repeated turtles-all-the-way-down metaphor is not a misreading but a misdirection, a legerdemain secret clue that something else is going on beneath the textual surface?

The central occlusion concerns the relation of politics and economics. Fukuyama early on fights off the idea of reducing political institutions to transactions, and yet the evidence mounts that the only viable generalization about our social behaviour is that it is dedicated to taking advantage of one another, usually with money. It is the corrupt *ancien régime* of eighteenth-century France that both invented the word and perfected the practice of *rente*, but every political system known to history has been dedicated to some form or other of legitimated extortion: polls, taxes, fines, bribes, and rents, together with their financial arms-race counterparts of evasion, loopholes, lawyers, and regulatory capture. The 2008 market collapse and subsequent government bailout of financial institutions hopped to levels of meta-transaction rent-seeking that make Hegel look like a piker in the abstraction department are just a late, supercharged refinement of the basic human desire to get one up—and remember to collect the vig as you go.

From this vantage, the institutions of politics are at best trailing-edge mechanisms for what we are doing anyway and, at worst, cynical and wafer-thin window dressings that justify the advantages of the few in terms that will be swallowed by the many. An untenable system like democracy under capitalism colonizes aspects of our own desire and experience to stitch together a narrative of legitimation, even as it generates numerous incentives for citizen-consumers to game the system. This pincer movement of postmodern capitalism means there is no longer any possibility of a great reveal in the standard tradition of *ideologiekritik*, the scales falling from our eyes with the aid of good philosophy. Instead we are locked in the no-exit condition of the character Nada in John Carpenter's *They Live*, the 1988 horror-action-comedy film that Jonathan Lethem has fondly described as "probably the stupidest movie ever to take ideology as its explicit subject." If this is stupidity, it is stupidity with a serious agenda, and a big payload. Itinerant worker Nada (Roddy Piper) arrives in a repressive Reaganite Los Angeles and discovers sunglasses that expose the reality of a stealthy alien invasion, complete with subliminal messages to consume and obey. Formerly a staunch believer in America as the land of opportunity, Nada is transformed into an instant resistance fighter. Even as he destroys the television signal that is broadcasting the ideological smokescreen (yes, it's 1982) in the film's climactic scene, he is shot down and, in a final act of will, gives the aliens the finger. It is not clear, though, what difference it will make to have the signal knocked out. Carpenter's film demonstrates that ideology has always been about consumption, not politics. Most people are pretty happy to consume and obey, even under alien overlords—why wouldn't they be, when it's the best possible way to tell who's winning?

Fukuyama rightly questions the accuracy of Lockean accounts of private property, which suggest that the institutions and rights of ownership result from a security-seeking bargain of individuals equal in their natural rights. In fact, he says, property is rooted in family life, religious observance, and common law. What the book fails to consider, or even mention, is a much more convincing account of family life, religious observance, and common law, namely Freud's in *Civilization and Its Discontents*. Property, Freud argues, is not the cause of envy but its symptom: when I see another better placed than myself (say, my older brother) I cry foul. That foul has a name: injustice; and it has a penalty: division of goods. Justice is here recast as a squabble among children, property a mechanism for facilitating envy and indicating status.

I called this envy-first theory of human life an emergent property of Fukuyama's book; he never fingers rent-seeking as the secret message of all politics, still less offers a desire-freighted account of politics. Nevertheless the property emerges, and with tremendous explanatory power, because the importance of money collection is everywhere implicit in the book's detailed accounts of regime-specific rises and falls. In David Foster Wallace's posthumous final novel, *The Pale King*, a character called DeWitt Glendenning Jr., Midwest Regional Examination Center Director of the Internal Revenue Service, offers this piece of wisdom: "The tax code, once you get to know it, embodies all the essence of life: greed, politics, power, goodness, charity." The line was quoted in many reviews of the novel; in fact, by a typical Wallace twist, it turns out the words were originally uttered by a non-fictional tax man, former IRS director Sheldon S. Cohen. Taxes, like death, are inevitable horizons of human meaning. And politics are inconceivable without them.

What this means for any student of political origins is that you play down the centrality of money at your peril. In a standard gesture offered early in *The Origins of Political Order*, Fukuyama notes that ancient Greek "classical republicanism did not scale well"—one reason he starts his account of politics in China, with its wide gap between rich and poor, entrenched bureaucratic elites, legacy-style education system, and elaborate positional-goods market for the distribution of honours and offices. All democratic self-congratulation aside, twenty-first-century America resembles Han-dynasty China a lot more than it does Percilean Athens.

What the shift from Greece to China ultimately shows is that the insistence of robust citizen-virtue found in, say, Aristotle's *Ethics* and *Politics*, cannot be applied to sprawling, diverse societies with their different conceptions of the good life. Calls for greater civic virtue fall on deaf ears in pluralistic societies, where there is no prior agreement about what makes for human flourishing; or, worse, the idea of virtue mutates into *Starship Troopers*-style fascism, where only soldiers are true citizens. A materialist explanation would note that, without the institution of slavery, the cost of cultivating Athenian ethical and political virtues is prohibitive. In any event, there is a simple reason that most contemporary democratic systems focus their energy, and their discourse, on how social services are delivered in exchange for taxes. Democratic citizens, with their well-stoked individual interests and priority for their own families, need not possess any conception at all of civic virtue. They need not participate with vigour in public life; they need not even vote. Systems of fining people for not exercising their franchise, as in Australia and thirty other democracies around the world, confess their basic futility. Such fines are just taxation by other means, a price I am willing to pay to be left alone. They are the equivalent of a parking ticket whose cost I will shoulder as a tolerable contract expense, not as punishment for a genuine violation.

The reduction of all fines to prices, and of all obligations to tax burdens, shows just how comprehensive is the transactional contamination of democracy. If citizens are really consumers, forever negotiating the shoals of tax avoision—that tricky territory between avoidance (licit) and evasion (illicit)—then it immediately becomes rational to game the system. Smarter players will take the contest up a level and realize that you can game the system's dominant myths as well as its material realities. From this vantage, the American Dream is the biggest long con in the history of politics, and the ultimate form of regulatory capture is not buying out a watchdog agency or tame subcommittee chairman; it lies in keeping the narratives of democratic legitimacy and economic opportunity alive even when all the facts are ranged against them.

———

Fukuyama's book stops just when the questions are emerging, that is, on the eve of the French and American revolutions: two historical events that were very much driven by philosophical ideas, not just material forces. On page 442 Fukuyama acknowledges that "[i]t is impossible to develop any meaningful theory of political development without treating ideas as fundamental causes of why societies differ and follow distinct developmental paths." This will come as a surprise to the faithful reader who has been doggedly pursuing the history-before-theory accounts of political systems in China and India, in Europe, in the Muslim world. But it turns out that the ideas in question, the ones without which development cannot be understood, are not to be confused with *theories*, which purport to explain everything. No, the ideas are—you guessed it—part of the chain of turtles. "[I]n turtle terminology, they are turtles far down the stack that do not necessarily stand on the backs of turtles related to the economy or physical environment." Of course.

One can only hope that the complex relation of theory and practice will emerge more clearly in volume two of Fukuyama's origins project, as he continues his detailed story, but the concluding passages of this volume, where he considers political decay, prompt worries about the clarity of his thinking. His comparative historical approach, so careful to fight off larger theoretical commitments, makes its own kind of theoretical commitment—let's call it anti-Whiggishness by principle. The idea that ideas are, even theoretically, separable from their applications in the economy and the physical environment, not to mention from political institutions, is itself an example of a concretely applied idea, albeit of a tendentious sort. One reason political commentators consistently fail to understand the social order is that they enjoy the habitual exercise of concept-separation: driving a conceptual wedge between politics and markets, between democracy and capitalism. Today's debates about the 'export' of democracy around the world, or its upsurge in the former Soviet Union or the Middle East, are mostly misguided. At their best they indulge an appreciation of televised populism—crowds in the streets! the people speak!—while ignoring any interrogation of actual political conditions. At their worst, they devolve into product-placement ads for social-networking websites.

Democracy is an unstable commodity, but there is a reason it has become the go-to answer to questions of political order—if not the very last word in history itself. That reason is not, however, what most people, including Fukuyama, would have you believe. Pious defenders of democracy point to the interests and desires of the people as the basis of legitimacy. This ignores not only the realities of democratic politics under capitalism, where those interests and desires are routinely bent into bargains, narrative sleight-of-hand, and self-defeating parlays; it also obscures the strange truth at the heart of democracy, what Hegel called "the magical transformation of quantity into quality." The lever of democratic legitimacy turns on a spectral pivot, a fiction we know as democratic premise of equal worth. But we are not, in fact, equal, before the law or otherwise. This awkward truth was clearly acknowledged by the first democrats, those ancient Greek eccentrics, who knew that a bare lottery was the only way forward when the choice of leaders had foundered on competing claims of virtue. If you cannot compare merits, you might as well just draw straws. (For more on this last point, see the following essay in this volume, "Throwing Dice.")

We have lost sight of the key lesson of all politics, which is that the origins of political order are either insupportable, mysterious, or both.

All stories of legitimacy, from the naturalism buried in Plato's noble lie to the optimism shading a presidential inauguration, are forms of mythmaking. Authority, as the late Jacques Derrida argued with reference to similar claims in Montaigne and Pascal, always has a mystical foundation: the force of law is not an institution whose history can be unearthed, even through careful historical study. To know everything about the Chinese legal system, for example, is still to know nothing about why such a thing as law should ever be binding, or why the state should ever have a monopoly on the unpunished use of lethal violence. Sooner or later, all politics is *realpolitik*. And here, as Derrida said, discourse "meets its limit" because there is "a silence walled up in the violent structure of the founding act."

But silence does not satisfy historians, those inveterate slingers of discourse. The irony of Fukuyama's book is that his fondness for the turtle story actually turns out to be on point, though not in the fashion he imagines. There actually is an infinite regress in the story of origin, and whether your response is a large-scale theoretical reduction or a studied refusal of theory in favour of evolutionary fact, the turtles keep on going all the way down, disappearing into a void of force without justification. This may be offensive to reason; but then, human action often is.

6

Throwing Dice:
Luck of the Draw and the Democratic Ideal

IS DEMOCRACY A GIFT ECONOMY—that is, one essentially distinct from, and opposed to, reduction to transactional exchanges such as those typical in a market economy? Beginning with a case study of success, let us consider the role of *scalable effects* in destabilizing the relationship between merit and reward. This opens up the question of how the general issue of 'title' functions in larger systems of merit and reward, crucially including politics. Pursuing Jacques Rancière's insights concerning *hatred of democracy* means that we can begin to see the importance of 'the drawing of lots' in mechanisms of political legitimation— the paradoxical 'title which is no title'.

The hidden force of lots is not their randomness, which is merely a device, but a matter of prior agreement to abide by their outcome, not their randomness. This *agreement to abide* is likewise the hidden force of all democratic devices of legitimation, whether they employ lots or not. The decisions issued by democratic electoral systems are both undeserved (because unconnected to intrinsic qualities or claims) and apparently binding (because accepted). This tension has consequences beyond thought-experiments, where randomness is sometimes explicitly in play; all real-world democratic systems remain dependent on disconnections between merit and success.

On this view, the capture of electoral processes by the moneyed interest is a perversion of the democratic ideal, a perversion which only a democracy of the gift can redeem. In other words, a claim to democratic legitimacy only functions if and when that legitimacy has no price, and is accepted as the undeserved gift it must be. And so:

1. The Gould Conundrum

In 2009 I published a philosophical biography of the pianist Glenn Gould. Since then I have been asked countless times to explain his peculiar appeal. Almost alone among twentieth-century classical players, Gould is revered and mythologized to a degree rivalling a sports hero or global film celebrity. He has inspired a cult following in many countries, notably Holland, France, and Japan, and has sustained a steady flow of interest in his recordings and short, strange life. Why?

One obvious reason is precisely the strangeness of that life. As is well-known, Gould withdrew from the life of public performance in 1964 and became almost a hermit. Though he continued to record and broadcast prodigiously, both in music and in the radio-documentary form he helped to pioneer, he never again appeared on stage, or boarded another airplane or, other than for urgent business, left his home in Toronto. Already at that time he was a legend of eccentricity, humming audibly during performances and going about even in warm weather clad in overcoat, muffler, flat wool cap, and gloves. His hypochondria drove him into a self-medicated regime of painkillers, anti-anxiety drugs, sleep aids and other cross-prescribed pharmaceuticals that likely hastened his death from bronchial failure in 1982, aged just fifty.

Such circumstances presumably enhance an aura of bewitching strangeness in a performer. Gould is widely considered to have suffered from Asperger Syndrome, lately a condition of almost cliché appeal for its mixture of high-functioning autism and alluring oddity. And in back of it all, of course, lies Gould's vast talent as an interpreter and player of the classical keyboard corpus, in particular his career-long engagement with the works of Johann Sebastian Bach—though he always claimed as his favourite composer the much less famous Tudor court musician, Orlando Gibbons. Gould's startling renditions of Bach, especially the difficult *Goldberg Variations*—recorded by him twice, first as his debut release and second as almost the last record he did—reveal an artist of deep intelligence and somewhat twisted emotion. This ability combines alchemically with his personal circumstances to create what might be considered a textbook narrative of genius.

Despite recent popular sociology to the effect that genius is merely a matter of devoting hours to a certain task, the category retains widespread appeal as a marker of transcendental specialness. And yet, we must also recognize that there are many performers just as talented as Glenn Gould who are not favoured with the title. Rather than debunk genius as simple hard work, I suggest a different lesson. What I will call the Gould Conundrum consists in the fact that Gould managed to garner more than his fair share of attention, musical and otherwise, because of the vagaries of luck. In other words, his specialness lies not in ability but in success, and that success is only partly a function of ability. Indeed, ability has far less to do with success than we often imagine.

This finding has wide implications but I will focus here on what I believe are the most important ones, namely those pertaining to the idea of democracy. If success is not 'earned' in the way common sense usually imagines, then we have to rethink not only baseline notions such as merit and responsibility, but also the claims elites make upon subordinates in structured systems. More profoundly still, the very idea of democracy may be shown to be without foundation—something at once revealed and concealed in its paradoxical ability to influence the founding and direction of systems and states.

2. Scalable Effects

The key to understanding the success of Gould, or any other example of an individual who manages to outstrip all competition for our attention, is what economists call scalable effects. That is, the manner in which, for certain fields of endeavour and under favourable circumstances, the same work can generate more and more results with no further work needed. The phenomenon of scalable effects in turn has implications for all attempts to link merit and reward—attempts which lie at the heart of democratic thought either as goals (the ideal of meritocratic entitlement) or as fears (the perversion of elite entitlement).

So let us consider scalable activities. Contrast writing books with baking loaves of bread—both honest forms of toil, at least if you listen to the writers of books. While it's true that each copy of the book needs to be produced, what makes books scalable is that no further work is required on the part of the author to do so. Indeed, as reproduction and dissemination technologies evolve, the costs of reproduction approach zero. By far the largest costs in the standard book economy of the modern era were related to the printing, binding, and shipping of the material objects we call finished books, which is one reason printers also used to be publishers. Baking bread, on the other hand, necessarily proceeds loaf by loaf. The baker has his reproduction costs but also his work costs; bread doesn't bake itself. In the relevant sense, books do make themselves because they are beneficiaries of mechanical reproduction— tokens of the original type, which is produced once and for all. This, incidentally, was Socrates' complaint about them in Plato's *Phaedrus*: the written or printed word just keeps saying the same thing over and over again, as we say, like a broken record.

But notice that even a non-broken record says the same thing over and over again, just at greater length than the one marred by a scratch or imperfection. Recorded music is a perfect example of scalable effect, because here a single performance—or, more accurately, a series of recording sessions executed to create the illusion of a single performance—are laid down on tape or computer and then reproduced, potentially to infinity. Whereas before a musician had to perform his music to every new audience, whether of one or of one hundred, he or she can now reach a potentially limitless audience with just one bout of effort. And if the recipients are willing to pay for the experience, which they surely will be, the profit from that single effort is likewise without limit. This willingness does not compete with, and hence does not rule out, their being also willing to pay, perhaps even more, for a live performance of the same piece; but it does compete directly with both rival recorded performances and rival live ones. Opportunity costs of access to musical pleasure are absorbed into recorded music, despite its clear difference from performed music. Thus, I will almost certainly pay $10 to purchase a Glenn Gould CD, which I listen to again and again, rather than pay the same $10 to hear a one-off performance by my local piano legend. Yet, given the chance, I might pay that $10 and a whole lot more to hear Gould perform live, but that does not affect the scalable success of the original recording.

Music is thus an almost perfect example of a scalable good, better than books (even bestsellers compete only with other books, not with troubadours or wandering lyric poets) or films (blockbusters blow away their Cineplex competition, perhaps, but there is no such thing as 'live' film). The irony, staying with Gould for a moment longer, is that he was a dedicated opponent of what he called the competitive streak in public performance; and yet, with his foresighted advocacy of recorded music over performance, he scored the ultimate competitive victory. No other classical artist could hope to compete with his sales over the years.

Now, as we know, ability must be present to work this particular trick, but it is not as determinative as we like to think. Gould's initial reputation enhances his sales, and his growing reputation for that elusive—in fact empty—category of genius, pushes them still further. Success begets success, in other words, and the harsh truth about most markets, but especially those that hinge on human attention, is that there can only be a small number of winners. The result is not quite a winner-take-all or zero-sum game, but it is close enough to make a big difference: Gould's success leaches attention away from others who might (we don't know) be as deserving of it. Scalable activities tend to create lots of losers and few winners. The same is not true of bakers, for example, who will tend to distribute their success more evenly because demand is steady and supply is toilsome.

There may appear slight exceptions to this: one might think of the celebrated bakery with a long lineup next to one that is oddly bereft of customers. Are the two loaves really that different? This sort of minimarket is functioning in a mode past ample supply, and so is driven more by reputation than actual product, even if the product in question is indisputably better than its rivals (it may not be). Reputation, as such, is of course the ultimate scalable good, and one that free-rides on well-supplied markets to create artificial scarcity. Historically, there hasn't been enough bread to go around, just as this was once true of music before the advent of recording. Now that those markets are unhindered by actual scarcities, reputational ones may take hold. The point remains that even the most widely reputed baker still has to bake the loaves one at a time—indeed, such artisanal attention to detail may be part of what is being purchased by those in the long line, who clearly exist at a point where bread is not the staff of life.

Background economic and technological conditions determine which effects are scalable and which not, and the categories are not fixed. Just as music had become scalable because of early recording technology, further advances in the very same technology since Gould's death have nearly obliterated the cost of access to music altogether—advances that he, ironically given his financial dependency on record sales, ardently advocated. Now the good of recorded music is virtually a free public one, non-rival and non-excludable in the world of MP3 downloads (strictly legal or otherwise). Under these conditions, the musician may choose to fight a rearguard action over copyright control and prosecution of piracy; or, more cleverly, he or she may try to monetize the difference—ideally, the exclusion—between general audiences and special ones. That is, he or she may choose to make an album available for free online (general audience) but then charge a profitable fee for concert appearances and other exclusive opportunities (special audience). The same effect is achieved by an author who gives away his book via digital file but collects large sums for speaking engagements. It is worth noting that advocates of this content-for-free culture generally are already in such a reputational position that they can achieve such leverage; the majority of 'content providers' are not.

Claims about a beneficial long tail in online markets—lots of virtual shelf space for everything, hence no need to bet on winners—do not square with the evidence. Worse, the claims are often self-serving. As one commentator has put it, the advocates of the long tail are cheering a divide between *attention economy* and *cash economy*—hooray, they say, there's room for everyone's claims in the former!—but doing so from the far side of the latter. Yes, the traditional gatekeepers on content have been, or are being, removed: editors no longer control which books get published, which articles run; producers no longer keep musicians from potential audiences. But a new class of overlord is arising, the ones able to derive profit from the widespread human desire to express ourselves as individuals. They do this by various soft-impact means, including mining data from freely offered preferences on Facebook and Google, or gathering advertising revenue from the margins of websites with nearly costless editorial centres. Chris Anderson, a leading voice for this form of digital sharecropping, summed up the position with admirable frankness: "There's a lot of Free out there, and a lot of money to be made off it."[1] Meanwhile, those generating the free stuff—Anderson and others disingenuously call this generation a gift economy rather than an uncompensated attention economy—still face the demands of living in the cash economy. "[N]o matter how much we might love attention, we can't use it to meet our basic needs," critic Rob Horning has pointed out. "I can't send my landlord some attention in the mail in lieu of a rent check."[2]

The key, as always in a capital economy, is to convert attention (or the other effects that accrue to an activity) into cash and its equivalents. The main point here is that the attention need not be deserved in any deep or 'intrinsic' sense—whatever intrinsic might be thought to indicate. In a heavily mediated culture, for example, we observe the curious phenomenon of the pure celebrity, which is to say, someone who is famous simply for being famous. Moralists may mock such people and cynics grow depressed by them but, in strictly economic terms, celebrities are the ones who have the last laugh. Indeed, they have that laugh over and over at absolutely no cost to themselves (unless we count possible mental breakdowns or stints in rehab). Not only is no *further* work needed to generate more success as a celebrity, there is no work or talent of any kind anywhere in view. Now there's an economy of scale.

3. The Seventh Title

What lessons should be drawn from the Gould Conundrum and its variations? Well, that can be hard to see, because (to paraphrase Walter Benjamin) we understand backwards even though we live forwards. Looking back over the career of Gould, we construct a narrative that explains his wild, one-in-a-million success. That narrative will, in his case, speak about genius and eccentricity, about unavailability and disappearance. But the basic fact about Gould's career was precisely availability. His music was widely reproduced, indeed to a degree unknown to any previous performer. Columbia Records, signing him in 1955, took at least two risks: one, that his choice of the *Goldberg Variations*, a relatively obscure and forbiddingly difficult work, would appeal to an audience; and two, far more significantly, that he would succeed *at all.* That he did so was a function at least as much of luck as of talent. We cannot quantify this luck precisely because our backcast narratives do not allow us to extricate talent from anything else.

Was Gould one in a million? Absolutely; his success is a matter of record, in all senses. Was he destined to be one in a million? Absolutely not; his success was never assured, no matter how much talent he had. One way we can alter our intuitions about such matters is to recall that human abilities, however esoteric, are likely to be distributed in roughly normal patterns. Obvious cases in point are physical characteristics such as height or weight. Though there is considerable range, such that basketball star Yao Ming (7'6") and jockey Angel Cordero (4'11") are both within it, the vast number of people cluster at or near the mean. Likewise with weight. As in all normal distributions, outliers become increasingly rare at the edges and simply do not appear past a certain point. Not so, however, with wealth or fame, which can increase potential without limit and hence tend to produce top-heavy distributions where a very small number concentrate the bulk. Although rare, extraordinary musical ability is closer to height than to wealth in the realm of distributions, since, despite claims about transcendental or god-given genius, it remains a function of the human species. No matter how much of an outlier Glenn Gould is in terms of talent, he still falls within a range defined by human ability. Musical *success*, on the other hand, is more like wealth than it is like height—and that is the point.

The moral of this perhaps over-long story—a narrative against narratives, if you like—is to loosen our intuitive shackling of success to merit. I do not suggest that Gould did not deserve his success, in the basic sense of having a right to it when it came. What I do suggest is that such success does not belong to him by some special right, or entitlement, placed under the sign of talent or, still less, genius. Not only do matters of fortune condition all narratives of success—Gould's birthdate, the material conditions of his society, his physical and psychological proclivities, etc.—but sheer randomness enters into all markets where human action is negotiated with other forces, such as attention, cash, and happiness. Though these markets may seem to exhibit somewhat stable outcome vectors (prices fluctuate with supply and demand, for example) they are subject both to pathologies and, more startling, to non-inductive random events.

In the former category belong all those surprising stories of how people fail to act according to rational economic interest: driving ten miles, and so spending a dollar in gasoline, in order to save fifty cents at a yard sale. Or, more seriously, the consistent position-effects that show people willing to accept less as long as others also have less (e.g., preferring to be one of ten people at $90,000, rather than one of the nine people at $100,000 when one person has $200,000). In the latter category belong those truly unpredictable events or effects where a market collapses unexpectedly or, more pleasantly, pays off big with a runaway bestseller or surprise blockbuster. The non-inductive nature of such events is often proved negatively: not only can we not predict them, we cannot replicate them in future because we cannot explain them via the past. Or more precisely: our explanations, while they sound accurate, are misplaced. And so the dispiriting spectacle of next season's book-list being dominated by what worked last year but never will again.[3]

To reiterate, my interest here is less to give an alternative account of success—there are enough of those circulating already—than to consider what follows *politically* if success and merit are not intrinsically linked. In particular, we can reveal a fundamental instability in the idea of democracy when we reflect on the possibility of unmerited (or only semi-merited) success. Furthermore, this forever renewed instability may turn out to be the real meaning of the idea of democracy.

Jacques Rancière has offered a provocative version of this argument. He analyzes the recurring hatred of democracy that runs from Plato's vivid denunciation in *Republic* Book VIII to fashionable postmodern critics of our day. While the two species of opposition may seem distinct—an appalled vision of licentious desire run amok, on the one hand, and a cynical awareness of sham promises in the rhetoric of freedom and individual rights, on the other—in fact the two critiques are one. That is, both are rooted in an awareness that the basic fiction of democratic politics, equality between persons, issues in pathological results. The vision of an orgiastic, rudderless state, ripe for the tyrannical picking, differs only in costume and technology from the hyper-mediated consumer society, full of brand-conscious purveyors of their own narcissism, that so exercises the ire of the contemporary pundit, left or right. Both mistake democratic society or democratic government for the idea of democracy, and so both denounce the symptom without regard for the underlying condition that makes it possible.

To see that condition, Rancière invites us to consider what Hannah Arendt identified as the founding act of all social movements and states, the *arkhé*, or commencement. But this is a commencement that both begins and, crucially, justifies. Indeed, as Rancière puts the matter, *arkhé* is crucially doubled: "It is the anticipation of the right to command in the act of commencing and the verifying of the power of commencing in the exercise of commanding."[4] Such a combination of anticipation and act, starting and seizing, is the essence of all politics, the violence necessary to the moment of founding which we likewise observe through Derrida's account of *force of law*.[5] Politics is distinct from other forms of human action-coordination and organization in making a claim, however disingenuous *post facto*, for legitimacy or entitlement. Those who govern trumpet, or perhaps just gesture towards, the reasons or qualities that make them suited to the guiding rather than guided position.

In fact, we can be more precise than this if we follow a debate within the Platonic *oeuvre*. In *Laws* Book III Plato attempts to order the natural facts that establish title, in part to counteract the lawlessness towards which desire inclines us. Lacking the transcendental guidance of a divine shepherd, lacking too the *ex cathedra* reliability of a genuine philosopher-king, how might we organize ourselves and avoid what Rancière calls the "perturbed natural relations" in democracy? The natural order suggests a "census of titles" that are at once aligned with how things are in the world around us *and* offer hierarchical power relations with prescriptive force. This census shows the following natural hierarchies:

    i. parents over children
    ii. the old over the young
    iii. masters over slaves
    iv. the high-born over the no-account
    v. the strong over the weak
    vi. the knowledgeable over the ignorant

Notice some revealing features of this array of power relations. The first four titles are species of kinship relation, whether directly or indirectly. Indeed, we may view them as nested rings of kinship, whereby the procreative relation is expanded concentrically from actual parentage (i) to generalized parentage (ii) and then to metaphorical (iii) and positional (iv) forms. But the latter two are, on this census, no less natural than the first two.

The last two titles in the list point to a more direct relation with the natural order, bypassing the biological order of parentage and birth. Here, qualities belonging to the superordinate group—strength and knowledge, however defined and no matter how controversial—are understood to confer a natural authority over the subordinate others.

We should be grateful, perhaps, that title (vi) even makes the list, since most political regimes have seemed content to leave it out of account. Naturally, too, most regimes, even or especially the most 'enlightened' ones, will in practice rely on a mixed bunch of these titles, such that pure types of gerontocracy, aristocracy, and epistemocracy will be hard to find, and even the baldest form of realist regime will feel the need to advert to other titles than mere strength. The key in all cases is the claim to title. "That is effectively when politics commences," Rancière notes, "when the principle of government is separated from the law of kinship, all the while claiming to be representative of nature."[6]

This is essential to the idea of politics. But what about democratic politics? Here we observe the seventh and most illuminating of the titles included in Plato's census:

vii. the drawing of lots

From where, suddenly, does this strange form of authority-claim arise? Lacking any connection to the natural order such as we observed in titles (i) through (vi), the idea of random selection would seem disqualified *prima facie* as a form of title. Worse, while it is certainly true that the luck of the draw can establish hierarchical distributions, is it not the case that the claim will always be challenged because it is so flimsy? That is, we seem to defer the justification problem forever. All participants may have had reason to enter the draw when the outcome was unknown, taking their chance on success, but what incentives do the losers retain for obeying the winners when the outcome is a function of mere chance? How can such authority be maintained *going forward*?

Such deferral is thus also, in its way, a return—to the moment before we initiated the draw in order to establish title. If we lack prior willingness to abide by the rules of the draw (to cooperate, in game-theoretic parlance), what is there to keep us from not playing along afterwards (defecting, in the same language)? And if that prior willingness to abide was indeed present, we are forced to wonder what it was based on. Surely *that willingness*, whatever it is, is the real source of the title, not the draw itself?

4. The Title That Is No Title

This suspicion concerning hidden prior willingness is indeed warranted. That would seem to make title (vii) a deception or illusion. And yet, accepting the truth of prior willingness can also, paradoxically, allay the worry that title (vii) is illegitimate. "The democratic scandal simply consists in revealing this," Rancière notes: "there will never be, under the name of politics, a single principle of the community, legitimating the acts of government based on laws inherent to the coming together of human communities."[7] The democratic legitimation crisis is a permanent one. But this 'scandal' may be another name for 'opportunity'. Once the dream of an "innate virtue of sociability" is abandoned, we can begin to see the prospects for salvaging the democratic ideal precisely as something without innate qualities, and without price.

To see how this might be, consider, first, the obvious but not always understood idea that the ancient Greeks viewed luck or fortune very differently than we do today. The modern conception emphasizes randomness, and hence lack of identity with reason or virtue, even (or especially) in colloquial expression such as "You have to be smart to be lucky and lucky to be smart." That is, luck is viewed as external to qualities of merit that might otherwise be considered decisive in success; you can cultivate these internal qualities, and indeed doing so may increase the chances of a superaddition of good luck, but luck itself remains distinct from them. But the colloquial expressions likewise acknowledge that the conception's roots are tangled in more searching early modern positions, notably Machiavelli's view in *The Prince* that *virtù* and *fortuna* are close but antagonistic cousins: the first stresses preparation, readiness and attention to opportunity; the second, while providing that very opportunity, retains elements of contingency and unpredictability that cannot be mastered.

Thus the famous passage where Machiavelli figures Fortune as a woman who must be briskly seduced: "I conclude, then, that so long as Fortune varies and men stand still, they will prosper while they suit the times, and fail when they do not. But I do feel this: that it is better to be rash than timid, for Fortune is a woman, and the man who wants to hold her down must beat and bully her. We see that she yields more often to men of this stripe than to those who come coldly toward her."[8] Or, in a slightly less abusive language, the familiar and very modern maxim that "Fortune favours the brave."

In fact Machiavelli's position here is, as so often, transitional. He straddles two worlds, the pre-modern and the modern, by combining two world views, the pagan and the Christian, and arrives at a conception of fortune that is also doubled, with a sense of brute luck mitigated by the sense of opportunity. "I think it may be true that Fortune governs half more or less of our actions," he says in the same chapter, "but that even so she leaves the other half more or less in our power to control."[9] There are elements here of the lingering fatalistic medieval *weltanschauung* which viewed Fortune as the bitch goddess and symbolized her workings on the famously inescapable wheel; but there is also a celebration of preparation and action, the warrior code of the Roman tradition who can tame the capricious woman. Hence the celebration of *virtù* in its basic etymology, as the masculine quality of boldness, over inherited notions of virtue as general good character. In this way Machiavelli becomes, though he and they may not know it, the patron saint of professional athletes and soldiers everywhere, with their precarious combinations of practice and training with superstition and voodoo. He is also, in his attention to war as the prince's primary concern, the essential bridge between Sun Tzu and the modern theorists of armed conflict. As the much-repeated paraphrase of Field Marshall von Moltke has it: "No battle plan survives contact with the enemy"— which is of course not an argument against planning but one in favour of adaptability.[10]

It would be left to Pascal and the other pioneers of probability to thematize luck in ways that both recognize and codify its principled randomness. This growing scientific account does not reduce the role of chance in human affairs, of course; nor does it, on the whole, prevent many people from guiding their views and actions according to erroneous conceptions of probability.[11] (There would be no gambling industry otherwise.) But it does shift the baseline account in an irrevocable fashion, such that when we think about fortune—assuming we think about it rather than stumble in slightly irrational fear of it—we see chance as a mute and implacable set of forces, like vectors in a gravitational field. There are in reality no luck streaks, or hot dice, or (still less) effective propitiatory gestures when it comes to the modern gods of chance—who are not gods, but factors. Thus the general view, at least in reflective positions, that lucky results are somewhat, if not entirely, undeserved. If, for example, one has the good luck to have wealthy parents, there is something unseemly, to the democratic mind, in considering that stroke of good fortune a matter of entitlement or merit. The old saw has it that the scion of a rich and well-connected family, such as might go on to Yale as a legacy of his father and then, perhaps, ascend to the United States presidency likewise, is someone who was born on third base and thought he'd hit a triple.

This generally sound mistrust of social luck is nevertheless tempered everywhere by traces of elite self-congratulation. Sometimes, indeed, there can be a fine line between deserved success and mere inherited privilege. Birthright lotteries—where an individual happens to be born, under what social and political conditions—determine a significant measure of future possibility, even when other factors (intelligence, resourcefulness, optimism) might be equal. Likewise, prevailing social and cultural conditions in local contexts will determine which elements of personality, which skills and aptitudes, will be most fully rewarded. A person of moderately high scholarly aptitude can earn a very comfortable living in a country with a public university system, for example, even as the same person might not be able to pass the gate in a smaller, private system or in a nation where higher education is less valued and so not publicly supported. That is purposely an example of fine distinction; when we imagine other differentials, say between those persons able to adapt to quick technological change versus those who are not, or between persons with enough food margin to allow any sort of education versus those who have no such opportunity, the point becomes starker.

All of this is familiar to theorists of democratic justice, of course, and there is no need to rehearse here the details of the various theoretical mechanisms devised to cope with the problems: Rawls's veil of ignorance, Dworkin's lottery, Nozick's contractual transfers, and so on. I want merely to highlight the underlying dynamic that motivates such theoretical moves, namely that luck enters the systems of political legitimacy at a very early point. Indeed it might be said that luck is the problem that democratic political theory is at pains to solve. Some have more than others (where 'have how?' and 'more of what?' are important subsidiary questions) and the basic problem is how to decide whether, and when, that more is justified or merely a matter of contingency. At the margins of all such theories will be a threshold question, too often unasked but nevertheless omnipresent: what is the difference between the kinds of luck that political theory should address, even control, and the kinds that remain beyond human (or at least theoretical) intervention? Physical beauty is a birthright lottery; so is height; so is cognitive quickness. Should we control for these, as we control for income level and competitive social mobility? One has only to recall Kurt Vonnegut's anti-utopian 1961 short story "Harrison Bergeron" to see, vividly, what a radically egalitarian Handicapper-General might generate in the way of perversions when faced with differences in ability generated by the genetic lottery: gifted 14-year-old Harrison, destined to wear weights on his wrists and ankles to temper his athletic ability, and a set of buzzing headphones to mute his searing intellect.[12]

The ancient *title that is no title* is not driven to such theoretical pathologies. It does not regard fortune as mere luck, or randomness in distribution; and so it does not commit the conceptual error of treating fortune as both inevitable *and* subject to intervention under the sign of justice. Instead, fortune is conceived as a divine force which, without governing to a specific cosmic purpose as in so-called 'intelligent design', takes matters out of the hands of men and places them in a region less contaminated by interest, confusion, and partial knowledge. The lottery has a mystic legitimacy that is greater, not lesser, than the rational choices of individuals. The result may be, as we say, *hard luck* on the recipient of the black ball—think only of the celebratory violence of Shirley Jackson's much-anthologized 1948 short story, "The Lottery," in which a bucolic New England town preserves itself through the random selection of an individual who is ritually stoned to death.[13] But it may, equally, be the wonderful *luck of the draw* that occurs when my number comes up, or my ticket is chosen. As the state-sponsored gambling ads have it, "You can't win if you don't play!"

In the Platonic census, drawing lots is the decision that lies beyond question precisely because it was made beyond choice—in fact, drawing lots generates not so much a decision as a founding judgment, external to and hence not to be assailed by the claims of reason. Legitimacy must acknowledge this mystical foundation, or invite an infinite regress of justificatory disputes. Note this apparently incidental paragraph from Jackson's story, for example:

The original paraphernalia for the lottery had been lost long ago, and the black box now resting on the stool had been put into use even before Old Man Warner, the oldest man in town, was born. Mr. Summers spoke frequently to the villagers about making a new box, but no one liked to upset even as much tradition as was represented by the black box. There was a story that the present box had been made with some pieces of the box that had preceded it, the one that had been constructed when the first people settled down to make a village here. Every year, after the lottery, Mr. Summers began talking again about a new box, but every year the subject was allowed to fade off without anything's being done. The black box grew shabbier each year: by now it was no longer completely black but splintered badly along one side to show the original wood color, and in some places faded or stained.

The lottery is here executed by a literal black box, a decision-machine whose very material origins are obscured in a sort of ship-of-Theseus identity mystery and local antiquity. The box is beyond question because it is entirely opaque, both in its workings and its beginnings. Then note, by contrast, how the lottery-like schemes of democratic political theory, which attempt to align reason with devices of justification, fail precisely because they try to combine transparency (of justification) with opacity (of the device). That is, by presuming that reason and chance can be reconciled, they only end up obscuring the fact that chance, so far from being a corrigible aspect of human affairs, is their very basis. Not just the luck of the draw, in other words; luck is the draw.

5. The Real World of Democracy

Lest one think the objection is restricted to imaginary, theoretical or thought-experimental exercises, consider that the very same point can be made against virtually all real-world mechanisms of distribution and decision. An election for representation, no matter its degree of stated or realized transparency, is always a device for (as Hegel put it) *transforming quantity into quality*. The numbers game of totting up votes to execute a majority decision—a decision which, to be sure, often falls well short of a population majority, or even a popular-vote majority—

is no less and no more than window dressing for entrenched interests, or perhaps, less cynically, a species of performance art gesturing in the direction of legitimacy.

We abide by these decisions according to nostrums of sanctioned representation, and accept the resulting power wielded by states, including the threshold power of holding a monopoly on unpunished use of force. But we do this not because we sincerely believe in the quantity-quality transformation, but rather because we realize that other sorts of mechanisms or schemas are likely worse, and that this one, despite its many failings, at least presumes to work in accordance with some supposed rational public sphere concerning 'debate on the issues' or, at least, with media exposure such that we can judge the 'leadership qualities' or 'democratic vision' of the contenders for supremacy. Let me hasten to add that I am here thinking of robust democracies—the United States, Great Britain, France, Canada—rather than cases at the margins, where the system just described is subject only to more corruption, abuse, and declension from anything like genuine legitimacy.

Nor, again, is the point absent in conceptions of social function that privilege markets. Every market with more complexity than primitive barter is structured and regulated to the benefit of some parties over others. It is in the nature of markets, however, to claim benefits from less regulation even if that means ignoring or covering over what regulation is actually present. The spectre of Adam Smith is invoked so often in defence of the 'invisible hand' function that it is easy to forget that Smith favoured highly regulated markets that would, not unlike a justificatory scheme of the liberal stripe, make people's inherently selfish individual desires redound to the benefit of the weaker and less able. At the same time, even a much freer market than this is subject to internal pathologies that skew its benefits. The introduction of capital, which is infinitely scalable because it is fungible and non-perishable, is, as Locke ascertained, the end of any hope for basic market parity. Pooled capital is not subject to any of the natural 'headwind' or 'gravity' effects on accumulation, such as the limits of human enjoyment or the contingencies of fortune-reversal. This is not to say that one cannot lose money just as one can gain it, often very quickly; it is, rather, to observe that money has the ability to expand to geometric proportions through transaction and accumulation, whereas other goods can only expand arithmetically.

When capital then is entwined with the zero-sum games associated with positional goods—goods whose enjoyment by you entails their absence to me—the resulting markets are, in effect, structured as winner-take-all economies. In effect, every aspect of human life is susceptible to a play of competitive status anxiety, and, human beings remaining after all primates highly sensitive to dominance, there is very little to countervail this complex of declensions. The rapid accumulations of wealth and status are tethered to privileged individuals, in other words, through a series of effects: (1) birthright, including especially inheritance; (2) enhanced personal opportunity; (3) preferential attachment from outside agencies; and finally (4) cumulative advantage. To see the drift here, consider a case drawn from cultural or social capital rather than capital *simpliciter*: academic reputation.

Other things being equal, a number of good articles are published each year in scholarly journals. The one written by the full professor at Harvard may be no better, though also no worse, than the one written by the assistant professor at Wesleyan. Blind reviewing procedures notwithstanding, there is a strong chance that the former article will find a place in a prestigious journal—the Harvard professor knows to aim high, and knows how to write in a certain approved style. There is then an even higher chance, post-publication, that her article will be 'taken up' by the profession, even as the Wesleyan professor's piece lies unnoticed (except perhaps by friends and a few loyal graduate students). Citation of the two articles now becomes a winner-take-all economy: every time the Harvard-produced article is cited, it becomes still more likely it will be cited again, and again. Citation indexes will then measure this effect as an effect of quality, which in some sense it genuinely is, and reward the Harvard professor accordingly. At some point, the given article may achieve the critical mass of an article which it is impossible not to cite.[14] At this point, there is no headwind or gravity on the article at all: its success is infinitely scalable.

It is not always easy to discern the relationship between quality and success. Glenn Gould or Dan Brown are the equivalents, in their markets, of the Harvard professor. The former was, arguably, a genius while the latter is, at best, an adept marketer of intrigue. The market both cares and does not care: it is not in the business of rewarding quality, only of maximizing success. In short, we do well always to uncouple any presumed connection between market achievement and worth—but also to uncouple the opposite connection, namely that prejudice which assumes market success to be incompatible with quality. The first prejudice might be called the *myth of meritocracy*; the second might be called the *hatred of democracy*. It is obvious that the two prejudices can often be entertained within the same political culture, if not sometimes the same person.

Matters are slightly more complicated, also more serious, when it comes to other kinds of economies, especially the entwined economy of capito-democracy. Here at least two important developments are generated by the market-distribution mechanisms, neither of which has directly to do with the usual justice-theory distribution issues and therefore cannot be addressed by their mechanisms, even supposing such mechanisms were effective. There are, first, the reduction to transaction of all social matters; and, second, the creation of entrenched rather than circulating elites. Each can be addressed only briefly here. (I will have more to say about entrenched versus circulating elites later in "What Are Intellectuals For?" and the "Wage Slavery" essay.)

Transactional reduction occurs when an aspect of human affairs is conducted under the presumption of contract. That is, every time we approach interactions as bargaining sessions, including those bargains where the others are not present (they may be competitors for a contested or positional good, for example), we reinforce the ideological dominance of the market over any other way of conceiving the situation—and hence ourselves. Markets and, within them, contracts are of course appropriate for all kinds of interactions, including the efficient exchange of goods and services. There may also be valid non-monetary contracts such as promises or oaths, which bind not because of force or threat of punishment. But such non-monetary contracts are a limit case that should highlight the issue of transactional reduction. If such a non-monetary contract can be reduced, in the event of dispute or non-compliance, to a monetary contract—as when a marriage becomes a battle for estates, or a person 'buys out' his promise—then the original force of the contract is obliterated, replaced by a different kind of constraint than the 'moral' one originally intended.

Indeed, this obliteration can be undertaken consciously, if perhaps cynically. As mentioned in the previous essay, I may decide to consider a fine for illegal parking as merely the price, high but bearable, of leaving my car somewhere. (We must assume the penalty does not involve towing.) On a larger scale, a corporation might shoulder the costs of state punishment for violating environmental standards as merely 'the cost of doing business', with no attendant regard for why the standards are there in the first place. This is distinct from 'greenwashing' costs which, however open to objection that they are paid grudgingly or just for show, do not seek to change one kind of cost into another. In taking on the parking ticket or the state sanction, these actions mutate *fines* into *prices*, in effect buying out the legal or ethical sanction.[15] Such mutations, so routine that we hardly notice them, or perhaps dismiss them even when noticed, collectively act to undermine the authority of the original obligation or constraint.

Naturally the largest such reduction comes with the monetary corruption of the electoral process in putatively democratic systems. Beneath the dark humour of that familar joke about "the best government money can buy" lies a bleak truth: the cost of seeking and gaining election in many systems is prohibitive. Those who can shoulder it incur many debts along the way, which leads to a further related reduction, namely regulatory capture. (Other examples of this process are analyzed in "The Tomist" and "'Fuck You'," in this collection.) Regulatory capture is the process by which an interested group, say a cartel of oil companies or investment banks, can influence government policy to reduce or relax the regulations that would otherwise constrain their actions (and profits). The agency created for the purpose of regulating a sector or commercial element has been 'captured' such that it, instead, promotes the interests of the dominant players. The gamekeeper has turned poacher, in the popular idiom; in my current terms, regulatory capture is the point where moneyed interests are not only converting fines into prices, they are actually buying out the fining mechanism before the fact.

Entrenched elites act to reinforce these aspects of transaction reduction because they tend to be precisely those who have incurred debts and obligations on the path to status and success. The common democratic complaint against elites is often wrong-headed or confused. In theory an elite is merely a subset of the given population whose abilities are best suited to the task at hand. There is nothing amiss about this efficient matching of skill to work; what bothers people about elites is the assumption of *other* forms of superiority: when gifted professional athletes assume an arrogant social manner, or scholars disdain popular taste, or politicians think they are above the law. None of these connections is warranted, but none is necessary either. Especially in the realm of the title that is no title, the elite in question is one of random generation: the ability here is really just availability. The unfortunate consequence of generalized complaints about elites is the cultivation of an opposite pathology which I have elsewhere labelled *Gumpism*: the celebration of ignorance and stupidity as virtues of 'honesty' and 'like-me-ness'.[16] Nowadays we might do better to call it something like the *Palin-drone Effect*.[17]

The democratic issue resides not with the bare fact of elites, then, but with entrenched elites, especially when they conjoin money and politics in capito-democracy. Elites are entrenched when they are reproduced over generations with little or no variance in cross-section identity. Circulating elites, by contrast, are those where pre-eminence is a reward of demonstrated ability—or even generated randomly, as when the leadership of a club rotates by lot. In general terms, elites tend to entrenchment precisely because their associated privileges work to confer advantage in successive iterations of distribution: they eliminate headwind by creating entitlement, as when the son of a wealthy father begins life with a competitive advantage that can be leveraged over and over. This need not be the case for non-monetary elites, as when they are generated by genuine meritocracy or in open competitions, but there is strong evidence that over time even such meritocratic systems tend to ossify, moving from general circulation (equal opportunity of success for the able) to entrenched (reproduction of a ruling class or type). Consider competitive college admission as one kind of allegedly meritocratic mechanism, intended to guarantee a circulating elite. Experience shows that the circulation effect is actually small, because those with capital advantages enjoy the conditions where those advantages can, as it were, be converted into competitive cognitive advantage in the form of better coaching for tests, closer schooling in the skills rewarded by the tests, and so on.

Can we sense again the allure of the seventh title? The only way to counter the entrenchment effects of elites is to make privilege a matter of randomness. If that privilege were to include the matter of being a democratic representative, an elected leader, then the incentives and disincentives associated with transactional reduction would disappear. Debts would not be incurred on the way to office, and regulatory capture would be rendered difficult if not impossible. As long as markets continued to function in some aspects of human affairs there would still be individual incentives to convert fines into prices, but only on a minor scale, and with reference to matters that were trivial enough that the resulting contaminations could be tolerated. The market would take its proper place as a mechanism of exchange rather than as an overarching presupposition of every human interaction, and politics would be free of the deleterious influence, now so pervasive, of the moneyed interest in all its forms.

Of course, none of this is ever going to happen in the world we know. So what can be said now?

Rancière, for his part, will say this: "We do not live in democracies." Instead,

> [w]e live in States of oligarchic law ... States where the power of the oligarchy is limited by a dual recognition of popular sovereignty and individual liberties. We know the advantages of these sorts of states. They hold free elections. These elections essentially ensure that the same dominant personnel is reproduced, albeit under interchangeable labels, but the ballot boxes are generally not rigged and one can verify it without risking one's life. The administration is not corrupt, except in matters of public contracts where administration is confounded with the interests of the dominant parties. Individual liberties are respected, although there are notable exceptions here to do with whatever relates to the protection of borders and territorial security.[18]

And so on, in a portrait that is all too familiar, and depressing, to most of us. What we routinely call 'democracies' are just oligarchies "that leave enough room for democracy to feed its passion."[19]

That passion is significant, however, and not always subject to domestication and perversion. As Rancière himself will go on to say: "To understand what democracy means is to hear the struggle that is at stake in the word: not simply the tones of anger and scorn with which it can be imbued but, more profoundly, the slippages and reversals of meaning that it authorizes, or that one authorizes oneself to make with regard to it."[20]

I am going to authorize myself to make this slippage and reversal: out of the ruins of the regulatory capture of democracy comes the gift of democracy, democracy as a gift.

6. Democracy's Gift

A gift economy is one that cannot be reduced to transactions. Though it is true that many gift exchanges fall prey precisely to transaction—one has only to think of the massive competitive-consumption market created each year for Christmas—true gifting is performed without expectation of return or recompense. A gift, to be a gift, must have no calculable value. That is why, in economic terms, gifts constitute *dead-weight losses:* the giver by definition commits more resources in the gesture of the gift than the receiver himself would have done. Even welcome gifts generate losses because they execute a transaction at higher than optimum cost; unwelcome gifts are *a fortiori* propositions in loss, since the costs are the same and the transaction values even lower. Conceived as an economic exchange, gifts are at best inefficient and at worst create negative value.

But that is not how they should be conceived, and the paradox of gift-as-dead-weight-loss shows us the limits of usefulness in the economic conception—a gift of its own sort, generating insight. The fact that gift economies can operate alongside, or beneath, even complex, capital-dominated market economies is a hint at what democratic politics could be like. Democracy's gift is twofold, turning on the double genitive of its 'of': the gift that democracy bestows, but also the bestowal of democracy itself. This doubling is the gift that keeps on giving: an economy without gravity or headwind, infinitely scalable not in generating wealth or consolidating position, but offering an infinite non-zero-sum game of justification, a game without an equilibrium that dominates either weakly or strongly.

To be sure, these remarks are offered in a spirit of optimism. Transactional reduction everywhere destroys the possibility of the democratic gift, making the incalculable precisely calculable, offering a finite game of winners and losers, dominant positions and exclusions. The spirit and the reality of democratic politics have ever been in conflict, and it is only the strength of the former that keeps the latter from a final cynical reduction. The tension between the two cannot be resolved, but perhaps it can be leveraged. What does this mean?

The first step should be the elimination of any professional political class, an entrenched elite whose susceptibility to influence by other interests, especially capital-fueled ones, is beyond argument. Practical measure: campaign finance reform, so that deep pockets are no longer a necessary condition of aspiring to public office. Practical outcome: circulating elites, bearing the title which is no title.

A more searching move would involve keener awareness of the birthright lottery, both within nations and between them, such that individuals who enjoy inherited benefits, including basic ones of being born in a wealthy nation rather than a destitute one, know that this enjoyment is a function of multiple contingencies. If the fact of the birthright lottery is taken seriously, new distributive justice measures acquire force. Practical measures: raising inheritance tax, or eliminating inherited capital transfer altogether; citizenship taxes to offset gross inequalities between nations. Practical outcome: global citizens with a sense of responsibility for more than just their own good fortune.

Next, a shift in conceptual derivation. For four hundred years, liberal-democratic politics has argued that the unit of justification in the game of legitimacy is the private individual, in particular that individual as the owner of actual property or at least of desires and projects which are beyond general question. But without attempting to challenge this edifice of modern thought, consider a shift in value that can change the game drastically: the public justification of the line between public and private. Not only does this shift insist that those spaces and things called private constantly call for justification, it means that those justifications, themselves public, generate a discursive community of citizens. Practical measure: more public spaces in which the priority of the public over the private is explicit. Practical outcome: engaged citizens maintaining a public realm rather than self-interested consumers exchanging taxes for services in a series of private transactions.

Finally, even a pluralistic liberal-democratic political order requires a shared ethical orientation at the baseline that, at a minimum, recognizes the other as a fellow citizen rather than a market competitor. I have argued elsewhere for a hybrid liberal-Aristotelian version of this baseline in the form of political virtues which at once sustain citizenship and defer to the fact of pluralism.[21] Whether that version is successful is not for me to judge; I will just note that it is consistent with an even less onerous baseline commitment to the value of *sympathy* in political life. I mean by this not empathy—actual identification with the pain of another, even supposing that possible—but what Smith meant in *The Theory of Moral Sentiments*, where he takes full measure of the innate selfishness of the modern individual even as he demonstrates how to leverage that selfishness to greater goods.

Consider again the striking passage from its opening pages, quoted earlier in the Introduction: "How selfish soever man may be supposed, there are evidently some principles in his nature, which interest him in the fortunes of others, and render their happiness necessary to him, though he derives nothing from it, except the pleasure of seeing it," Smith notes. "Of this kind is pity or compassion, the emotion we feel for the misery of others, when we either see it, or are made to conceive it in a very lively manner." But the exercise of compassion actually turns on another cognitive ability, namely imagination, which requires a kind of ethical and political cultivation. Otherwise, we have the perverse ability to remain unmoved by the suffering of others, even those close to us. "Though our brother is on the rack, as long as we ourselves are at our ease, our senses will never inform us of what he suffers. They never did, and never can, carry us beyond our own person, and it is by the imagination only that we can form any conception of what are his sensations ... By the imagination, we place ourselves in his situation." This ethical imagination is itself a kind of gift, both in the having and in the exercise of it—another doubled 'of'. Imagination is its own reward, but it also makes for the ability to see the other as relevantly like me, vulnerable and contingent, and so to see myself for the first time.

The practical measure here? Nothing less than the cultivation of human possibility. And the practical outcome? Just democracy, more or less.

Notes:

1 Chris Anderson, *Free! The Future of a Radical Price* (Hyperion, 2009); see also Anderson, *The Long Tail: Why the Future of Business Is Selling Less of More* (Hyperion, 2006). Anderson was heavily criticized for cribbing large parts of the former book from Wikipedia, though one could view that as costless content-provision in action.

2 Rob Horning, "Your Brain is the New Factory Floor," at *PopMatters*, 10 August 2009; http://www.popmatters.com/pm/column/109584-your-brain-is-the-new-factory-floor/P0/

3 A very funny narrative dissection of this phenomenon can be found in Steve Hely's recent novel, *How I Became A Famous Novelist* (Black Cat; Grove/Atlantic, 2009), which includes a notional *New York Times* bestseller list with pitch-perfect parodies of the sorts of books found there.

4 Jacques Rancière, *Hatred of Democracy [La haine de la démocratie]* (trans. Steve Corcoran; Verso, 2006), p. 39.

5 Jacques Derrida, "Force of Law: The Mystical Foundation of Authority," in Drucilla Cornel, ed., *Deconstruction and the Possibility of Justice* (Routledge, 1992); see also his *Rogues: Two Essays on Reason* (Stanford University Press, 2005).

6 Rancière, *Hatred of Democracy*, p. 40.

7 *Ibid.*, p. 51.

8 Machiavelli, *The Prince*, ch. 25.

9 *Ibid.*, ch. 25.

10 As so often, the original version is not quite as pithy: "No plan of operations extends with certainty beyond the first encounter with the enemy's main strength." Originally in Graf Helmuth von Moltke, *Militarische Werke*. vol. 2, part 2., pp. 33-40; English trans. found in Daniel J. Hughes, ed., *Moltke on the Art of War: Selected Writings* (Presidio, 1993). p. 45-47.

11 See Ian Hacking, *The Taming of Chance* (Cambridge University Press, 1990) for a lucid and bracing account of these developments.

12 The opening paragraph of Vonnegut's story goes like this: "The year was 2081, and everybody was finally equal. They weren't only equal before God and the law. They were equal every which way. Nobody was smarter than anybody else. Nobody was better looking than anybody else. Nobody was stronger or quicker than anybody else. All this equality was due to the 211th, 212th, and 213th Amendments to the Constitution, and to the unceasing vigilance of agents of the United States Handicapper General." Harrison is taken away from his parents by agents of the Handicapper General; they do not notice.

13 Shirley Jackson, "The Lottery"; first published in *The New Yorker* (June 26, 1948).

14 See John Rawls, "Two Concepts of Rules," *Philosophical Review* 64:1 (January 1955): 3-32.

15 I owe this way of making the point to discussions with Mark Migotti. Migotti imagines a region where the towns of Fineville and Priceburg share a border; in the former, the law's sanction for illegal parking is $10, while in the latter the cost of a parking space is likewise $10. Is there a difference between the two costs, and if so, what is it exactly? The possibility of that difference is the aperture or liminal space of the current argument.

16 See Mark Kingwell, *Dreams of Millennium* (Viking, 1996), chs. 1 and 3.

17 Sarah Palin's extended genius at playing this game makes her a democratic phenomenon of a particular postmodern sort: the mangled English, the flat contradictions, the complaints of 'gotcha' questions from the 'lamestream' media, the post of aggrieved outsider—all lend her campaigns the status of performance art. "Washington was stunned by the emergence of this feisty outsider from the North," one columnist noted. "For decades, political leaders had seduced voters with their fancy talk and pretty words. But Palin refused to be a slave to oratory or grandiloquence or basic syntax. She liberated the English language from the rigid orthodoxy of meaning, because in America even words should have freedom: the freedom to appear wherever they'd like, almost as if emerging by chance or random draw." A sample: "My concern has been the atrocities there in Darfur," Palin once said, "and the relevance to me with that issue as we spoke about Africa and some of the countries there that were kind of the people succumbing to the dictators and the corruption of some collapsed governments on the continent." As the columnist concluded: "Words truer been have spoken never." (Scott Feschuk, "Sarah Palin's no slave to syntax," *Maclean's* (16 October 2009).)

18 Rancière, *Hatred of Democracy*, p. 73.

19 *Ibid.*, p. 74.

20 *Ibid.*, p. 93.

21 See Kingwell, *A Civil Tongue: Justice, Dialogue, and the Politics of Pluralism* (Penn State University Press, 1995) and *The World We Want: Virtue, Vice, and the Good Citizen* (Viking, 1999).

7

Intellectuals and Democracy

YOU MIGHT THINK JUDGES would make diverting dinner companions, but I can tell you that on the whole they don't. The judge sitting next to me, who shall go nameless, condemned all modern art as overpraised child's play. She railed against graduated income tax. She told me I would outgrow my socialist tendencies (I was 48 at the time). She left without contributing to the bill.

So I was not at all surprised when, after hearing what I did for a living, she said, "But what will your students *do* with that?"

There is a special intonation to this use of the verb 'do', familiar to anyone who has studied classics or considered a graduate degree in mathematics, with its long vowel of contempt honeyed over by apparent concern. When I was in my second postgraduate year, a woman in an Edinburgh bus queue delivered the best version I have so far encountered: "Philosophy! Really! Do you have any idea what you'll *do* with that?" (Poor sod: useless *and* out to lunch!)

I could have told the judge something she ought to have known already, which is that *philosophy students usually rock the LSAT*. They get into prestigious law schools, even sometimes make it onto the bench. Statistically speaking, there is no better preparation for success in law than an undergraduate degree spent thinking about the nature of knowledge, the meaning of being and, especially, what makes a valid argument.

But even though this is itself a valid argument, it is not a good one. I mean that the success of the argument actually concedes a greater failure; it gives away the game of justification to a base value. A degree in philosophy, or humane study more generally, does not require validation in the court of do-with usefulness. It is a convenient reality that such validation is sometimes gained, but the victory is really a surrender performed on the enemy's ground.

What's surprising is how many of today's university administrators are rushing to do just this, hyping the 'competitiveness' and 'pragmatism' of higher education. The annual higher education supplement published by *Maclean's*, the Canadian weekly news magazine, is ground zero for the transactional reduction of learning. The latest version of the supplement included this representative claim from Robert Campbell, president of Mount Allison University in Sackville, New Brunswick. Parents of prospective students, he told a reporter, "are looking for a return on investment" in their child's tuition.

And so professors are told that they need to justify their activities according to a market model of 'research effectiveness', where quantifiable 'impact indicators' and 'external research use values' can be totted up and scanned. Students respond by assuming a consumer stance to their own education, swapping tuition dollars not for the chance to interact with other minds but to acquire a postgraduate market advantage. When a 2010 survey of 12,500 students asked, "What was the single most important reason in your decision to attend university," just 9% picked "a good general education" as their answer, while almost 70% had enrolled to "get a good job" or "train for a specific career."

Historically, median earning power for university graduates is indeed higher than that of college or high school grads, and over their lifetimes university graduates earn substantially more—75% by some estimates—than non-graduates. And yet, paradoxically, recent years have witnessed an avalanche of over-qualification. "[M]ore than a quarter of a million Canadian university students are about to graduate into the workforce this spring," *Maclean's* noted. "Yet studies show that fifty percent of Canadian arts and science grads are working in jobs that don't require a university credential two years after graduation."

All is not lost, however. "As the knowledge economy continues to grow—and manufacturing jobs disappear—there's more demand for university grads in the workforce than ever." Rest easy, parents. Pony up, students. There's still a reason to get an education! It's just not anything to do with education.

Call this familiar mixture of doom and market optimism the *standard position*. It can be summarized this way: university education must be judged according to its ultimate usefulness. That usefulness will be understood as career success of one sort or another, especially as measured by wealth. The position then adds the *soft option*: get a degree because the "knowledge economy" will otherwise crush you.

The soft option is favoured by presidents as well as university presidents. Barack Obama, giving a speech at a college in 2011, noted that America's need to 'remain competitive' was an argument for higher education: "If we want more good news on the jobs front then we've got to make more investments in education." He offered no other arguments in its favour.

—

For all its currency, the standard position strikes me as wrong-headed, if not dangerous. It is a philistine position, obviously; it works to hollow out the critical possibilities of education. Holders of this position regard real humanistic education as a dispensable luxury of idiosyncratic and purely personal value, and that makes them, in turn, dangerous.

They are correct, however, that the standard position is now so deeply presupposed that even calling attention to it can be enough to brand one an ivory-tower whackjob, tilting at windmills. The 2011 *Maclean's* authors noted with some satisfaction that nobody would nowadays express the indignation that greeted similar reductive accounts of education a decade ago, not apparently aware of the role *Maclean's* and its consumer-style surveys have played in that reduction.

As far as I'm concerned the judge and all those in the standard-position camp are the enemy. They are not enemies of philosophy, or me, or my students; they are enemies of democracy, and insofar as we refuse to admit that—insofar as we soft-pedal the value of the humanities when confronted by a scale of value keyed only to wealth—we are not being serious about what democracy means. As with the democratic narratives discussed in relation to Francis Fukuyama (see "The Tomist," in this collection) and the electoral system (see "Throwing Dice"), we are witnessing nothing less than the regulatory capture of universities under the general influence of a market model that can only be challenged by arguments rooted in another, human code of value.

Most defences of the humanities fall back on preaching to the choir: they assume the value of the very thing they need to defend, namely the cultivation of self and world that marks genuine study, what Aristotle called *skholé*, or leisure (hence the word 'school'). At that point, there is usually a predictable spinoff into denunciations of elitism and counter-denunciations of its reverse-snobbery evil twin, anti-intellectualism. The net result is either an impasse or a trail into absurdity: witness the 2006 *National Post* reader poll which concluded that bombastic hockey commentator Don Cherry was the nation's "most important public intellectual"—a fact that will exercise the duelling voices of "What Are Intellectuals For?" later in these pages.

But there's no need to go through any of that, because the standard position is actually self-defeating.

Let's do a little casual philosophical analysis. What are the unspoken premises of the standard position?

Most obviously, it assumes (1) that we know what *use* is. Something is useful when it has instrumental value. Things of instrumental value serve needs other than their own, either some higher instrumental value or an intrinsic value. And yet, in practice 'use' almost always comes down to money, which is itself a perfect example of a *lower* instrumental value. Money is just a tool, but we talk and act as if it were an end in itself.

So the position likewise assumes (2) that we know how to value things that contribute to use. We can convert any activity or human possibility into some quantified assessment, and thus dispose of the question of whether it is worth doing. Not only does this make a mockery of human action, quickly narrowing the scope of what is considered worth doing, it simultaneously narrows the scope of argument about the nature of worth. This leads to a market monopoly on the notion of the 'real': anything that is not in play in a market is irrelevant or imaginary.

The position in turns presupposes (3) that education is in thrall to this 'real world' of market value—actually a massive collective delusion as abstract as anything in Hegel's *Phenomenology*—because according to (2) all human activities are. The market's monopoly on reality reinforces the dominant value of competition and selfishness, incidentally converting education into a credential-race that can (and rationally should) be gamed rather than enjoyed in itself.

Lurking nearby are two other implicit ideas about life after graduation: (4) education must be intimately linked to work; and (5) doing work while 'over-qualified' is a bad thing. This link between education

and work is a nifty piece of legerdemain which preys on the uncertain-
ties all humans have about the future, even as it leaves untouched the
general presumption that one must have a job to be human. Parents
and children alike fall for it.

Finally, at least in the soft option, there is (6): the assumption that
education can find its match in white-collar work of the knowledge
economy, and so justify doing a degree after all. This completes the regulatory capture of education. What was once considered a site of challenge to received ideas and bad argument, even to entrenched power
and pooled wealth, is now a not particulary successful adjunct to the
pursuit of that power and wealth.

Unfortunately the facts do not bear this out, and this is where the
entire arrangement collapses.

While the number of jobs asking for a degree has increased over the
past two decades, the fact is that, since 1990 or so, the North American
job market has not been characterized by a smooth rise in demand for
cognitive skills to match growth in technology. Instead, there has been a
hollowing out of the market's middle, such that top-level jobs (creating
technologies, playing markets, scoring touchdowns) have risen in overall
wealth but not numbers, while low-end jobs (fixing pipes, driving semi-
trailers, pouring lattes) have remained steady or grown slightly. In between,
there is a significant depression of the very middle-class occupations that
most university graduates imagine will be their return on investment.

The consequences of this economic reality are twofold. First, it
explodes the assessment of education in terms of economic reality.
There is no prospect of the competitive 'knowledge economy' future to
underwrite a decision to go to university. The soft option is gone.

Second, and more profoundly, the standard position now exhibits
its full contradictions. If you cannot value education in terms of money,
then education has no value. That means that, if you decide to pursue
such an education, it has to be for reasons other than value. But that
would mean doing something that has no use, and surely that is silly.

There is an ironic benefit to this collapse. Sure, some people will
conclude that university is not for them: it doesn't confer the market
benefit it used to, so to hell with it. For others, though, the land beyond
use might continue to beckon, a place where there is no easy decline
into the disengagement of merely personal interests.

The standard position was founded on a paradox: university graduates are overqualified for the jobs they do; but you should still go because there is a statistical link between a degree and higher income. This is now replaced with a new paradox, the paradox of philosophy in the general sense: there is no use in pursuing a university education; but you should pursue it anyway because it's the only way to see any use beyond what is everywhere assumed.

—

What does any of this have to do with democracy? Again, a twofold conclusion. First, wider university admission isn't going to result in prosperity for everyone. If we want to have more equitable distributions of wealth and opportunity, we can't rely on markets to do it, even or especially markets flooded with dazed graduates looking for work in a depression created, in part, by high-flyers gaming the abstract markets. And no, more business schools are not the answer.

Second, though, we actually need graduates more than ever precisely because democracy depends on a population of engaged, critical thinkers who have general humane knowledge of history, politics, culture, economics, and science, citizens and not consumers who see that there exist shared interests beyond their own desires. Once the link between higher education and work has been broken, the value of the humanities and non-applied sciences become clear. Education is not there to be converted into market value, it is there to make us better and more engaged citizens, maybe even better and more virtuous people. There, I said it! The entailed benefit is that these citizens are ones who will challenge the reduction of all consideration to the price of everything and the value of nothing.

Aristotle again: usefulness is not virtue. He meant to ask us each to consider how and why we come to value things, to consider them relevant, to think them worth doing. "What are you going to do with that?" asks the concerned fellow diner or transit passenger.

But as Socrates said, philosophy concerns no small thing, just the tricky matter of *wondering how best to live.* So the answer is: I'm already doing it. And you should be too.

8

What Are Intellectuals For?
A Modest Proposal in Dialogue Form

Q: So who are considered the important ones in this country?
A: Any simple list will be controversial, a form of special pleading both for who's on and who's not. But Marshall McLuhan and Northrop Frye, obviously. And Harold Innis. You could add George Woodcock and George Grant. I think Glenn Gould should be in there. Jane Jacobs for sure, though she was actually American. Margaret Atwood. Charles Taylor, too, but he's different because he just did good scholarship and left it to percolate into the wider world. Not quite the same thing. Then he chaired that commission in Quebec, ran for office. Oh yeah, so also Michael Ignatieff.

Q: Is he the guy some people call The Torturer?

A: He never actually tortured anyone, and for the record when Americans are in charge it's not torture, it's "enhanced interrogation technique." But Ignatieff did defend the Iraq war, and its attendant depravities, over and over in the *New York Times Magazine*. Tony Judt, an important English public intellectual in his own right, who died not long ago, classed him with Thomas Friedman and Peter Beinart as the "useful idiots" of the Bush regime, "America's liberal armchair warriors."

Q: Whoops. That's when he was calling himself an American, right? What's he doing now?

A: Don't ask.

Q: Okay, but is there anyone younger?

A: Sure, but what's the point of mentioning them?

Q: Don't they do some interesting things, especially on television?

A: Television. Listen, a few years ago one of the national newspapers ran an extended poll to find the country's favourite public intellectual. The clear winner: Don Cherry.

Q: That deranged hockey guy with the, uh, special clothing sense? You're joking.

A: I wish I was. So there you go—the hockey guy, who is by any rational standards an incoherent blowhard, is the country's favourite *intellectual*. You can't blame television itself, though. It's no better or worse than the people who produce it. But anyone who tells you this country is less anti-intellectual than, say, the United States or Britain hasn't been paying attention. The hockey guy as public intellectual is a one-line joke on the country as a whole.

Q: I get it. It's an updated version of the egghead-meathead conflicts of times past. Instead of mocking eggheads as hopelessly inept, or domesticating them by having them, say, learn how to surf and dance to rock 'n' roll in a beach-blanket movie, you just collapse the distinction.

A: Exactly.

Q: Where does that leave us?

A: It could leave us with a fairly interesting question, like what do we even think intellectuals are for, anyway? I mean, what do we imagine is the point of them? The newspaper poll assumed that the concept of 'public intellectual' was clear enough to use without further ado. But then the generated answer actually begs the question, since it's clear that the concept is not clear.

Q: That's all a bit finely spun, isn't it? A sort of meta-intellectual question for intellectuals about intellectuals.

A: You started it. Anyway, there's something here for everyone.

Q: What do you mean?

A: Consider the standard defences of intellectuals. From the time of at least Socrates and Lao Tzu, they saw themselves as performing a necessary function, chiding those in power for their blindness and ambition, warning the rest of us about the dangers that cling to power. Intellectuals were, in this tradition, essential barriers to tyranny. And when they tried to work on the side of power, as Plato disastrously did when he accepted Dion's invitation to tutor Dionysius in Syracuse, things go badly wrong. Even Aristotle, an altogether more rational intellectual, was frustrated by Alexander the Great, an altogether greater ruler. Real kings are always a disappointment to philosophers.

Q: But wait! Didn't Plato actually advocate that there should be philosopher-kings? It's somewhere in the *Republic*.

A: Book VII, 473c-d. Socrates says this to his young friends, especially Glaucon and Adeimantus, the brothers: "Until philosophers rule as kings or those who are now called kings and leading men genuinely and adequately philosophize, that is, until political power and philosophy entirely coincide, while the many natures who at present pursue either one exclusively are forcibly prevented from doing so, cities will have no rest from evils … nor, I think, will the human race." Socrates said it, but you have to see that Plato himself *didn't mean it*. There is all kinds of evidence in the text that the idea is being set up as a deliberate provocation. Some people even think the whole discussion about the philosopher-king is meant as a warning, to readers smart enough to catch on, that real philosophers shouldn't even think of ruling. It's a dialogue, not a treatise.

Q: Hey, is this why we're having a dialogue right now, instead of this being an essay? So we can toss ideas around without being bound to them?

A: I don't know. Sure.

Q: Back to Plato. So, despite his own project with Dionysius, Plato thinks philosophers should stay out of politics?

A: Despite, or maybe because of. Plato had also seen the Thirty Tyrants nearly destroy Athens, after all, not to mention witnessing the staged trial that convicted Socrates for corrupting youth and celebrating false gods. He knew exactly what happened to intellectuals when they got on the wrong side of politicians. But he also knew that, without intellectuals to harass and scold them, and to awaken at least some of the people, there would be no curb at all on power.

Q: So you're saying that people like Karl Popper, who blame Plato for initiating a utopian urge that always ends in totalitarianism, are wrong?

A: Not wrong that this happens, but wrong that Plato didn't realize that. He's not seriously calling for an ideal city in the *Republic*, he's telling us that any desire for an ideal city is going to entail force and deception—and hence will cease, by definition, to be ideal. Notice that even the basic claim about the philosopher-king is haunted by a spectre of force: philosophers are not going to be allowed to go on just philosophizing, any more than kings are going to be able to rule without philosophy. Elsewhere there are defences of lying for political purposes, and a blithe suggestion that all the adults of any actual society will need to be exterminated to begin creating an ideal one. And then we're told that philosophers are lovers of wisdom? No, Plato was too smart to miss the contradictions, or to be making them inadvertently. Popper wasn't paying enough attention to the text. It's all in there.

Q: Okay, but at one point Plato himself still felt "the lure of Syracuse," as Mark Lilla called it.

A: Yeah. I'm not sure any really great thinker can deny the temptation, even if they should always resist it. An intellectual looks at society and thinks: I could do better than *that*, for crying out loud.

Q: But not without some violence. And that would make them, and society, worse. Also, they're probably wrong. The basic building blocks of politics are people, not ideas. Of course ideas are in the mix, sometimes with real power, but it really all comes down to the mysteries of human desire. What do the miserable creatures want? They hardly know themselves.

A: That's it. The whole "crooked timber of humanity" business. No such thing as an ideal state, or even a very rational one, when you're dealing with the humans. They're pretty hopeless.

Q: So philosophers, or intellectuals, should not aspire to rule. But where does that leave them? Seems like depression, or cynicism, would be their natural fate. I mean, you're right, looking at the humans, trying to make them better or anyway not worse, constantly being disappointed, is bound to make anyone depressed.

A: It happens. We could say this, though: just as it is an intellectual's job not to rule, it's also his job not to be too cynical. Or, since we've been talking about ancient Greece, we could say they should be Cynical. The original Cynics were social critics, really, not defeatists. They used sarcasm and satire, but they never gave up. Hope for the best, expect the worst.

Q: I like that idea, and yet satire can become a bad habit. It seems to breed misanthropy.

A: I don't think you're right. Or maybe I believe there's a good kind of misanthropy, a humanistic kind. Frye himself defined satire as "militant irony," and that militancy is as important as the irony. You can be militant only if you believe in something, if you have a mission. You pursue the mission aslant, but you still pursue it.

Q: And what is the mission?

A: I guess the simplest way to put it would be to say that it's calling out the best of ourselves, our highest possibilities, while acknowledging that we are really sad and limited, even sometimes downright nasty. We invent astonishing art forms like contrapuntal music, with geniuses like Gould to play it, and then we use the same ingenuity and creativity to think up ways to torture each other.

Q: Misanthropic humanism. Isn't that a contradiction in terms?

A: It's not a contradiction, it's an irony. The tension contained in the phrase—how can one be saddened by human foible while celebrating the value of the human?—wedges open a gap in the self-congratulation typical of liberal humanism, its blithe confidence in the idea of the individual. Misanthropic humanism is a *grenzbegriff,* a limit concept. It asks us to question the illusions of human existence even as it acknowledges that same existence as the only source of meaning in the world.

Q: Can you give me some examples?

A: I could—Hobbes maybe, Nietzsche for sure, Michel Foucault at times. But rather than discuss their specifics, or even try to define the rigid extension of the concept of intellectual—a fool's errand—let's consider four types of modern public intellectual to see what they tell us about their role of today. This would be the beginning of the modest proposal up there in the title.

Q: I thought we had established that role: criticism of power, and reflection on human possibilities.

A: But you're far too trusting! That sounds good, but it only sounds good *to intellectuals.*

Q: To intellectuals? I don't think I understand.

A: Of course not! That's why I'm here. Look, most intellectuals, public or otherwise, assume what most ordinary people do not really see, namely, that what they do is important. A public intellectual presumably imagines that he or she is performing some useful, even indispensable, service. That service may be to ideas themselves, to public discourse, to democracy, or to some other large abstraction: in an excitable version of this, to justice, or humanity, or the future. The reality is a lot more complicated, and depressing. These days, there are four forms that public intellectual engagement typically takes.

Q: Four?

A: Yes, four. Stop repeating what I say. The four types are: (1) the savvy media don, what Pierre Bourdieu dismissively labelled *le fast-thinker;* (2)

the political pundit or professional contrarian, with an ideological axe to grind; (3) the tame cleric, selling soft soap on behalf of the current arrangement; and (4) what I would like to call the persistent xenocyst.

Q: You're kidding.

A: No, really, it's the right term and I'll explain why.

Q: Okay, go on.

A: So *le fast-thinker* is the guy—it's usually a guy—who opines about this, that, and everything at the drop of a chase producer's phone call. Specializes in the near-instant generation of a TV 'quote', mostly about features of the passing scene: pop stars, movies, clothing and education trends, sexual mores, generational differences. And so on.

Q: Didn't you use to do this sort of thing all the time?

A: Nah, that was the smiley bald guy in the suit. He's gone now.

Q: Right. Okay, so this popular culture business is trivial and constant, but is it really bad? I mean, what's the problem?

A: The problem is that the producer always wants you to explain 'what it means' or 'what it says about us'. And the only valid answer to these questions is, very little if not nothing. Meanwhile, the various answers offered to the questions only serve to torpedo themselves. We can call this the 'white lipstick conundrum'.

Q: How's that?

A: Here's Frye, in *The Modern Century*: "Thus if there appears a vogue for white lipstick among certain groups of young women, that may represent a new impersonality in sexual relationships, a parody of white supremacy, the dramatization of a death-wish, or the social projection of the clown archetype. Any number may play, but the game is a somewhat self-defeating one, without much power of sustaining its own interest. For even the effort to identify something in the passing show has the effect of dating it, as whatever is sufficiently formed to be recognized has already receded into the past."

Q: Sounds like he's mocking McLuhan there.

A: Yeah.

Q: Okay, so by this reasoning, today's vampire fixation, say, or obsession with celebrity drunkorexia, or, going back a bit, the metrosexual backlash—remember that?—are already yesterday's reality. It's like calling something 'cool'. As soon as you do, it no longer is, it no longer can be. Classic self-collapse of positional goods.

A: Which means that, as so often happens when it comes to the pursuit of speed, you cannot succeed; *le fast-thinker*, no matter how nimble, can never be fast enough. His comments themselves consign cultural phenomena to the dustbin of so five minutes ago.

Q: Pundits surely are better, then?

A: Yes and no. The pundit, as I consider him—and again, they are usually guys—is essentially a shill for a particular position, or cluster of them. They are the ones you see on the Sunday morning television shows, being angry and interrupting each other.

Q: Sure. Again, though, what's wrong with that?

A: The word pundit is from Sanskrit, and means an expert in Sanskrit. The pundits we see now are not experts in anything, except punditry. That is, they speak authoritatively but not necessarily, or at all, from a position of authority. Eric Alterman, who long ago lamented the rise of a 'punditocracy' in American politics, even set out the rules for success in this sphere. The two most important are these: (a) remember that it is better to look right than to be right; and (b) blanket the media with a contrarian view about an argument already in progress.

Q: That's a bit reductive, isn't it?

A: That's the point! Reductionism rules! Shouting down your opponent is nobody's idea of valid argument, and yet that's precisely what most of these people do, even in print. Mockery goes a long way, passing itself off as satire even while being in the service of power. There is no external burden of proof: you can say anything, even if it's wrong, without fear of comeuppance. And most telling of all, simply assuming the stance of an aggrieved minority—the besieged conservative battling gamely against the mainstream liberal media that provides him with a stage and princely salary, the lone courageous supporter of an allegedly unpopular but massively funded war—is enough to generate an aura of moral righteousness.

Q: Stop shouting, I get it. That's why these people sometimes change positions so radically, no?

A: Yes, exactly. You can't be a contrarian when the wind shifts and your formerly outsider position is now widely held. That's the moment to cross the ideological floor, denounce your once courageous but now sadly sheep-like former comrades, and get some new fill in your disputatious sails.

Q: Christopher Hitchens?

A: Christopher Hitchens.

Q: Okay, so I agree that a blustering punditocracy is a danger to democracy. It hollows out public discourse by reducing all sallies to carriers of ideological position, and it probably erodes civility too, understood as a general willingness to engage in meaningful political dialogue. But surely it was ever thus?

A: Maybe. Television has been a huge enabler of these erosions, because it rewards certainty and appearance. But print is actually not much better, despite our romanticizing of the written argument. When it comes to new media, who the hell knows? Lots of incivility and nonsense, to be sure, sometimes at a level hard to imagine among civilized people; but also some really smart and effective content-strategy interventions. No room for optimism, I'd say, but certainly room for hope.

Q: Huh. I want to get back to that distinction in a minute, but meanwhile explain category three, the tame cleric.

A: Obviously I borrow the noun from Julien Benda's 1927 polemic, *La trahison des clercs*. It's usually translated as "The Betrayal of the Intellectuals" or "The Treason of the Learned," but I prefer the more general and suggestive idea of *the taming of the clerics*. The real treason comes when intellectuals accept their status as adjuncts to the order of things, and today that almost always means accepting a system whereby they are warehoused in institutions dedicated to the 'training' of the 'workforce' of 'tomorrow'.

Q: I've heard you rant about this before, but explain 'clerics' first.

A: Cleric just means someone in holy orders, eventually contracted to 'clerk' and expanded to mean any learned person. The French *clercs* means intellectuals or academics, but I like to translate it as 'clerics' because it reminds us, even if we're secular, that scholarship is a kind of holy order. We don't wear those gowns for nothing.

Q: What about Benda then?

A: Benda's point was both specific and general. He attacked certain French and German intellectuals of his day, especially Charles Maurras and Maurice Barres, for their abandonment of Enlightenment ideals of intellectual life, embracing instead toxic forms of nationalism and racism. These articulate men had reduced themselves, and their learning, to mouthpieces for power. Benda considered this move, which certainly brings prestige and even the double-edged gift of influence, a crime against the true vocation of intellectuals.

Q: Which is?

A: Benda was an optimist. For him, intellectuals were "all those whose activity essentially is not the pursuit of practical aims, all those who seek their joy in the practice of an art or a science or a metaphysical speculation, in short in the possession of non-material advantages." Because such people existed, he said, "humanity did evil for two thousand years, but honoured good. This contradiction was an honour to the human species, and formed the rift whereby civilization slipped into the world." According to him, this delicate balance of force and thought shifted in the first part of the twentieth century. Intellectuals gave up on serving philosophical ideals and became masters of justifying the status quo.

Q: Still true?

A: Certainly still relevant. I would say that the problem today is less intellectuals abandoning the Enlightenment in favour of nationalism, though that still happens, and more the embrace of capitalism as the only framework of meaning. The most successful are the ones who parrot sociological evidence in smooth deployment of 'ideas' that sound kind of neat, a little obvious, but are given catchy new labels, and so manage to challenge nothing and nobody even while creating the illusion of being 'smart'. Never mind if there are jaw-dropping errors here and there.

Q: Malcolm Gladwell?

A: Malcolm Gladwell.

Q: But this doesn't apply to most university-based intellectuals, does it? I mean, if anyone is working in the field of Benda's 'non-material advantages', it's them.

A: Yes and no. In this country they are paid pretty well, and from the public purse at that. Still, we should always be prepared to argue for the value of the things they do *especially* when those things seem to have no value as the market understands the notion. I'm more worried about something else, namely self-delusion.

Q: Lost me again.

A: This is the trap in Benda's idea of 'non-material advantages'. Intellectual rewards may be non-material, but they're still advantages.

Intellectuals mask their own privilege even as they claim to expose privilege elsewhere. That's their problem: their thought is limited precisely by the illusion of thought having no limits. Their representation of themselves is therefore askew, even more than such representations usually are, because they believe they are above such representations. And they're stuck in these representations, usually based on 'superior taste' or 'excellent critical judgment' or some such, just as much as their egghead-mocking opponents are stuck in representations of the intellectual as a dork.

Q: I think I see that. Anti-intellectualism is a conceptual and political dead end, but so is this kind of pro-intellectualism. Pro-intellectualism leads to elitism, in particular to an outcome where there are entrenched rather than circulating elites, a privileged *classification class* in fact.

A: There you go.

Q: Again, though, where does it leave us?

A: Well, to avoid the endgame of fully entrenched intellectual elites, you have to be on guard all the time. You can't escape class position entirely, nobody is able to do that, but you can cultivate better awareness of its follies and limits. You need master self-investigators like Adorno and Žižek and Houellebecq and Ballard around. You have to be HiLobrow rather than Highbrow.

Q: Hmm. Still not sure I totally get this. Anyway, what happened to the fourth type of modern public intellectual.

A: It's all related. Here, look at Frye again, in *The Modern Century*. He's comparing the experience of critical awareness, what Martin Amis called *the war on cliché*, to that of looking out the window of a railway carriage as the sun goes down. "Even the most genuinely concerned and critical mind finds itself becoming drowsy in the darkening carriage," Frye says. "[T]he very ability to recognize the cliché works against one's sense of full participation. Self-awareness thus operates like a drug, stimulating one's sense of responsibility while weakening the will to express it."

Q: Right. You become your own worst enemy—though only just.

A: Yes, good. And there's no way out, no transcendence possible. But what you can do is hold on to an awareness of that fact. Frye once more, capturing the larger stakes of critical intellectual engagement:

"Democracy is a mixture of majority rule and minority right, and the minority which most clearly has a right is the minority of those who try to resist a passive response, and thereby risk the resentment of those who regard them as trying to be undemocratically superior." Hence anti-intellectualism, which is really a resentment against assumed claims of elite status. *Who do you think you are, being so critical?*

Q: Yeah, that sounds familiar.

A: But the real issue is the interior tension, not the external hostility. Frye nails it: "I am speaking however not so much of two groups of people as of two mental attitudes, both of which may exist in the same mind. The prison of illusion holds all of us; the first important step is to be aware of it as illusion and as a prison."

Q: I do like that, it sounds right. But if that's the first important step, what's the second?

A: Now we finally get to the fourth type. The second step is: *make yourself indigestible.*

Q: Uh ...

A: Make yourself indigestible. Refuse to be assimilated or domesticated, tamed or bought out. I called this the persistent xenocyst role, right? A xenocyst is just a lump of foreign matter, a speck of something that doesn't belong. Any organism, sensing the presence of a xenocyst, will work to solve the problem it poses. The commonest recourse is rejection: refuse the challenge, expel the alien matter via whatever mechanism or orifice will serve. Next in popularity comes assimilation: make what was foreign conform to the organism's dominant patterns. Rarely, if ever, does the host organism respond by rearranging its own patterns to accommodate the foreign particle, though if the xenocyst is large enough, sometimes that's the only option. You know: Bartleby *would prefer not to.*

Q: Uh ...

A: You see it. My proposal here is modest—it is not entirely pessimistic, though it is misanthropic, hopeful without being optimistic. Optimism is about expectations, reasons to believe. Hope operates beyond reasons, it is a kind of openness without expectation.

Q: So?

A: So the best public intellectuals can hope for themselves is to be good citizens, and to engage the semi-conscious majority with as much self-awareness, wit, and eloquence as they can muster. But they cannot expect to be thanked for this, nor should they take refuge in the soft tyranny of 'non-material advantages'. Especially in an age when there is no such thing as real public discourse, they will always be in danger of being consumed by the system they inhabit. More insidiously, they may find themselves doing the consuming, calculating the costs and benefits of their buy-ins of the mind, their mental self-cannibalizing. At that point, the best strategy—the only alternative—is to be as indigestible as possible.

Q: Uh ... Modest proposal? Consumption? Has this whole discussion been an example of the militant irony you were talking about before? Do you really mean any of it?

A: Not for me to say.

Q: But come on, this is important! Don't you worry that we live in an age where irony is out of fashion, lost equally on militants who don't care about reason and on those autistic narcissists who spend all their time checking email on their phones?

A: Yes. Yes, I do. But you have to keep trying, and by any means necessary. Because if you give up, the system will eat you alive. It might do that anyway, but you can at least make it hurt a bit going down. Do you know Michael Foot? A British politician. He said this about intellectual engagement, in a campaign speech for an election his party went on to lose: "We are not here in this world to find elegant solutions, pregnant with initiative, or to serve the ways and modes of profitable progress. No, we are here to provide for all those who are weaker and hungrier, more battered and crippled than ourselves."

Q: Yes.

A: Yes. Never worry about those on top—they will always find a way to take care of themselves. And never try to be on top yourself—you won't like it there. No, worry about those stuck at the bottom, speak and provide for them as best you can. There's no other point to being here.

Q: Thanks.

A: As we say, you're welcome. And everybody should be welcome.

9

"Fuck You" and Other Salutations: Incivility as a Collective Action Problem

For as laws are necessary that good manners may be preserved, so there is need of good manners that laws may be maintained.
—Machiavelli, *Dei Discorsi*

CALLS FOR CIVILITY STRIKE a keynote in the current political moment. Greater civility is urged for public discourse, both on-air or online, in shared spaces, whether physical or virtual, and in common undertakings ranging from the mundane (whether or not to recline your airline seatback) to the essential (whether or not to pay taxes). Civility is thought especially important in those areas where there is no explicit regulation, such that citizens themselves must act to coordinate their actions, or in the spaces that run between explicit regulation and its application in the real political world, such that citizens must negotiate the precise details of regulatory execution. The urgency of these calls rises in direct proportion to the amount of everyday conflict that is encountered in social life, from shopping malls and corridors to online encounters and Twitter feeds.

As Machiavelli perceives, the ideal relationship between law and manners is symbiotic. I take "manners" here to mean more than just table manners, say, or the other largely conventional systems of coordinating social behaviour. Hence they should be understood at least to include, if not to indicate, civility as understood in the typical demands for more of it; though more on that later. Each term of this distinction reinforces the other after the fashion of the rules ("laws") of an organized sport such as football insofar as they relate to the unwritten norms ("manners") of good sportsmanship in the executed iterations of the game.[1] The trouble comes when this symbiosis generates systematic deformations by (legal) advantage-taking within the game that runs contrary to the norms but is nevertheless exempt from punishment. Such advantage then generates incentives for further violations of the norms. This is what I will call, following the usage introduced in earlier essays, the regulatory capture of civility. In normal usage, as we have seen, regulatory capture is what happens when a government agency becomes dominated, through aggressive lobbying and influence-peddling, by the sector or industry the agency is meant to regulate. This results in a failure of the public good. Regulatory capture in effect privatizes allegedly public interests, allowing pools of moneyed interest to obviate individual citizen interest; civility will offer a parallel case, not in the capital markets or the public education system but in the market of public discourse itself.

If nothing else, this approach offers the immediate benefit of novelty. Most defences of civility proceed along positive lines: that is, they argue for civility as a virtue of citizens and/or dialogic participants; or they enumerate goods and outcomes that civility can generate. These arguments, while well-intentioned, tend to fall into that peculiar form of comforting uselessness known as preaching to the choir.[2] They do not succumb to lack of validity, only lack of effectiveness. In this essay, I propose to reverse the polarity of civility defences by providing a negative argument. My claim is that civility can be defended best by demonstrating that incivility generates a collective action problem (CAP) along the lines of the standard race to the bottom. I will further explore how incivility CAPs generate wider democratic deficits in the form of political-dialogue CAPs. I conclude with a suggestion that democracy under capitalist conditions is structurally prone to CAPs, and that the recovery of democratic deficits can only be pursued via a revitalized political economy of the gift, in particular the invaluable gift of silence.

1. Smith's Conundrum

We must appreciate the somewhat unexpected presence of Machiavelli, usually considered a political realist, on this field of argument. His controversial position on virtue suggests the stakes, and the difficulties, of the debate. Another realist can be invoked on the same point, though to be sure he is here speaking in his pragmatic-liberal mode. "By manners, I mean not here, decency of behaviour; as how one man should salute another, or how a man should wash his mouth, or pick his teeth before company, and such other points of the small morals," Hobbes avers in *Leviathan*, "but those qualities of man-kind, that concern their living together in peace, and unity."[3] Hobbes's and Machiavelli's manners mean the same thing: something very like the social virtue of civility, in fact, and not just a set of behavioural rules and conventions without special (or much) ethical significance. Hobbes and Machiavelli likewise both want to insist that such manners matter in making higher-order law operative in the social order.[4]

One might begin an account of civility as a political virtue in more than one place. My choice here is directed by the special problems generated by the relationship between such accounts and emergent capital-dominant economies. Thus, instead of Aristotle or the Latin civic republicans, we begin with Adam Smith. Smith's version of the positive civility defence is a key moment in the growing inability of such defences to be effective. Smith, following the lead of Hume and other Scottish Enlightenment apostles of "the polite society," argued that politeness was a virtue of social interaction. It encouraged good feeling among citizens, and worked to smooth the rough edges of persons when they entered the company of others or, more to the point, shared social spaces. The special strain of "the polite society" as a defence may be captured in the etymological note that polite comes not, as many people suppose, from the Latin *polis*—city, politics—but from the phonetically similar but semantically distant *politus*, polish. A polite society is a polished one, and while it is the case that the cycles of social life might work like a rock-polishing device, rounding off sharp points in repeated tumbles, there is no sense here of an independent moral value. The connection between politeness and Smith's most powerful moral sentiment, sympathy, is present but tenuous.

Precisely this is what allows him to defend politeness thus even as he limns the influential defence of market reliance after observing the workings of a Scottish pin factory. Smith holds an explicit brief for the inherently rational workings of the market, including its ability to tolerate marginal corruption and free riders; which means—though this is never set out in so many words—that he must abandon any strong republican account of civic virtue calling for deep commitment to the political order. The two positions are not compatible: any enjoinder for the latter would suggest, perhaps demand, limits on one's behaviour in the former, and that means so much the worse for the republican account. The republican citizen does not make an effective or cooperative producer-consumer—something clear, perhaps, at least since Plato distinguished producing and consuming from "higher" functions of the soul in the ideal-city sections of the *Republic*.

The time has passed in which such ideas of the soul could be seriously maintained, and in any event they do not answer to the new economic realities of mercantile production, free trade, and cash-based consumption. Smith is among the first philosophers to recognize this particular early-capitalist reality check on moral-philosophical ambition; but, at the same time, he is unwilling to defend that which his many post-mortem admirers have imagined he called for, namely an entirely unregulated market. He knows, in fact, that there can be no such thing as an unregulated market. All markets are regulated by some mechanism or mechanisms of exchange: regulated exchange is just what a market is. The important question is always how the market is regulated, and for whose benefit. Smith is sincere in his defences of sympathy; on the question of present concern, he salvages moral sentiment by, in effect, downgrading civic-republican character to cooperative social nicety. Civility as a political virtue is reformed and becomes the social virtue of politeness.

The difficulty, in my terms, is his failure to recognize the immediate prospect of a CAP in such an account. This is what I will call *Smith's Conundrum*. Smith follows Daniel Defoe (in, e.g., *Everybody's Business is Nobody's Business*), Bernard Mandeville (in *The Fable of the Bees*), and David Hume (in his *Treatise of Human Nature*) by concluding that republican accounts of virtue are excessively demanding and, hence, unrealistic given the basic selfishness of humans. Instead, society could in effect bank on that selfishness to produce, under certain conditions, a functional civic order. Commercial transactions, driven by personal interest, would generate public goods in the form of working markets and, crucially, fair players within those markets. The fairness of play would be guaranteed by the allocations of costs and benefits through the market itself. In an important twist on the Machiavellian nostrum relating laws and manners, Smith further argued that there need not be any deep connection between private virtue and the public good. Private vice, in the celebrated formula, could generate public virtue. Manners, insofar as they were maintained as a matter of personal cultivation, were valuable; but the market could function quite well without them.

The difficulties of this view were visible to Smith himself, and he is at pains to nuance the general claims against a general account of moral sentiments. The Conundrum lurks despite his efforts. The reduction of public virtue to a transactional function, because it tolerates some corruption, cannot ward off systemic corruption. Transactional reduction follows no logic other than its own, and will be constrained only by market failure, as when a price is refused or a sharp practice taxed. There are some clear upper limits in a market game—I cannot assassinate my competitors, or destroy their wares—but below the threshold of failure lies a great terrain of vicious possibility, and only isolated and incidental patches, if any, of virtue. Think of a game which has rules but no norms of fair play or culture of sportsmanship. In such a game, any move can be calculated entirely on a risk/reward scale of what it will cost. Even "prohibited" moves may then be executed, providing the price of any resulting penalties can be absorbed without crippling loss.

By displacing the once-public virtue of civility to the private realm of politeness—even though good manners are still publicly displayed and valued, they have no particular political significance—Smith has in effect transformed the constraints of virtue into incidental costs. What once was an ethical fine or penalty now can be recast as a market price. The desiderata of politeness do not function as constraints because they can now be assessed according to relative expense. And so we witness the regulatory capture, now, of civility. As with other forms of regulatory capture, a supposedly public interest is in fact dominated by private interests. Smith's privatization of virtue, when set against a background of general commercial freedom, cannot halt any trend toward total transactional reduction in his system.

We can see how it was that, dancing on this uncertain terrain, Thomas de Quincey could offer one of the most famous inversions of conventional morality in English. I mean his much-quoted slippery-slope argument from the essay "On Murder Considered as One of the Fine Arts," published in *Blackwood's Magazine* in 1827: "For if once a man indulges himself in murder, very soon he comes to think little of robbing; and from robbing he comes next to drinking and

Sabbath-breaking, and from that to incivility and procrastination." Usually heralded as a vanguard sally in the kind of decadent topsy-turvy wit that Oscar Wilde would bring to lapidary perfection, even as the essay itself is considered one of the enabling texts of the murder-mystery genre, a sort of theoretical *ur*-text for the aesthetics of the "perfect crime," de Quincey's formulation can also be read as a devastating reverse commentary on the emptiness of surface virtues. His own reactionary political views tend to pull even farther away from the proto-Wilde interpretation, even as his celebrated opium indulgence suggests a libertine of a high order. At all events, whether decadence and right-wing politics naturally mix must remain a matter of debate—and taste. What is clear is that de Quincey is not simply fooling around; he has a serious ethical and political point to make.[5]

Incivility and procrastination are here understood as social vices, and social vices having been disjoined from a deeper ethical sensibility and elevated to the level of necessary conditions of civilized life, their violation of decorum must be condemned as worse than murder and robbing. Murder, indeed, becomes in de Quincey's inverted scale of wrongdoing the gateway drug of norm-breaking that leads by swift and frightening stages to breakdowns in polite behaviour. The reversal carries the message: in a society where mere politeness is of seeming greater value than true virtue, its moral status is no more than a smokescreen for traditional vice. To put the point clearly (and so, alas, drain it of the author's elegant irony): only a madman would consider that incivility is worse than murder, and only a mad world would concentrate its attentions on disruptions of superficial expectations over the deathly depredations of real theft and destruction of life.

By the time of the essay's composition, the Hume-Smith philosophical formulations of civility had, as so often, hardened into mere social carapaces that commanded "appropriate" public deportment without regard for any deeper qualities of interpersonal consideration, let alone general personal virtue. Even the minor element of ethical substance had been drained from civility and so had rendered it, via a surprising reverse-polarity version of the Machiavelli/Hobbes distinction, into no more than politeness, the small morals. This sort of politeness is neither robust enough to perform the positive task of bolstering law, nor independent enough to exert the defensive pressure needed to curb selfish interest in the market. Politeness, however pleasant, cannot forestall a general reduction of the shared aspects of ethical life to processes of cost-benefit calculation performed according to instrumental reason. Indeed, we might begin to suspect that for Smith, as for some of his more extreme followers, there is no such thing as "shared aspects of ethical life." (Compare Margaret Thatcher, speaking as prime minister of Britain: "There is no such thing as society."[6] The claim performs a twofold function: it (1) denies any state responsibility for individuals or their outcomes; and by extension (2) denies the existence of non-individual public goods.)

At this stage, we are not far from Schopenhauer's celebrated hedgehogs, who struggle to reconcile their need for warmth (prompting proximity to each other) with their dislike of being pricked (prompting recoil from each other), and so find "[t]he mean distance which ... enables them to endure being together [in] politeness and good manners (*feine sitte*)"[7]; or Emerson's tart observation that "politeness was invented by wise men to keep fools at a distance."[8] But in fact matters are worse than that. After all, a wise man—or indeed, any person, wise or otherwise—may well feel happy to take advantage of the refuge politeness offers us from unwanted social contact. And surely there is a similar sort of advantage in evolving mechanisms of social order such that our repulsive qualities may be held (somewhat) at bay even as we enjoy the benefits of cooperation. Every realm of social life, not just the traditional scenes of eating and dressing, might well generate its own manuals of etiquette. (A recent example: a pamphlet concerning good behaviour at art openings called *I like your work: art and etiquette*.[9] One contributor noted that "bad manners" in this realm could be defined as "violence, passing out, vomiting, hoarding all the beer"—which somehow sounds like just one thing.)

Such etiquettes will never suffice, however. The deeper problem is a matter of systematic distortions in the very idea of advantage. In short, the full thrust of Smith's Conundrum is not that he defended politeness instead of civility; it is rather that the defence of politeness that he offers, because it is in fact ultimately market-based, opens the door to progressive abuses of civility. Worse, these abuses have no theoretical end because their advantages always seem evident to the abusers.

2. *"Fuck You"*

The standard argument in favor of civility as a political virtue is something like the following. At least since Aristotle, it has been obvious that a thriving political order—let us call it a just society—happens only when there is a significant store of fellow-feeling between citizens. Aristotle was an ethical monist, of course: when there is just one best way to live, one singular (if multi-part) manner in which to flourish as the human form of life, there can be no serious argument about good citizenship, only a nuanced account of the *eunoia*, or good will towards others, necessary to achieve it. Strictly speaking, Aristotle has no need of civility insofar as it is understood as a restraint on bad behaviour. Good behaviour is, instead, an emergent property of a polity in harmony with its own ends.

Under conditions of ethical pluralism—that is, where there is more than one answer to how one should live—we quickly see that conflict, not harmony, is the basic condition of human affairs. You do not need to be a confirmed Hobbesian to acknowledge that it is not all sweetness and light at the polling station or on the debating floor. Somewhere in the seventeenth century, civility emerges as a signal virtue of politics precisely because it allows diverse views to be debated with tolerance and respect—at least some of the time. The basic insights of Locke's *Letter on Toleration* and Spinoza's *Tractatus Theologico-Politicus* is obvious: we need not agree, especially on the specific routes concerning salvation, if we can agree to disagree. "Truth," Locke argued in the former text, "has no such way of prevailing, as when strong arguments and good reason, are joined with the softness of civility and good usage."[10] Indeed, from the perspective of modernity, that rational-civil background of agreement concerning disagreement is a major achievement of human civilization. Not only does it allow a minimal cohesion, staving off the anarchy of war between all and everyone, but the conditions of rational disagreement actually indicate a significant upgrade in human intelligence. Even vehement argument, if it replaces outright violence, marks a big step forward in the march of reason and civilization.

Not that it is all about reason. Smith would, in *The Theory of Moral Sentiments*, argue persuasively that the recognition of shared human vulnerability is the real glue of social structure. Contractual theories, like the ones popularized a century earlier by Hobbes and Locke, miss a crucial point that the hero of the free market actually discerned with typical acuity. We would not make a contract with another, still less hold to it, unless we already recognized the other as an entity worthy of our consideration in some sense. There may be fear woven into the heart of all contracts, and comprehensive selfishness may be compatible with reason (as Hume had memorably asserted[11]), but not all of that fear and selfishness is personal nor is fear all that is so woven. Civility is the expression of regard for the other when discussing matters of shared political concern. That is why it is both more and less than the mere politeness with which, as we have seen, it is often confused: more because it extends well beyond the niceties of interpersonal behaviour, but less because it is not rule-governed or explicit. Civility is, on this account, something like the political air we must all breathe to negotiate our differences and—maybe—serve the cause of justice.

This is an optimistic picture; worse for present purposes, it is one that is justified using arguments that are themselves optimistic: namely, that people will smoothly discern a personal interest in being cooperative. Hence the standard objections to a political virtue of civility, which run the gamut from the claim that civility stifles dissent or obscures power relations to the brisker claim that civil talk, in common with all talk, changes nothing. None of these objections is ever far from sight. In 2007, the collection of intellectual anarchists known as The Invisible Committee published their manifesto, *The Coming Insurrection*, and argued that "All the incivilities of the streets should become methodical and systematic, converging in a diffuse, effective guerrilla war that restores us to our ungovernability, our primordial unruliness ... [R]age and politics should never have been separated. Without the first, the second is lost in discourse; without the second the first exhausts itself in howls."[12]

That is, if nothing else, an elegant piece of dialectical reasoning. Rudeness now! The only trouble is that, though passion may sometimes fuel good change, rage is a distinct modality of human conduct. Rage and politics really should be separated, or there will be no such thing as discourse—just shouting. Even anarchists demonstrate this, otherwise they would not bother penning manifestos that make studied factual claims and offer rational arguments. (The calm, scholarly tone of *The Coming Insurrection*, with its reasoned demands to destroy families and even couples—"the utopia of autism-for-two"—is ironically hilarious, possibly by design.) But the argument for civility based on the presuppositions of discourse is valid only if we already accept, however tacitly, those presuppositions. And clearly many people do not. So what, if anything, can we say to them?

Consider the theoretically minimalist possibility that incivility is nothing except a species of collective action problem. A collective action problem is generated whenever a situation's rational opportunities at the individual level generate, at the systemic level, outcomes that are bad for everybody. Take, as an all-too-familiar example, status-seeking via acquisition of name-brand consumer goods, let's say a high-end athletic shoe currently considered 'cool'. The shoe and its cool-conferring powers are not materially separable, so I have to buy it to achieve positive status. As we compete for this positional good, however, we accrue mounting opportunity costs; moreover, every move to advance my position creates a new incentive for you to invest more in order to pursue the motive good, which is the status and not the shoes themselves. Because this good functions by position, there is no theoretical upper limit to the ratcheted spending of our competition. We cannot win for losing. We all end up poorer—except for the shoe manufacturers.

These competitive-consumption races to the bottom and tragedies of the commons have been much analyzed for their prisoner's-dilemma-style paradoxes, which demonstrate how and when the exercise of rational self-interest generates system-wide defeats that leave everybody worse off. It is now amply clear that individual rationality in the form of profit-seeking, amped by greed, cleverness, and forms of derivatives that even their ardent traders did not fully understand, led to the collective self-defeat we know as the economic meltdown of 2008—though this says nothing about the uneven distribution of the costs of that meltdown, in which the greediest ended up losing the least. But relatively little attention has been given to discursive versions of collective action problems, perhaps because we assume discursive transparency— unlike competitive dilemmas, we know what the other is going to do. This assumption is false, though. Discourse, no less than consumption, has positional and hence competitive aspects. Indeed, winning the argument—or rather, being seen to win it—is the essence of many discursive exchanges.

The philosophical defence here has always been that some arguments just are better than others, and so they carry the day justifiably, not just factually. This may be true in some idealized sense, though there are certainly people who would doubt even the idealized claim. The trouble is that there are still many ways that the worse argument can win factually, and incivility is one of these. So I therefore have a clear incentive to resort to incivility, especially if my argument is weak: "You jackass." Now, however, you have an incentive of your own. In fact, merely repeating the incivility would only return us to the starting position, so you actually have an incentive to raise the rudeness stakes: "Where do you get off calling me a jackass, you moron?"

Rising incivility is thus like other forms of competition over position. Rudeness is parasitic on civil talk, because only by contrast to that talk does it achieve its argumentative advantage. Now it becomes rational—it makes sense, from the perspective of maximizing expected utility—for me to adopt the same tactical advantage in pursuit of victory. But as soon as I do, I give you a reason to adopt and exceed my rudeness. Which then gives me further reason to go farther. And so on. The result is that the goal we sought, carrying the discursive day, has been obliterated. Nobody can win now, because the well is poisoned; it no longer contains the fresh justificatory water that drew us here in the first place.

So much for Locke's reason-plus-civility, not to mention what Jürgen Habermas labeled "the unforced force of the better argument," that fanciful lodestar of rational discourse. Even Mill's "marketplace of ideas," where good arguments are supposed to emerge as evolutionary winners, has a hard time surviving the rigours of real life. In actual discursive markets, bad money tends to drive out good, not the other way around. Birthers and Tea-partyers can effectively cloud the truth by flooding the market with misinformation, the discursive equivalent of shoddy but cheap merchandise; and corporate donations to election war chests are effectively limitless, especially given the five-four U.S. Supreme Court decision in *Citizens United* (2010), skewing the electoral process in favor of their interests. As noted earlier, the Court held that restrictions on independent corporate expenditures in political campaigns, as opposed to direct political contributions, are unconstitutional restrictions on the freedom of speech.

This decision at once inhibits democracy by quantifying (and then hiking) the opportunity costs of participation, even as it reduces the idea of such participation to money itself. Corporations have been granted some of the rights of citizens in American law for some decades.[13] But this decision does more than extend such rights. By means of a spectral metaphysics of plutocracy, it effectively delivers the electoral process over to the moneyed interests whose pools of capital are now instantly transformed into pools of influence. As one critic of the decision noted: "Much of the judicial literature on the subject, including Justice Anthony Kennedy's majority opinion in *Citizens United*, simply substitutes the words 'speech' and 'speak' for the words 'spend' and 'buy'."[14]

Amazingly—amazing, that is, only if you have not been paying attention to the outraged sense of grievance typical of the Wall Street lobbies—the Court's majority decision saw nothing dangerous in the transformation. Justice Kennedy argued that "it is well understood that a substantial and legitimate reason, if not the only reason, to a cast a vote for, or to make a contribution to, one candidate over another is that the candidate will respond by producing those political outcomes the supporter favors. Democracy is premised on responsiveness." He then went further, tipping the decision into the realm of sick fantasy: "The appearance of influence or access, furthermore, will not cause the electorate to lose faith in our democracy."[15] Will *not*? It *will not*? This last is a sentence one must read several times to be sure it is not the result of an editing gaffe. (The dissenters were wry, if ineffective, in their objections: "While American democracy is imperfect," Justice John Paul Stevens wrote in his minority decision, "few outside the majority of this Court would have thought its flaws included a dearth of corporate money in politics.")

All the while, in every jurisdiction and most vividly in that public sphere beyond all jurisdiction which we know as the virtual, there is widespread de-individuation—adopting an online nickname, for example, or hiding behind a political action committee so that uncivil moves can be made with impunity—that tends to exacerbate the general damage by snapping the bonds of personal responsibility for what people say. It is a small irony of the digital world that John Rawls's "veil of ignorance," behind which imagined anonymous citizens rationally choose fair principles of justice, has been actualized in the real world as the get-out-of-jail-free card of nameless flaming. Under extreme conditions, the instrumental rationality that dominates current discursive spaces issues the general imperative, familiar from less salubrious realms such as public-house violence, of instant escalation. That is, when there is no rational curb on the swapping of rising incivilities, it makes strategic sense to take your game to maximum on the first move. In my title's parodic terms, "Fuck you" becomes the salutation of choice, even if it eviscerates the possibilities of the discursive space at the outset.[16]

The argument I am offering here is the oppositely-charged companion to the traditional one of moral sentiment. In short, instead of (or in addition to) saying that civility is a good thing for a pluralistic society, respecting difference and disagreement, we can say just why incivility is a bad thing along the lines of thought established by realist-liberal Hobbesianism, where minimal self-interest is considered adequate to generate and legitimate a political *modus vivendi*, without appeal to metaphysical or otherwise non-political motives for cooperation.[17] And that reason is simple: incivility is self-defeating. Ultimately, all recourse to advantage via incivility works against everyone's individual interests, including the individual who made the first non-cooperative move. Being rude might look like a good discursive tactic in the short run, but sooner or later it is revealed as a loser's move because it destroys the goods we sought to gain in the first place.

You might be thinking—and poised to e-mail or text me—that surely nobody sane considers anonymous discussion boards or even outrageous attack campaigns to be genuine forums of democratic debate. True, but it is nevertheless instructive to watch how our fellow citizens talk to each other over the issues of the day. And consider the more serious case of political attack ads: though widely decried by citizens, polls demonstrate that they are still sometimes effective, which gives all parties a strong motive to use them. Once the last resort of a dying election campaign, attack ads are now business as usual even for the party in power, launched pre-emptively in place of the former convention of ads that outline competing platforms. Remember platforms? Where parties would set out what they believed in, rather than attacking the competing guy as a doofus, a cynic, an opportunist? Those were the days.

The claim that negative ads excite political energy, and hence are good for discourse—yes, some people say they believe this—collapses when we observe that their effect is spiraling nonsense from the start. An attack ad is a deliberate appeal to unreason—fear or suspicion or hatred—which can only mean that the party fashioning the ad has nothing rational to offer. If we let discursive idiocy of this order succeed, we really would be a sad lot. The fact is that attack ads do not even work reliably, which means a party resorting to them is being stupid as well as rude, because you never know when they will backfire, damaging the hand that threw the first stone. This is true even when the bearer of that hand will try (as he will) to blame the other party for starting it. And so on, of course, until the incessant name-calling blankets a miasma of disgust over the entire public sphere. If you still doubt that these incivility ratchets can also disable forums of democratic debate more important than television—well, surely your cable package includes C-SPAN.

3. Civility as a Public Good

Unfortunately, the CAP argument against incivility is imperfect, especially in the short term, which means that its corollary implicative argument in favor of civility is serially weakened. Game theory research has shown that optimal results in many games can be achieved with a combination of cooperation and defection—that is, the best strategy is neither to work together all the time nor to cheat all the time, but to mix it up so your competitors cannot predict your moves. Under competitive conditions, equilibria that involve the risk of self-defeat but also generate greater rewards than cooperation will always dominate, sometimes strongly.

At this point in the general argument, the risk of self-defeat may be offset by a number of possible bolstering moves, all more or less controversial. One may, for example, extend the narrow range of rationality associated with the game-theoretic approach and appeal to forms of interest that are not constrained to personal profit. The rules/norms distinction introduced in the first section is one example of how this may be done. Yes, it is within the rules always to seek advantage, even sometimes to bend the rules to that advantage; but constant play of this sort may begin to rankle other players, threatening future rewards even below the threshold of self-defeat. This side-constraint of good sportsmanship is then structurally similar to familiar game-theory advantages concerning trustworthiness or sincerity, which come into play in any multiple-iteration game—though these constraints too can be gamed, if one is clever enough.

Other possible bolsters include enforced bargains, which effectively act as miniature social contracts within a larger framework of competition. Traffic rules fall under this heading, at least in their more arbitrary deployments (e.g., whether to drive on the left or the right side of the road, a non-disputable decision with no cost to anyone). As we have seen, though, the difficulty with such bargains is that they can be gamed at the margins by converting fines into prices. The same limit holds for all game-generated disincentives, provided they are small or rare enough to be absorbed into one's overall cost-benefit analysis.

Naturally we must rule out, on present grounds of argument, more searching forms of bargain and disincentive, such as appeals to general goods, overall welfare, categorical imperatives, self-policing in the name of virtue, and empathy. Though all of these may be, indeed have been, used as curbs to the lurking escalations and self-defeats of incivility, none of them is free from the controversial commitments to those wider values than self-interest and more expansive accounts of reason that we cannot, for the moment, allow ourselves to indulge.

What I want to suggest instead is that the incivility CAP reveals civility to be a public good in the economic sense explored earlier in the essay "Masters of Chancery," with respect to public space. The benefits of civil discourse are free of charge because they cannot be gated: the good is non-excludable. It is also non-rival in that engaging in civil behaviour does not, in itself, generate a competition. It is only when incivility is viewed as conferring a competitive advantage that the public good of civility is weakened and progressively destroyed by the unstoppable incursions of runaway private interest. The solution is not to enforce civility but to show that there is an equilibrium always already generated by the public idea of civility. Not only is this equilibrium more beneficial in its overall effects, it is more efficient at the level of the individual player as long as that player thinks even two moves ahead. Casting civility as a public good removes it from merely private interests *for the sake of* those interests and public ones both.

More significantly, the public-good thesis shows that civility must be seen as an infinite rather than a finite game. A general objection to game theory is that, even over many iterations, the games it posits are always and inevitably competitive. To be sure, this is no valid objection within the stated purview of such theory (i.e., competitive games). But we can note here, and without excessive commitments concerning value or rationality, the many non-competitive games which excite our interest, and serve our ends, just as comprehensively as competitive ones. Transfinite games are ones whose general ludic goal is the game's continuance, not a definitive outcome. For example, transfinite games resemble James Carse's notion of infinite games but without the attendant religious or existential perspective. "The rules of the finite game may not change; the rules of an infinite game must change," Carse argues. This is so because, with its general goal of continuance, an infinite must not cease, and so any move that seeks or even merely generates the effect of an approach to resolution must result in changes to guarantee continuance. "Finite players play within boundaries; infinite players play with boundaries," Carse goes on. "Finite players are serious; infinite games are playful."[18] The difference in transfinite games is that they are not, as Carse's infinite game is, identical with life itself. ("There is only one infinite game," he says.)

Transfinite games offer the same playful possibilities as highlighted in the Carse distinction, but they also serve definable ends. In the case of civility, the continuance of the game has the effect not only of allowing the productive disagreements of politics to proceed without degeneration into competition and, eventually, self-defeat; it also underlines the need for a general orientation to publicness as a presupposition of any pursuit of private ends. The public good of civility is (must be viewed as) this type of game—a result that we can appreciate fully by experiencing the self-cancelling negative results of multiple incivility CAPs in political life.

4. The Rest is Silence

Are civil citizens true friends, or just friendly competitors in various games, some of them zero-sum? In a striking passage from *The Politics of Friendship*, a book that takes apparently infinite pains to query the links (and the gaps) between politics and friendship, Jacques Derrida makes this striking claim: "Friendship does not keep silence, it is preserved by silence."[19] This silence preserves friendship because it leaves unarticulated the troubling truth that friendship is always and already inverted, the claim of non-sanguine kinship ever a spectre and an invitation to enmity. This is not the "companionable silence" of "true friends" but rather the unspeakable knowledge that social association is fraught with vulnerability and incalculable value. Also ignorance: "We knew nothing of each other, / being friends," notes the speaker of an Adam Zagajewski poem ("The Light of the Lamps").[20] Such silence is a gift in two senses: first, it preserves and holds the fragile construction that binds two persons, a bond which cannot bear too much articulation; and second, because it demonstrates, like all gifts, a structural refusal of reduction to calculable value. There can be no regulatory capture of silence because, as a gift, it lies beyond all economies of exchange. We do not trade with our friends. Friendship's transfinite game is played under the sign of silence.[21]

We may compare this Derridean silence with another, even more controversial version that figures in his thought, namely the "mystical" and "rather Wittgensteinian" silence found in the violence of authority's opaque foundation: "Discourse here meets its limit—in itself, in its very performative power. It is what I propose to call here the mystical. There is here a silence walled up in the violent structure of the founding act; walled up, walled in because this silence is not exterior to language. Here is the sense in which I would be tempted to interpret, beyond simple commentary, what Montaigne and Pascal call the mystical foundation of authority ... I would therefore take the use of the word mystical in a sense that I would venture to call rather Wittgensteinian."[22] Discourse "meets its limit" in this case because there is no further articulate gesture to be offered, no extension of the range of performative speech acts. Nothing more can be communicated. And yet, the resulting silence is not exterior to language; it is, rather, a potentiality or violence that lies coiled within ("walled in") language itself. Political authority's foundation is mystical because it must be so: any other sort of foundation would fail in its foundational task. The lawgivers in Plato's *Republic* offer a myth of distant origin precisely so that the clay-footed realities of social order may be naturalized and, hence, sent beyond question.

In fact this silence is not, despite some notable affinities between Derrida and Wittgenstein, anything like the silence enjoined by those things whereof we cannot speak.[23] *That* silence is a limit of language in the technical sense of possible extension, not of discourse in its justificatory performance—Derrida's meaning. But the limit-concept engages our attention for the present argument. The debates generated in defending civility, in particular the looming prospect of regulatory capture in the form of transactional reduction and zero-sum finite games, show us that we have, in effect, reached the limits of discursive constraint, if not of discourse itself. One premise of standard political defences of civility was that such constraints were needed to order and direct the abundance of claims, desires, and interests in play in diverse polities. Now we can see that there is no such solution to that abundance which is in fact, on any competitive model, a self-defeating superabundance. No account of civility constraints, even (or especially) those found in the virtue literature, can motivate the kind of political friendship that civility indicates, and infinitely demands. We cannot regulate by rules alone, because rules tell us only how to play, not why we do or what the game is for.

Sometimes the only civil thing to say is nothing.

And so, my friends, enough.

Notes:

1   The idealized relation also allows for, even encourages, critical interplay between rule and norm, with the result that both the game and its rules may evolve over time. In some cases, the rules will be modified to account for changes in the culture of the game (e.g., instituting an anti-spearing rule in football when helmet-on-helmet tackles become the norm); in others, the rules will gestate new innovative "moves" within the game (e.g., the offside rule in soccer allowing for the invention of the "offside trap" tactic). I explore these issues further in "Keeping A Straight Bat: Cricket, Civility and Postcolonialism," in *C.L.R. James: His Intellectual Legacies* (University of Massachusetts Press, 1995), pp. 359-87. It is worth noting here that cricket's governing body, the Marylebone Cricket Club, keeps written 'laws', not rules. Perhaps they knew their Machiavelli.

2   I do not exempt myself from this charge. Again, see *A Civil Tongue* (Penn State University Press, 1995) and *The World We Want* (Viking, 1999). The problem surfaces embarrassingly in some campus- or community-based civility campaigns, which gamely try to make civility "cool." My favourite was a recent campaign centred on the sadly uncool slogan "CIVILITY ROCKS!"

3   Thomas Hobbes, *Leviathan*, I.11 (capitalization modernized). I explore the distinction and its political implications in *A Civil Tongue, passim.*

4   These claims are thus consistent with the arguments, usually offered in the prefaces of etiquette manuals, that even the "small morals" are an expression of regard for the other—not to distress another with the sight of one's teeth-picking, for example. But for present purposes, that line of argument collapses the civility/politeness distinction too quickly, and would seem to invite a version of what I am here calling Smith's Conundrum.

5   None of this is to deny, by the way, that de Quincey may also have been keenly interested in the aesthetics of murder, a matter of some note given developments in the genre since. One has only

to think of the many thousands of novels and many dozens of films and, especially, television series that make the taking of life a matter of special-effects spectacle and cathartic satisfaction. American television at the turn of the millennium is literally unimaginable without the highly developed technological representation of murder in all its bizarre variety—perhaps a subject for some future anthropologist's own keen second-order interest. It is, rather, to suggest that the manner in which he formulates that interest is ranged along a scale of vices, and their implied virtues. Worth mentioning is that de Quincey himself was a procrastinator of a high order who repeatedly failed to answer letters and to pay bills, often to this own detriment. The projected publication of his collected works, by the American publisher Ticknor and Fields, was delayed and almost aborted because of his inability to answer letters from editor James Thomas Fields. The edition was published anyway, in twenty-two volumes appearing between 1851 and 1859, though even at that size it was incomplete. De Quincey was that most tortured of souls: the procrastinator who must nevertheless be prolific to survive. One can only imagine that he grew irritated at being condemned for such a relatively unserious crime against human life.

6   From an interview with *Women's Own Magazine* (31 October 1987).

7   Schopenhauer, *Parerga and Paralipomena*, Vol. II (1851), ß396.

8   Quoted by Phillip Lopate ("Between Insanity and Fat Dullness," *Harper's Magazine* [January 2011], p. 70), as found in *Emerson: Selected Journals 1820-1842*, Lawrence Rosenwald, ed. (Library of America, 2010).

9   *Paper Monument*, 2009.

10 John Locke, *A Letter Concerning Toleration* (Filiquarian, 2007), p. 20 (capitalization modernized).

11 "'Tis not contrary to reason to prefer the destruction of the whole world to the scratching of my finger. 'Tis not contrary to reason for me to choose my total ruin, to prevent the least uneasiness of an Indian or person wholly unknown to me. 'Tis as little contrary to reason to prefer even my own acknowledged lesser good to my greater, and have a more ardent affection for the former than the latter. Reason's only purpose is to help us to satisfy our desires. Reason is, and ought only to be, the slave of the passions." David Hume, *A Treatise of Human Nature*, II.3.3. p. 415.

12 *The Invisible Committee, The Coming Insurrection* (Semiotext(e), 2009), pp. 110-11.

13 In the United States corporations were recognized as having the rights to contract as natural persons in *Dartmouth College v. Woodward*, decided in 1819. In the 1886 case *Santa Clara County v. Southern Pacific Railroad*, 118 U.S. 394, the Supreme Court further recognized corporations as persons for purposes of the Fourteenth Amendment, which guarantees due process and equal protection.

14 Roger D. Hodge, *The Mendacity of Hope: Barack Obama and the Betrayal of American Liberalism* (HarperCollins, 2010), p. 220. Despite its somewhat tendentious title and subtitle, Hodge's book is a useful and witty popular primer on the hollowing out of civic republican virtue under conditions of capito-democracy circa 2010.

15 *Citizens United v. Federal Election Commission*, 130 S. Ct. 876 (2010), pp. 43-44. Here Kennedy is quoting his own dissenting opinion in *McConnell v. Federal Election Commission*, 540 U.S. 93 (2003), a 68-page document in which he (joined by then-Chief Justice William Rehnquist) argued that reforms to limit campaign contributions forced "speakers to abandon their own preference for speaking through parties and organizations."

16 There is of course a good joke lurking here, captured in an old cartoon contrasting rude-but-friendly New York with sunny-but-insincere Los Angeles. In the first frame, two Angelenos greet each other with speech bubbles that read "Have a nice day!" even as their thought bubbles record an unspoken "Fuck you!" In the second frame, two Gothamites reverse the alignment of speech and thought: *Fuck you! = Have a nice day!*

17 Compare Carl Schmitt on this issue, especially in *The Concept of the Political* (George Schwab trans.; University of Chicago Press, 2007). Schmitt argues that liberalism is a denial of real politics, occluding the existential stakes of friend and enemy with a defence of abstract individual rights. Leo Strauss's pointed "Notes on Carl Schmitt, *The Concept of the Political*" shows that Schmitt's blanket condemnation of liberalism, as an endlessly discursive antithesis to the political as such, misses the mark when we consider realist liberals such as Hobbes. (This above and beyond any intrinsic difficulties with Schmitt's notion of the political.) For the purposes of the present argument, I am adopting a stance similar to that of Hobbes; but see the final section of the essay, where friendship is thematized after a different fashion.

18 James P. Carse, *Finite and Infinite Games* (Ballantine, 1987), *passim*.

19 Jacques Derrida, *The Politics of Friendship* (George Collins, trans.; Verso, 2005), p. 53.

20 Included in Adam Zagajewski, *Canvas: Poems* (Renata Gorczynski, C. K. Williams, and Benjamin Ivry, trans.; Farrar, Straus and Giroux, 1994), p. 199.

21 Some readers may be interested to know that the famous line from Shakespeare's play is rendered this way in an uproariously foul-mouthed parody called *The Skinhead Hamlet*: "I'm fucked. The rest is fucking silence." See Richard Curtis, "The Skinhead Hamlet: Shakespeare's play rendered into modern English," in Simon Brett, ed., *The Faber Book of Parodies* (Faber, 1984), p. 320.

22 Jacques Derrida, "Force of Law: The 'Mystical Foundation of Authority'," in Gil Anidjar, ed., *Acts of Religion* (Routledge, 2001), p. 242.

23 "What we cannot speak about we must pass over in silence"—proposition 7 of Ludwig Wittgenstein, *Tractatus Logico-Philosophicus* (D. F. Pears and B. F. McGuinness, trans.; Routledge & Kegan Paul, 1961), p. 74. For a clear and engaging account of the affinities between deconstruction and Wittgensteinian philosophy of language, see Henry Staten, *Wittgenstein and Derrida* (University of Nebraska Press, 1982).

10

The Philosopher President Sets Forth:
A Monologue

AND SO YOU WOKE UP one morning and it was finally over. Victory. A triumph. Your acceptance speech was deliberately subdued, more effective in its withheld power than the barnburners of the early days. The crowd surged and wept. Your wife and daughters exited the windswept stage smiling, leaving you there, tall and handsome, a new man for a new millennium.

And what you thought then was not what people think. It was not the relief or joy of having won. It was not the burden of that same win. It was not even a mixture of the two, the smart pundit's comment of choice. He's got a lot on his mind now, Anderson. The reality is starting to sink in, Tom. Heavy lies the head, Campbell.

It was none of that. Instead you kept thinking of that moment on the late-night talk show, the funny one, when you were asked to recite a random text as if it were a speech. And you did that, because it was the funny one, and it's important to show you have a sense of humour and you're not stiff or elitist or dull. You did it. And it was weird, it was eerie, it was actually kind of creepy. The banal words came out of your mouth with the same intonation, the same building crescendos of inspiration, that floated hope and change and *yes we can* across crowds and screens and that made people, even hardened cynics, tear up a little, because even they believed it might be true or just really wanted it to be true. Or maybe because of some mysterious neurobiological response from a deep part of the primate brain that responds, physically and emotionally, to certain rhythms and stresses recalling the happiness of dancing, the beatific content of polyphonic harmony or Fibonacci curves, the line of beauty. As basic and as meaningless. As content-free.

No, worse—not content-free, content-neutral. You could say anything at all, and if it was said right it would sound right. It would *be* right. There you'd been, reciting the phone book or whatever, and it sounded *awesome*. And the host was kind of freaked out, and you were a bit freaked out too. Because what was going on anyway? If inane sentiments, random word-strings, could sound almost as certain, almost as impressive and commanding, as your real message, your message of hope and change and yes we can, what was that? Your message was real. The other wasn't. And yet they sounded the same.

But now, making another speech, accepting the office, inaugurating the new era, you thought: wait a second. This is crazy, you thought, there on the stage in front of the people shouting and waving and weeping at the mere sight and sound of you. The difference is obvious, it's *obvious*. Anyone watching you, hearing you, recite the phone book or whatever could tell the difference—that was what made it funny, the incongruity of making the meaningless sound meaningful, the contrast between appearance and reality, between acted and meant, between insincere and sincere, fake and authentic. Anyone, everyone, knows the difference. The difference is obvious!

And in fact, *in fact*, look how smooth you are, playing with this difference in such an assured way, meeting objections that you were an underqualified rhetorician, a pretender, by turning right around and taking them head-on, showing off your rhetorical skills to put them in their proper place. Not with the truth. Not with the message. Just the technique. Just the vehicle for delivering the message. One cool customer, you thought briefly to yourself there on the stage, one deft operator, being able to play around like that, to be so comfortable, so at ease with the difference that you could jump over the difference and back. You had command. It was obvious.

Was it really? Yes it was. Of course you had it, it was in your grasp, you knew in your heart, your faith was strong, your purpose true, your aims noble, and your character fine. Of course they were. You had it. Everyone said so. Everyone agreed. Everyone celebrated your command of the difference. But did you really have command? You kept wondering, and the wondering was hard to quell because that wondering was part of your having it. Your certainty came from doubt, your courage from trial, your resolve from pain. The command was earned, you'd been trying to show that for months and months now. And everyone agreed, everyone said so. The wondering remained, though, and you wondered in turn about that. If you had command, if everyone said so and everyone agreed, how come you kept wondering, how come you had moments of doubt that did not resolve into certainty, moments of trial that did not bolster courage, pains that would not go away because they were part of you.

Okay, okay—just a human being here. Not a saviour. Not a god. Not a devil either, or an evil genius. Just one man, risen to the top. Risen to the top of a system where the oneness of one man, the oneness of one woman, was the whole idea. Each one counts for one. That's the basis of the whole shebang, that's the fundamental tenet. Seven billion of us, almost, and in theory every single one counting for one. Everything flows from that, everything. Even though right now it was just 300 million or so, the ones with the right photo ID and bank accounts.

We actually know it's not true, it's a fiction, this counting for one. A *necessary* fiction, you thought, standing there. It's one of those fictions that serve a crucial purpose and therefore are accepted, their untruth converted to value. You might call it a noble lie, a lie with moral sanction. Because nothing would work without it. The whole system would crash if we stopped agreeing to suspend disbelief about this one thing, this basic idea. The whole business would come tumbling down. One counts for one. Even though it doesn't. And it doesn't because we're not equal, in opportunity or access to justice, let alone wealth, any more than in talent or good looks. Because nobody without hundreds of millions of dollars to spend could even think seriously of standing where you were now. Because one man with dark skin was not about to change the fact that who your parents were accounted for most of what your life would be like—despite the constant claims directly to the contrary.

Those claims had to keep coming, though, and we had to go on believing them, or else everything would falter. You wondered: did we play at democracy the way we play at cards or dice, evening out differences with the mechanisms of chance, with fictional order and accepted rules? Or perhaps as children play, imagining and taking on roles, switching them around, acting them out, *pretending*? A magical system, a brilliant invention, the best one so far?

People talked a lot about cheating as a threat to the game's sanctity. It wasn't really. Whether we like it or not, cheating is still a way of playing the game. Cheating is second-order pretending within the first-order pretending of the game itself. Cheating is pretending to play the pretending which is the game itself. Cheating is entirely compatible within the game, maybe even called out by the gamesmanship of the game. That's why those congressional harangues of hypo-happy baseball players sometimes seemed so bizarre: they were just acting the way the game encouraged them to act. Which is good, or anyway convenient, since cheating seemed pretty common in this largest game, the game of the system. Sure, people disagreed about what counted as cheating— but that was actually a big part of the game! You couldn't assassinate your opponent, yes, but was it cheating for two political parties to burn through $2.4 billion in order to enact the two-year drama of decision, the endless narrative of mandate, that got you here? You didn't think so, or at least you weren't prepared to say so.

And was it cheating for the nation's Treasury to toss more than $1 trillion after the failing health of financial ventures, those losing bets they called "institutions" or "pillars" of the economy? Or $775 billion to the myopic makers of automobiles, the crystallized worst selves of your nation, the supercharged producers of consumption, the great demons of desire? Was that cheating? It had better not be, because in a few minutes it would be you standing there, holding the ticket, guarantor of the loan, chaser of your predecessor's cheques, pre-compromised, shameful, the biggest mark in the whole game. A deficit of $1.2 trillion. A debt of $10.3 trillion. How easily the word *trillion*, the concept of *a trillion dollars*, rolled around the mind and off the tongue.

But even if any of that *was* cheating—which it wasn't, you thought, standing there, not really, maybe incompetence and poor judgment but not cheating—the main thing to remember was that it was still *inside the game*. What nobody could do, least of all you, now, standing there, was spoil the game by acknowledging the fictions at its heart. To refuse the collective illusion of the game is not to cheat; it is much worse. It's to be a spoilsport.

"It is curious to note how much more lenient society is to the cheat than to the spoilsport," you recalled reading, or having quoted to you. "This is because the spoilsport shatters the play-world itself," the argument went, while the cheat "pretends to be playing the game and, on the face of it, still acknowledges the magic circle."[1] The word *illusion*, you realized then, or perhaps later, actually means *in play*. They said irony was dead. It is not, you thought, as long as we keep playing at this endless round, this generalized confidence game, we call democracy.

———

And so you held firm to your belief as you stood there, risen to the top, the bearer of the message, commander of the difference, tall handsome harbinger of change and hope and yes we can.

Not to gratify your ego. Not to aggrandize yourself. But to serve. To serve a great nation and a great people, one perhaps lately fallen on hard times and bad decisions, and to remind them of their greatness, the sweet promise of their republic. You thought fleetingly of Whitman, though you never quoted him in speeches—too difficult, too weird, too gay. "Here at last is something in the doings of man that corresponds with the broadcast doings of the day and night. Here is not merely a nation but a teeming nation of nations. Here is action untied from strings necessarily blind to particulars and details magnificently moving in vast masses. Here is the hospitality which forever indicates heroes."[2]

You wanted to be that hero, the hero of openness. To embody the endless hospitality of a nation that has always, always—well, always until now, until these late dark days—made a place at the hearth for the stranger, the unaccommodated, the barren and rootless. "The proof of a poet is that his country absorbs him as affectionately as he has absorbed it," the poet concluded. And you wanted to be that poet, thought perhaps you could be that poet. You wanted to be absorbed in just that way. You had the command, everyone said so, everyone agreed.

But then the wonder, the doubt. Were you perhaps a poet the way an advertising copywriter is a poet? A genius of desire? Not merely a shill, not a crude hawker. Not some tired drummer knocking on doors or pushing knife-sets and shammies at state fairs and travelling midways. Rather a purveyor of aspiration, a dream merchant, a wizard of longing and its satisfaction. They projected their desires onto you, the good ones and the bad ones, and you mirrored them back. Yes! And yet you knew, somewhere in the back of your fine, subtle, highly trained mind that the only way to satisfy one longing is to replace it with another, to shuffle the dreams and desires along using the skill of your ideas. They weren't just any ideas, empty ideas. They were good ideas, ideas of substance! Big and moving ideas, about hope and change, about justice and truth.

There was another writer, also dead. He had covered your opponent's campaign in an earlier election, how strange, and he killed himself exactly seven years and one day after the terrorist attacks that brought such power to the executive you were ousting. The same executive your current opponent had failed to best for his party's nomination eight years ago. The writer was a young man still when he took his own life—only a little younger than you, with a mind as fine, as subtle, as highly trained as your own.

He had said this about political writing: "The rhetoric of the enterprise is fucked. Ninety-five percent of political commentary, whether spoken or written, is now polluted by the very politics it's supposed to be about. Meaning it's become totally ideological and reductive: The writer/speaker has certain political convictions or affiliations, and proceeds to filter all reality and spin all assertion according to those convictions and loyalties. Everybody's pissed off and exasperated and impervious to argument from any other side. Opposing viewpoints are not just incorrect but contemptible, corrupt, evil."[3]

He went on: "There's no more complex, messy, community-wide argument (or 'dialogue'); political discourse is now a formulaic matter of preaching to one's own choir and demonizing the opposition. Everything's relentlessly black-and-whitened. Since the truth is way, way more gray and complicated than any one ideology can capture, the whole thing seems to me not just stupid but stupefying."

He went on: "[This] simply abets the uncomplicatedly sexy delusion that one side is Right and Just and the other Wrong and Dangerous. Which is of course a pleasant delusion, in a way—as is the belief that every last person you're in conflict with is an asshole—but it's childish, and totally unconducive to hard thought, give and take, compromise, or the ability of grown-ups to function as any kind of community …

Implicit in this brief, shrill answer, though, is obviously the idea that at least some political writing should be Platonically disinterested, should rise above the fray."

You remember reading that, or having someone tell you about it on the plane, or anyway knowing it was there, and you thought: you could be that disinterested voice, that focus for dialogue. That could be your role, your part to play. You had, to be sure, said some things during the campaign that were ideological and reductive, spun and even demonizing. But that was part of playing the game, moving the agenda forward, contesting the mandate. Now we could move toward justice and the truth, and the hope for change would be justified. But right away you wondered: How would you know? How would you ever know that your dialogue was tracking the truth, moving toward justice, unless you already knew what justice and truth were! And knowing those things, or claiming to know them, would put you right back into the frame as *right* versus those who were certainly wrong, if not necessarily contemptible, corrupt, evil.

In fact, you thought, standing there, isn't the idea of Platonic disinterest really a contradiction? Right? Because the Platonic philosopher *knows* things, he doesn't just suspect or hope about them. He's in possession of the truth, about truth and justice and all the rest of it. Possession, knowledge; not hope, not belief. In fact, he's the only one who does know, that's what makes him the right person—the one and only right person—to be in charge. And yet, you don't buy that really, do you, even if you do think you're the right answer for right now. That idea of the transcendental telescope, the possession of the ultimate truth. That was not the command you claimed. You were not a philosopher-king, even if some people accused you of believing it, of craving that status. No, your command was over something else: a story, a narrative, a sense of possibility.

That's why you peppered every speech, every rhetorical moment, with a fistful of mini-narratives, about ordinary people and their ordinary desires. The single dad working two jobs. The mom and pop trying to make their small business grow. The laid-off steelworker trying to learn how to be a daycare provider. You gathered those lives and compressed them into bites and sent them back out into the political ether, and it was good. It was good because everyone said so, everyone agreed, they were uplifting and human and engaging. The way a philosopher could never be. And when people derided you and said you had only stories, and no real ideas or proposals, you told them about the idea of justice that was buried in those stories, the hope for change that the narratives carried. The stories were the ideas, the narrative *was* the justice.

Justice. You weren't about to define it in terms of some Big Idea, some capital-J vision. Because that would trap you, it would hold you back in your way of playing the game, your strategy of "post-partisan pragmatism," a phrase everybody seemed to like, seemed ready for. Also it would risk seeming like a Platonic claim after all, to have *knowledge* of what justice is. A praised novel of the day expressed the spirit of the times clearly, if a little brutally—more brutally than you would. "After the ruinous experiments of the lately deceased century, after so much vile behaviour, so many deaths, a queasy agnosticism has settled around these matters of justice and redistributed wealth. No more big ideas. The world must improve, if at all, by tiny steps. People mostly take an existential view—having to sweep the streets for a living looks like simple bad luck. It's not a visionary age. The streets need to be clean. Let the unlucky enlist."[4]

You liked the idea that the previous century was deceased, making way for a new life, but the language of bad luck was not yours. Instead, after the fashion of your time and place, you spoke of faith. Faith in a providential Lord, and in the wisdom of your fathers, and in the greatness of the nation and its people. But most importantly, faith in markets and taxes. "The market," you had said to the man with the notepad, "is the best mechanism ever invented for allocating resources to maximize production." You also said, "There is a connection between the freedom of the marketplace and freedom more generally."[5] People asked you what your vision of the nation was, and the answer was simple and obvious: people should be free to do whatever the market allows.

But then, to make sure things didn't get out of hand—which they had over the past few years, everyone now agreed, which they would if there were no constraints at all—you wanted to tax people. Yes, tax

them. Everyone, but very rich people more than others. And that tax-
ing would be just, would be all that justice meant. You didn't like the
word "redistributive," you had told the reporter, but now growth would
benefit everybody again and everybody would be happy. They would
be happy because their desires for things could be met, mostly, by the
market's genius at allocating resources. And then the new desires they
had would spur them on to more and more things.

What was it for? What was it in the service of? Well, nothing, really.
At least nothing beyond itself, nothing bigger than the desires themselves. Deep down, you thought that someone's having a desire was
enough to make that desire legitimate. You thought, standing there,
that this was basic. That's what you meant by freedom, and that's why
you thought markets were so good at doing what they do. That was
your vision. In this vision, there is no beyond—that was the point of
being free.

Well, there is God, obviously. You couldn't imagine standing here
without talking about God. Not even you, with your many gifts, of
hope and charisma and racial novelty, could have been standing there
had you not talked about God. This was, it's true, a God almost entirely
without program or demands, without risks or rewards, pretty much
without content. This God offered comfort when you had to ask young
men and women to kill the nation's enemies or when you and everyone
else had to confront the finitude of life. Maybe not surprisingly in this
land of the game, It or He seemed designed for pointing to after field
goals or home runs—the doubled We're-Number-One gesture that
defined the era. But that was about it.

You talked about faith, and you were sincere when you did, but
the faith you talked about never sounded like the infinite task that you
had read about in old books, maybe the kind of books that were on the
mind of that still-young man, the writer, when he killed himself. How
hard it is, how not even possible, to remain convinced of the value of
here, this nation and this earth, this mortality.

You were not like that. You were the post-partisan pragmatic, after
all, and in secret moments you figured people should not be surprised
when those principles extended to God as well. The truth is just what
works, pragmatism says, and what works better than that as an answer
to any demand for the truth? Game on.

——

Your speech was almost over. It had been a good one, of course, uplifting but realistic, emotional but hard-headed. You were really very good at this. You wanted everyone to know you were ready, that they had made the right choice. You promised oversight and stimulus and the double lever of free markets and higher taxes. You reminded the nation of the grave challenges ahead, the need for goodwill and courage. You called them to their better selves.

You did not specify what those better selves might be, except in general terms of family and so on, the usual stuff, because specificity would not respect the desires of this great democratic nation, where each one counted for one, where freedom was everything. Everyone here gets to dream! And if the dream is empty, that's a *good* thing, that's a positive. That's what makes the dream everyone's dream.

You realized then something that had nagged at your fine mind, your subtle mind, throughout the many months leading to this moment, to this speech. The hopes you had spoken of, over and over, the changes you called for, they were just like the dream. In fact, you saw now, they were the dream. And it followed that they, too, were free of content. They were empty categories, levers without purchase.

But now, you thought, now that you were almost in the big chair, that was okay. That, in fact, was your special genius. Not your height and good looks and racial category. Not your fitness and charisma. Not your fashion sense, your magazine covers, your comic-book appearances, bobble-head dolls, and action figures. Not your ability to succeed where others had failed. Certainly not your will to change the system, or to articulate any bold new vision. None of that was going to happen. Not just because the system was too big for anyone to change it, though that was certainly true.

Yes, everyone was going to be disappointed. That was inevitable, you thought, not for the first time. The expectations were too great to avoid disappointment. You recalled, with an inward smile, the fake newspaper headlines in the parody issue of the *New York Times*. Remember? The one distributed the week after the election and dated Independence

Day 2009. *Nation sets its sights on building sane economy. Pentagon ends secret budget. USA Patriot Act repealed. Public relations industry forecasts a series of massive layoffs. Court indicts Bush on high treason charge. Torture, rendition "not such good ideas after all."* It was funny because it wasn't true. And it wasn't going to be true, not even close, though you couldn't say that, especially not now, not here.

No, despite everything you had said, despite your command of the difference, your awareness that everyone said so, everyone agreed, your special genius was not change. Your gift was not even political—it was more metaphysical, more spectral. You saw that, oddly enough, you were bound to become a sort of philosopher-king after all. Not in your decisions or actions, not because of your special vision, but by your example. In the very fact of you and your inevitable failure, the inescapable disappointment, the pre-compromised nature of the whole undertaking, the entire game. You didn't tell the noble lie, you were the noble lie. Your special genius was to show that democracy is impossible but that *we have to play it anyway*.

Hope was the right word all along, because it is nothing more or less than the unresolved remainder of politics. Hope is that which will not submit either to policy analysis or to dialectic reasoning. Hope forever extends and remains, it is always not yet, always to come. You can make speeches about it, but you can't bring it to the mat later on, you can't *implement* it. There are no policy implications, no legislative measures, that move hope from theory to application. But—and here was the crux of the thing, the gist of the matter—without that hope, we would surely be lost to the same despair as the still-young man, the writer who took his life. The emptiness of our desires and our dreams, the paltry contours of our lives and efforts, the smallness of our vision, would swallow us up. Without hope, we would see that the bleakness of the world is not that it is unjust but that it is meaningless.

You would not change that. Nobody would change that, ever. No we can't! But you would make your own specific failure into hope's success. And then someone else, pointing up at another God, would have to try.

Notes:

1 Johan Huizinga, *Homo Ludens: A Study of the Play-Element in Culture* (R. F. C. Hull, trans.; Beacon Press, 1955; orig. 1938), p 11.

2 Walt Whitman, from the Preface to the 1855 edition of *Leaves of Grass*.

3 This and the subsequent quotations are taken from an interview between David Foster Wallace (R.I.P.) and Dave Eggers in *The Believer* (November 2003); available at http://www.believermag.com/issues/200311/?read=interview_wallace

4 Ian McEwan, *Saturday* (Jonathan Cape, 2005), p. 74.

5 All quotations are from David Leonhardt, "Obamanomics," *New York Times Magazine* (20 August 2008), *passim*.

11

Wage Slavery, Bullshit, and the Good Infinite

BEFORE OCCUPY WALL STREET and its various offshoots took centre stage in the fall of 2011, it was remarked, if not exactly often then at least poignantly, that there had not been, in the wake of 2008's economic meltdown, any sustained political critique of the system or individuals responsible for the collapse. No general strikes. No riots or mass demonstrations. No protest songs, angry novels, or outbreaks of resistant political consciousness. In contrast to the Great Depression of the 1930s, the 'recession' or 'correction' or 'setback' (choose your *status quo* euphemism) of 2008 had barely impinged on the popular media.[1]

Even the special class of idleness-under-duress fantasy film has disappeared without a trace: there is no contemporary equivalent of the heroes of those great 1930s and 40s freedom-from-work Hollywood comedies: Cary Grant and Katharine Hepburn in *Holiday* (1938, d. George Cukor) or Joel McCrea in *Sullivan's Travels* (1942, d. Preston Sturges). "I want to find out *why* I'm working," says the Grant character, a self-made man, in the former film. "It can't be just to pay the bills and pile up more money." His wealthy fiancée—and her blustering banker-father, seeing a future junior partner in his son-in-law—thinks it can be just that. Which is why Grant goes off with the carefree older sister, Hepburn, on what might just be a permanent holiday from work. In *Sullivan's Travels*, Hollywood honcho McCrea goes in search of the real America of afflicted life—only to conclude that mindless entertainment is a necessity in hard times. Childlike joy and freedom from drudgery is more, not less, defensible when unemployment rates rise. But there is no Preston Sturges for our own day.

The reasons are puzzling. The collapse proved every anti-capitalist critic right, though without anything much changing as a result. The system was bloated and spectral, yes, borrowing on its borrowing, insuring its insurance, and skimming profit on every transaction.

The FIRE sector—finance, insurance, real estate—had created the worst market bubble since the South Sea Company's 1720 collapse and nobody should have been surprised when that latest party balloon of capital burst. And yet everybody was. It was as if a collective delusion had taken hold of the world's seven billion souls, the opposite of group paranoia: an unshakeable false belief in the reality of the system. As a result of that, in the wake of the crisis, awareness of the system's untenability changed nothing. The government bailout schemes—known as stimulus packages, a phrase that belongs easily in the pages of porn—effectively socialized some failing industries, saddling their collapse on taxpayers, even as it handed over billions of dollars to the people responsible for the bloat in the first place. Unemployment swept through vulnerable sectors in waves of layoffs and cutbacks, and 'downturn' became an inarguable excuse for all manner of cost-saving action. Not only did nothing change in the system, the system emerged stronger than ever, now just more tangled in the enforced tax burdens and desperate job-seeking of individuals. Meanwhile, the role of gainful occupation in establishing or maintaining all of (1) biological survival, (2) social position and, especially in American society, (3) personal identity was undiminished.

Capitalism is probably beyond large-scale change, but we should not waste this opportunity to interrogate its most fundamental idea: work. A curious sub-genre of writing washed up on the shore of this crisis, celebrating manual labour and tracing globalized foodstuffs and consumer products back to their origins in toil.[2] The problem with these efforts, despite their charms, is that they do not resist the idea of work in the first instance. The pleasures of craft or intricacies of production have their value; but they are no substitute for resistance. And no matter what the inevitabilists say, resistance to work is not futile. It may not overthrow capitalism, but it does highlight essential things about our predicament—philosophy's job ever.

My contention in this essay is that the values of work are still dominant in far too much of life; indeed, that these values have exercised their own kind of linguistic genius in creating a host of phrases, terms, and labels that bolster, rather than challenge, the dominance of work. Ideology is carried forward effectively by many vehicles, including narrative and language. And we see that this vocabulary of work is itself a kind of Trojan Horse within language, naturalizing and so making invisible some of the very dubious, if not evil, assumptions of the work idea. This is all the more true when economic times are bad, since work then becomes itself a scarce commodity. That makes people anxious, and the anxiety is taken up by work: *Don't fire me! I don't want to be out of work!* Work looms larger than ever, the assumed natural condition whose 'loss' makes the non-working individual by definition a loser.

—

Consider the nature of work. In a 1932 essay called "In Praise of Idleness," Bertrand Russell is in fact more incisive about work than he is about idleness, which he seems to view as the mere absence of work (in my terms, defended elsewhere, that is slacking rather than idling).[3] Russell defines work this way:

> Work is of two kinds: first, altering the position of matter at or near the earth's surface relatively to other such matter; second, telling other people to do so. The first kind is unpleasant and ill paid; the second is pleasant and highly paid.

Russell goes on to note that "The second kind is capable of indefinite extension: there are not only those who give orders, but those who give advice as to what orders should be given." This second-order advice is what is meant by *bureaucracy*; and if two opposite kinds of advice are given at the same time, then it is known as *politics*. The skill needed for this last kind of work is not, Russell says, "knowledge of the subjects as to which advice is given, but knowledge of the art of persuasive speaking and writing, i.e. of advertising."

Very little needs to be added to this analysis except to note something crucial which Russell appears to miss: the *greatest work of work* is to disguise its essential nature. The grim ironists of the Third Reich were exceptionally forthright when they fixed the evil, mocking maxim *Arbeit Macht Frei*—work shall make you free—over the gates at Dachau and Auschwitz. One can only conclude that this was their idea of a sick joke, and that their ideological commitments were not with work at all, but with despair and extermination.

The real ideologists of work are never so transparent, nor so wry. But they are clever, because their genius is, in effect, to fix a different maxim over the whole of the world: work is fun! Or, to push the point to its logical conclusion, *it's not work if it doesn't feel like work.* And so celebrated workaholics excuse themselves from what is in fact an addiction, and in the same stroke implicate everyone else for not working hard enough. "Work is the grand cure of all the maladies and miseries that ever beset mankind," said that barrel of fun, Thomas Carlyle.[4] "Nothing is really work unless you would rather be doing something else," added J. M. Barrie, perhaps destabilizing his position on Peter Pan. And even the apparently insouciant Noël Coward argued that "Work is much more fun than fun."[5] Really? Perhaps he meant to say, 'what most people consider fun'. But still. Claims like these just lay literary groundwork for the *Fast Company* work/play manoeuvre of the 1990s or the current, more honest compete-or-die productivity language.

Work deploys a network of techniques and effects that make it seem inevitable and, where possible, pleasurable. Central among these effects is the diffusion of responsibility for the baseline need for work: everyone accepts, because everyone knows, that everyone must have a job. Bosses as much as subordinates are slaves to the larger servo-mechanisms of work, which are spectral and non-localizable. In effect, work is the largest self-regulation system the universe has so far manufactured, subjecting each of us to a generalized panopticon shadow under which we dare not do anything but work, or at least seem to be working, lest we fall prey to an obscure disapproval all the more powerful for being so. The work idea functions in the same manner as a visible surveillance camera, which need not even be hooked up to anything. No, let's go further: there need not even be a camera. Like the prisoners in the perfected version of Bentham's uber-utilitarian jail, workers need no overseer *because they watch themselves.*[6] There is no need for actual guards; when we submit to work, we are guard and guarded at once.[7]

Offshoots of this system are somewhat more visible to scrutiny, and so tend to fetch the largest proportion of critical objection. A social theorist will challenge the premises of inevitability in market forces, or wonder whether economic 'laws' are anything more than self-serving generalizations. These forays are important, but they leave the larger inevitabilities of work mostly untouched. In fact, such critical debates tend to reinforce the larger ideological victory of work, because they accept the baseline assumptions of it even in their criticisms. Thus does work neutralize, or indeed annex, critical energy from within the system. The slacker is the tragic hero here, a small-scale version of a Greek protagonist. In his mild resistance—long stays in the mailroom, theft of office supplies, forgery of time cards, ostentatious toting of empty files—the slacker cannot help but sustain the system. This is resistance, but of the wrong sort; it really is futile, because the system, whatever its official stance, loves slackers. They embody the work idea in their very objection.[8]

None of that will be news to anyone who has ever been within the demand-structure of a workplace. What is less clear is why we put up with it, why we don't resist more robustly. As Max Weber noted in his analysis of leadership under capitalism, any ideology must, if it is to succeed, give people reasons to act.[9] It must offer a narrative of identity to those caught within its ambit, otherwise they will not continue to perform, and renew, its reality. As with most truly successful ideologies, the work idea latches on to a very basic feature of human existence: our character as social animals jostling for position. But social critics are precipitate if they argue that all human action was motivated by tiny distinctions between winner and loser. In fact, the recipe for action is that recognition of those differences *plus* some tale of why the differences matter and, ideally, are rooted in the respective personal qualities or 'character' of winner and loser.

No tale can be too fanciful to sustain this outcome. Serbs and Croats may engage in bloody warfare over relatively trivial genetic or geographical differences, provided both sides accept the story of what the difference means. In the case of work, the evident genius lies in reifying what is actually fluid, namely social position and 'elite' status within hierarchies. The most basic material conditions of work—office size and position, number of windows, attractiveness of assistant, cut of suit—are simultaneously the rewards *and* the ongoing indicators of status within this competition. Meanwhile, the competition sustains itself backward via credentialism: that is, the accumulation of degrees and certificates from 'prestigious' schools and universities which, though often substantively unrelated to the work at hand, indicate appropriate elite grooming. These credentialist back-formations confirm the necessary feeling that a status outcome is *earned*, not merely conferred. Position without an attendant narrative of merit would not satisfy the ideological demand for action to seem meaningful.

The result is *entrenched* rather than *circulating* elites. The existence of elites is, in itself, neither easily avoidable nor obviously bad. The so-called Iron Law of Oligarchy states that "every field of human endeavor, every kind of organization, will always be led by a relatively small elite."[10] This oligarchic tendency answers demands for efficiency and direction, but more basically it is agreeable to humans on a socio-evolutionary level. We like elite presence in our undertakings, and tend to fall into line behind it. But the narrative of merit in elite status tends to thwart circulation of elite membership, and encourage the false idea that such status is married to 'intrinsic' qualities of the individual. In reality, the status is a kind of collective delusion, not unlike the one that sustains money, another key narrative of the system.

At this stage, it is possible to formulate 'laws'—actually law-like generalizations—about the structure of a work-idea company, which is any company in thrall to the work idea, including (but not limited to) bureaucracies. Parkinson's, Pournelle's, and Moore's Laws of Bureaucracy may be viewed as derivatives of the Iron Law, understood as ways in which we can articulate how the system sustains itself and its entrenched elite. While expressly about bureaucracies, these generalizations speak to the inescapable bureaucratic element in all workplaces, even those that try to eschew that element. In short, they explicate the work idea even as that idea works to keep its precise contours implicit.

Parkinson's Law is minimalist in concept but wide in application. It states: "There need be little or no relationship between the work to be done and the size of the staff to which it may be assigned."[11] This despite the lip service often paid to the norm of efficiency. Parkinson also identified two axiomatic underlying forces responsible for the growth in company staff: (1) "An official wants to multiply subordinates, not rivals"; and (2) "Officials make work for each other." The second may be more familiar as the Time-Suck Axiom, which states that all meetings must generate further meetings. And so at a certain threshold we may observe that meetings are, for all intents and purposes, entirely self-generating, like consciousness. They do not need the humans who 'hold' them at all, except to be present during the meeting and not doing anything else.

Examining the company structure at one level higher, that is, in the motivation of the individuals, the science fiction writer Jerry Pournelle proposed a theory he referred to as Pournelle's Iron Law of Bureaucracy. It states that "In any bureaucracy, the people devoted to the benefit of the bureaucracy itself always get in control and those dedicated to the goals the bureaucracy is supposed to accomplish have less and less influence, and sometimes are eliminated entirely."[12] In other words, just as meetings become self-generating, so too does the company structure as a whole. *The company* becomes a norm of its own, conceptually distinct from whatever the company makes, does, or provides.

Once this occurs—most obvious in the notion of 'company loyalty', with the required 'team-building' weekends, ball caps, golf shirts, and logos—there will be positive incentives for position-seekers to neglect or even ignore other values ostensibly supported by the company. More seriously, if Pournelle's Law is correct, then these position-seekers will become the dominant position-holders, such that any norms outside 'the company' will soon fade and disappear. The company is now a self-sustaining evolutionary entity, with no necessary goals beyond its own continued existence, to which end the desires of individual workers can be smoothly assimilated.

Moore's Laws take the analysis even further. If a bureaucracy is a servo-mechanism, its ability to process an error signal, and so generate corrective commands and drive the system away from error, is a function of the depth of the hierarchy. But instead of streamlining hierarchy and so making error-correction easier, bureaucracies do the opposite: they deepen the hierarchy, adding new error sensors but lessening the system's ability to respond to them. Large bureaucracies are inherently noisy systems whose very efforts to achieve goals makes them noisier. Thus, Moore concludes, (1) large bureaucracies cannot possibly achieve their goals; as a result, (2) they will thrash about, causing damage.[13]

He suggests five further laws. The power wielded by bureaucracies will tend to attract above-mean numbers of sociopaths to their ranks. Hence (3) large bureaucracies are *evil*. Because the mechanism of the system increases noise as it attempts to eliminate it, system members in contact with the rest of reality will be constrained by rigid, though self-defeating rules. Thus (4) large bureaucracies are *heartless*. They are also (5) *perverse*, subordinating stated long-term goals to the short-term ambitions of the humans within the system; (6) *immortal*, because their non-achievement of goals makes them constantly replace worn-out human functionaries with new ones; and finally (7) *boundless*, since there is no theoretical limit to the increased noise, size, and complexity of an unsuccessful system.

—

So much for elites looking backward, justifying their place in the work idea, and finding ever novel ways of expanding without succeeding. Pournelle's and Moore's laws highlight how, looking forward, the picture is considerably more unnerving. The routine collection of credentials, promotions, and employee-of-the-month honours in exchange for company loyalty masks a deeper existential conundrum—which is precisely what it is meant to do.

Consider: It is an axiom of status anxiety that the competition for position has no end—save, temporarily, when a scapegoat is found. The scapegoat reaffirms everyone's status, however uneven, because he is beneath all. Hence many work narratives are miniature blame-quests. We come together as a company to fix guilt on one of our number, who is then publicly shamed and expelled. *Jones filed a report filled with errors! Smith placed an absurdly large order and the company is taking a bath!* This makes us all feel better, and enhances our sense of mission, even if it produces nothing other than its own spectacle.

Blame-quests work admirably on their small scale. At larger scales, the narrative task is harder. What is the company for? What does it do? Here, as when a person confronts mortality, we teeter on the abyss. The company doesn't actually do much of anything. It is not for anything important. The restless forward movement of companies—here at Compu-Global-Hyper-Mega-Net, we are always *moving on*—is work's version of the Hegelian Bad Infinite, the meaningless nothing of empty everything.[14] There is no point to what is being done, but it must be done anyway. The boredom of the average worker, especially in a large corporation, is the walking illustration of this meaninglessness. But boredom can lower productivity, so a large part of work's energy is expended in finding ways to palliate the boredom that is the necessary outcome of work in order to raise productivity: a sort of credit-default swap of the soul. Workaholism is the narcotic version of this, executed within the individual himself. The workaholic colonizes his own despair at the perceived emptiness of life—its non-productivity—by filling it in with work.[15]

It can be no surprise that the most searching critic of work, Karl Marx, perceived this Hegelian abyss at the heart of all paid employment. But Marx's theory of alienated labour, according to which our efforts and eventually our selves become commodities bought and sold for profit to others, is just one note in a sustained chorus of opposition and resistance to work.[16] "Never work," the Situationist Guy Debord commanded, articulating the baseline of opposition.[17] Another Situationist slogan, the famous graffito of May 1968, reminded us that the order and hardness of the urban infrastructure masked a playful, open-ended sense of possibility that was even more fundamental: *Sous les pavés, la plage!* Under the paving stones, the beach!

Between Marx and Debord lies the great, neglected Georges Sorel, a counter-enlightenment and even countercultural voice whose influence can be seen to run into the likes of Debord, Franz Fanon, and Che Guevara; but also Timothy Leary, Jack Kerouac, and Ken Kesey. Like many other radical critics, Sorel perceived the emptiness of the liberal promise of freedom once it becomes bound up with regimentation and bourgeoisification of everyday life. Sorel was a serial enthusiast, moving restlessly from cause to cause: a socialist, a Dreyfusard, an ascetic, an anti-Dreyfusard. In the first part of the twentieth century he settled on the labour movement as his home and proposed a general strike that would (in the words of Isaiah Berlin, who had tremendous respect for this against-the-grain thinker):

call for the total overthrow of the entire abominable world of calculation, profit and loss, the treatment of human beings and their powers as commodities, as material for bureaucratic manipulation, the world of illusory consensus and social harmony, or economic and sociological experts no matter what master they serve, who treat men as subjects of statistical calculations, malleable "human material, forgetting that behind such statistics there are living human beings."[18]

In other words, late capitalism and all that it entails.

One might wonder, first, why such resistance is recurrently necessary but also, second, why it seems ever to fail. The answer lies in the evolutionary fact of *language upgrade*. In common with all ideologies, the work idea understands that that victory is best which is achieved soonest, ideally before the processes of conscious thought are allowed to function. And so it is here that language emerges as the clear field of battle. Language acquisition is crucial to our evolutionary success because it aids highly complex coordination of action. But that same success hinges also on the misdirection, deception, control, and happy illusion carried out by language, because these too make for coordinated action. Thus the upgrade is at the same time a downgrade: language allows us to distinguish between appearance and reality, but it also allows some of us to persuade others that appearances are realities. If there were no distinction, this would not matter; indeed, it would not be possible. Deception can only work if there is such a thing as truth, as Socrates demonstrated in the first book of Plato's *Republic*.

Jargon, slogans, euphemisms and terms of art are all weapons in the upgrade/downgrade tradition. We should class them together under the technical term *bullshit*, as analyzed by philosopher Harry Frankfurt. The routine refusal to speak with regard to the truth is called bullshit because evasion of normativity produces a kind of ordure, a dissemination of garbage, the scattering of shit. This is why, as Frankfurt reminds us, bullshit is far more threatening, and politically evil, than lying. The bullshitter "does not reject the authority of the truth, as the liar does, and oppose himself to it. He pays no attention to it at all. By virtue of this, bullshit is the greater enemy of the truth than lies are."[19]

Work language is full of bullshit. But by thinking about these terms rather than using them, or mocking them, we can hope to bring the enemy into fuller light, to expose the erasure that work's version of Newspeak forever seeks. Special vigilance is needed because the second-order victory of work bullshit is that, in addition to having no regard for the truth, it passes itself off as innocuous or even beneficial. Especially in clever hands, the controlling elements of work are repackaged as liberatory, countercultural, subversive: you're a skatepunk rebel because you work seventy hours a week beta-testing videogames. This, we might say, is meta-bullshit. And so far from what philosophers might assert, or wish, this meta-bullshit and not truth is the norm governing most coordinated human activity under conditions of capital markets. Thus does bullshit meet, and become, filthy lucre; and of course, vice versa.

As the work idea spins itself out in language, we observe a series of linked paradoxes in the world of work: imprisonment via inclusion; denigration via celebration; obfuscation via explanation; conformity via distinction; failure via success; obedience via freedom; authority via breezy coolness. The manager is positioned as an 'intellectual', a 'visionary', even a 'genius'. 'Creatives' are warehoused and petted. Demographics are labelled, products are categorized. Catchphrases, acronyms, proverbs, clichés, and sports metaphors are marshalled and deployed. Diffusion of sense through needless complexity, diffusion of responsibility through passive constructions, and elaborate celebration of minor achievements mark the language of work.

And so: Outsourcing. Repositioning. Downsizing. Rebranding. Work the mission statement. Push the envelope. Think outside the box. Stay in the loop. See the forest and the trees. Note sagely that where there is smoke there is also fire. Casual Fridays! Smartwork! Hotdesking! The whole nine yards! Touchdown! You-topia!

These shopworn work-idea locutions have already been exposed, and mocked, such that we may think we know our enemy all too well. But the upgrade/downgrade is infinitely inventive. The work of language-care is never over.

You might think, at this point, that a language problem naturally calls for a language solution. The very same inventiveness that marks the ideology of work can be met with a wry, subversive counterintelligence. Witness such portmanteau pun words as 'slacktivism' or 'crackberry' which mock, respectively, people who think that forwarding emails is a form of political action and those who are in thrall to text messages the way some people are addicted to crack cocaine. Or observe the high linguistic style of office-bound protagonists from Nicholson Baker's *The Mezzanine* (1988) and Douglas Coupland's *Generation X* (1991) to Joshua Ferris's *Then We Came to the End* (2007) and Ed Park's *Personal Days* (2008).

These books are hilarious, and laughter is always a release. But their humour is a sign of doom, not liberation. The 'veal-fattening pen' label applied to those carpet-sided cubicles of the open-form office (Coupland) does nothing to change the facts of the office. Nor does calling office-mateyness an 'air family' (Coupland again) make the false camaraderie any less spectral. Coupland was especially inventive and dry in his generation of neologisms, but reading a bare list of them shows the hollow heart of dread beneath the humour.[20] Indeed, the laughs render the facts more palatable by mixing diversion into the scene of domination—a willing capitulation, consumed under the false sign of resistance. This applies to most of what we call slacking, a verb at least as old as 1530, when Jehan Palsgrave asked of a task-shirking friend "Whye slacke you your busynesse thus?"

That is the main reason it is essential to distinguish idling from slacking. Slacking is consistent with the work idea; it does not subvert the idea, it merely gives in to its overarching through the complicit tactics of evasion. As John Kenneth Galbraith pointed out a half-century ago in *The Affluent Society* (1958), such evasion is actually the pinnacle of corporate life:

> Indeed it is possible that the ancient art of evading work has been carried in our time to its highest level of sophistication, not to say elegance. One should not suppose that it is an accomplishment of any particular class, occupation, or profession. Apart from the universities, where its practice has the standing of a scholarly rite, the art of genteel and elaborately concealed idleness may well reach its highest development in the upper executive reaches of the modern corporation.[21]

Galbraith's 'idleness' is not to be confused with genuine idling, of course; the 'concealed' that modifies his use of the word shows why. A slacking executive is no better, and also no worse, than the lowliest clerk hiding in the mailroom to avoid a meeting. But neither is idling, which calls for openness and joy.

And so here we confront again the Bad Infinite at the heart of work. What is it for? To produce desired goods and services. But these goods and services are, increasingly, the ones needed to maintain the system itself. The product of the work system is work, and spectres such as 'profit' and 'growth' are covers for the disheartening fact that, in Galbraith's words, as "a society becomes increasingly affluent, wants are increasingly created by the process by which they are satisfied." Which is only to echo Marcuse's and Arendt's well-known *aperçus* that the basic creation of capitalism is *superfluity*—with the additional insight that capitalism must then create the demand to take up such superfluity.[22] Galbraith nails the contradiction at the heart of things: "But the case cannot stand if it is the process of satisfying wants that creates the wants. For then the individual who urges the importance of production to satisfy the wants is precisely in the position of the onlooker who applauds the efforts of the squirrel to keep abreast of the wheel that is propelled by his own efforts."[23]

Still, all is not lost. There is a treasure buried in the excess that the world of work is constantly generating: that is, a growing awareness of a *gift economy* that always operates beneath, or beyond, the exchange economy. Any market economy is a failed attempt to distribute goods and services exactly where they are needed or desired, as and when they are needed and desired. That's all markets are, despite the pathological excrescences that lately attach to them: derivatives funds, advertising, shopping-as-leisure. If we had a perfect market, idling would be the norm, not the exception, because distribution would be frictionless. As Marcuse saw decades ago, most work is the result of inefficiency, not genuine need.[24] This is all the more true in a FIRE-storm economy. Paradoxically, idling is entirely consistent with capitalism's own internal logic, which implies, even if it never realizes, the end of capitalism. This insight turns the Bad Infinite of work into a Good Infinite, where we may begin to see things not as resources, ourselves not as consumers, and the world as a site not of work but of play.

The great Marxist and Situationist critics of work hoped that critical theory—accurate analysis of the system's pathologies—would change the system. The latest crisis in capitalism has shown that it will not. But a system is made of individuals, just as a market is composed of individual choices and transactions. Don't change the system, change your life. Debord's "Never work" did not go far enough. Truly understand the nature of work and its language, and you may never even think of work again!

Notes:

1 There are some important exceptions. I will note just three here: Jonathan Dee's novel *The Privileges* (Random House, 2010), a sly satire of the blithe arrogance of one couple who swim through the economic collapse; Chris Lehmann's collection *Rich People Stuff* (OR Books, 2010), which lampoons the favoured tropes and preoccupations of one-per-centers; and Roger D. Hodge's angry screed about the Obama Administration's complicity with minimizing the responsibility of Wall Street for the collapse, *The Mendacity of Hope* (HarperCollins, 2010). One complicated example is the hit 2010 film *The Social Network* (d. David Fincher), which tells the story of Facebook 'inventor' Mark Zuckerberg in the unspoken context of the early-2000s bubble. But the film can't decide whether it is a revenge-of-the-nerds celebration or a moralistic slam of internet-age sharp dealing.

2 See, for example, Matthew Crawford, *Shop Class as Soulcraft* (Penguin, 2009) and Alain de Botton, *The Pleasures and Sorrows of Work* (Pantheon, 2009). Andrew Ross summarizes the political puzzle posed by these two well-meaning but witless books: "It is an unfortunate comment on the generous intellects of these two authors that they do not see fit to acknowledge, in their respective surveys of working life, the nobility of those who resist" ("Love Thy Labor," *Bookforum*, Fall 2009, p. 16).

3 Bertrand Russell, *In Praise of Idleness: And Other Essays* (Routledge, 2004). I argued for a distinction between idling and slacking in "Idling Toward Heaven: The Last Defence You Will Ever Need," *Queen's Quarterly* 115:4 (Winter 2008): 569-85; later adapted as the Introduction to Kingwell and Joshua Glenn, *The Idler's Glossary* (Biblioasis, 2008).

4 From Carlyle's 1866 inaugural address as rector of the University of Edinburgh. Published later in *Critical and Miscellaneous Essays*, vol. 6 (Chapman, and Hall, 1869).

5 Quoted in *The Observer's* "Sayings of the Week" (London, June 21, 1963).

6 The working principle behind Bentham's "panopticon"—that subjects under surveillance will become their own agents of discipline—garnered much attention in the later writings of Michel Foucault, who saw the same principle at work across the institutions of modern capitalist society. In *Discipline and Punish: The Birth of the Modern Prison* (as *Surveiller et Punir*, 1975; David Hurley trans. Vintage, 1977) he writes, "[Bentham's panopticon] set out to show how one may 'unlock' the disciplines and get them to function in a diffused, multiple, polyvalent way throughout the whole social body ... It programmes, at the level of an elementary and easily transferable mechanism, the basic functioning of a society penetrated through and through with disciplinary mechanisms."

7 One could cite, in support here, the analysis of Gilles Deleuze in "Postscript on the Societies of Control," *October* 59 (Winter 1992), pp. 3-7; reprinted in *Negotiations* (Martin Joughlin, trans.; Columbia University Press, 1995). Deleuze notes three modes of social structure: sovereign states (pre-modern); discipline societies (modern); and control societies (postmodern). Whereas a discipline society moulds citizens into subjects through

various carceral institutions—schools, armies, prisons, clinics—a control society can be radically decentred and apparently liberated. The difference in the world of work is between a factory and a business. A factory disciplines its subjects by treating them as a body of workers; this also affords the opportunity of organizing and resisting in the form of unionized labour. A business, by contrast, treats employees like hapless contestants on a bizarre, ever changing game show—something like Japan's "Most Extreme Elimination Challenge," perhaps—where they are mysteriously competing with fellow workers for spectral rewards allocated according to mysterious rules. The affable boss who invites you over for dinner is a paradigm case: Is it business or pleasure? Who else is invited? Does it mean a likely promotion, or nothing at all? Thus does business invade and control the psyche of the worker, precisely because obvious mechanisms of discipline are absent.

8   Corinne Maier's otherwise excellent *Bonjour Laziness* (Greg Mosse, trans., Orion, 2005), especially on the language of work, is unstable on this point. She acknowledges that the work system is impervious to challenge, and yet finally urges: "rather than a 'new man', be a blob, a leftover, stubbornly resisting the pressure to conform, impervious to manipulation. Become the grain of sand that seizes up the whole machine, the sore thumb" (p. 117). This confused message would seem to indicate insufficient grasp of the slacker/idler distinction.

9   In *The Protestant Ethic and the Spirit of Capitalism* (as *Der Protestantische Ethik und der Geist des Capitalismus*, 1905; Talcott Parsons, trans., Scribners, 1958), Weber suggests that puritan ideals—particularly, the "Protestant work ethic" of hard labour as a sign of salvation—were highly influential in the development of capitalism.

10 See Murray N. Rothbard, "Bureaucracy and the Civil Service in the United States" in *Journal of Libertarian Studies* 11:2 (Summer, 1995): 3-75, p. 4. The "Iron Law of Oligarchy" was first proposed by German sociologist Robert Michels in *Political Parties: A Sociological Study of the Oligarchical Tendencies of Modern Democracy* (1911, English trans., Hearst International, 1915; see also Transaction, 2009).

11 C. Northcote Parkinson, "Parkinson's Law," *The Economist* (November 19, 1955).

12 From Pournelle's weblog, "Chaos Manor," (December 14, 2005) < http://www.jerrypour nelle.com/archives2/archives2mail/mail392.html#iron>

13 From Moore's weblog, "Useful Fools," (October 15, 2000) <http://www.tinyvital.com/ Misc/Lawsburo.htm>

14 In his *Science of Logic* (1812-1816), Hegel characterizes the "bad infinite" as that which is "never-ending" (such as an extensively infinite series of numbers—or, more appropriately, the never-ending toils of Sisyphus in Camus's novel). This is contrasted against conceptions of infinity as being "end-less" (such as a closed circle) which, for Hegel, represents a totality insofar as it incorporates both the infinite and the finite.

15 More extreme measures can be imagined. In J.G. Ballard's novel *Super-Cannes* (HarperCollins, 2000), bored executives at a sleek French corporate park are advised by a company psychiatrist that the solution to their lowered output is not psychotherapy but psychopathology: once they begin nocturnal sorties of violence on immigrant workers and prostitutes, productivity rates soar.

16 In his *Economic and Philosophical Manuscripts* (1844), Marx characterizes four types of alienation of labour under capitalism: alienation of the worker (1) from the product of labour, (2) from the act of labouring, (3) from him/herself as a worker, and (4) from his/her fellow workers.

17 "Ne travaillez jamais" was inscribed on Rue de Seine's wall in Paris by Debord in 1953 and was later, much to Debord's disappointment, reproduced en-masse as a "humorous" post-card. <http://www.marxists.org/reference/archive/debord/1963/never-work.htm>

18 Isaiah Berlin, *Against the Current: Essays in the History of Ideas* (Hogarth Press, 1979), p. 320.

19 See Harry Frankfurt, *On Bullshit* (Princeton University Press, 2005), a huge international bestseller which was in fact a repurposed version of a journal article Frankfurt had published many years earlier, included in his collection *The Importance of What We Care About: Philosophical Essays* (Cambridge University Press, 1988).

20 See, for example, http://www.scn.org/~jonny/genx.html.

21 John Kenneth Galbraith, *The Affluent Society* (Houghton Mifflin, 1958), p. 95.

22 Arendt famously distinguishes work, labour, and action—the three aspects of the *vita activa*—in her magnum opus, *The Human Condition* (1958; University of Chicago Press, 2008). In this schema, labour operates to maintain the necessities of life (food, shelter, clothing) and is unceasing; work fashions specific things or ends, and so is finite; and action is public display of the self in visible doings. Work as we are discussing it in the present essay is obscurely spread across these categories. As a result, Arendt could indict the emptiness of a society free from labour—the wasteland of consumer desire—but could not see how smoothly the work idea would fold itself back into that wasteland in the form of workaholism.

23 Compare a more recent version of the argument, in the nihilistic words of the Invisible Committee, the group of radical French activists who published their anti-manifesto, *The Coming Insurrection*, in 2009 (anon. English trans., Semiotext(e)): "Here lies the present paradox: work has totally triumphed over all other ways of existing, at the same time as workers have become superfluous. Gains in productivity, outsourcing, mechanization, automated and digital production have so progressed that they have almost reduced to zero the quantity of living labor necessary in the manufacture of any product. We are living the paradox of a society of workers without work, where entertainment, consumption and leisure only underscore the lack from which they are supposed to distract us" (p. 46). It is perhaps no surprise that the authors, viewing this superfluous majority as set off against the self-colonizing desires for "advancement" in the compliant minority, suggest that the current situation "introduces the risk that, in its idleness, [the majority] will set about sabotaging the machine" (p. 48).

24 In his *One-Dimensional Man* (Andy Blunden, trans., Ark Publishing, 1964), Marcuse distinguishes between "true needs" (i.e., those necessary for survival; food, clothing, shelter) and "repressive needs" (superfluous commodities; luxury items, status symbols, etc.), arguing that a worker's ability to purchase "repressive" items gives him or her a false sense of equality to oppressors and, more seriously, turns individuals away from recognizing the true inequalities of society.

12
Ways of Not Seeing

Discussed in this essay: Deyan Sudjic, *The Language of Things: Understanding the World of Desirable Objects* (Norton, 2009)

THE WORST GLOBAL ECONOMY in six decades would hardly seem to offer a sterling opportunity for the social bloodsport known as conspicuous consumption. Surely now in the downturn we all avert our eyes from the excesses of full-blown competitive spending, regretting the Gucci bags and Manolo Blahniks of yore, the Burberry shawls and Patek Philippe timepieces. The very names have a shopworn sound, the tattiness of last year's embarrassing enthusiasms. Now we hunker down, economize, carry our lunch in paper sacks and grow our own vegetables. We repair into repentant Thoreauvian retreat, contrite over the quiet desperation that fueled our dead-eyed zombie staggers from boutique to boutique.

Well, we do and we don't. The still-reigning genius of consumer economics, Thorstein Veblen, understood that the central goal of humans is not actually wealth, but distinction; and both boom and bust can happily enable this pursuit. Although frequently expressed as judgments of high-end taste, our "pecuniary interest" is actually motivated by a desire for relative advantage, achieved by conspicuous excess or by conspicuous economy as the times demand. The 'leisure class' moniker dominating his most famous book is misleading: Veblen's intention is nothing less than a comprehensive analysis of class as it is carried out by practices and things.

How so? True, the gentleman of leisure, as Veblen writes in a characteristic passage of *The Theory of Leisure Class*, "becomes a connoisseur in creditable viands of various degrees of merit, in manly beverages and trinkets, in seemly apparel and architecture, in weapons, games, dances, and narcotics."[1] Familiar enough; lucky him. But then the revealing paradox: "This cultivation of the aesthetic faculty requires time and application, and the demands made upon the gentleman in this direction therefore tend to change his life of leisure into a more or less arduous application to the business of learning how to live of ostensible leisure in a becoming way."[2] The gentleman is in fact a prisoner of his preoccupations, owned by rather than owning these outward tokens of his social position. And there is no escape for him or anyone else.

Increases in wealth cannot resolve our need to jockey for position. "However widely, or equally, or 'fairly', it may be distributed," Veblen notes, "no general increase of the community's wealth can make any approach to satiating this need, the ground of which is the desire of everyone to excel everyone else in the accumulation of goods."[3] Sudden decreases in wealth, meanwhile, show how overextended that accumulation has become among those who can least afford it. Conspicuous consumption is bad for everybody, but especially bad for the poor, who have to invest larger proportions of their income to stay in the game. Cheap credit, obtained to chase the American Dream of a house and car, is the ultimate enabler of the human addiction for distinction: when sub-prime mortgages go bust, envy is to blame, not greed. "[P]eople will undergo a very considerable degree of privation in the comforts or the necessaries of life in order to afford what is considered a decent amount of wasteful consumption," Veblen tartly concludes.[4] Yes; and given their disproportional investment and lack of hedge, even greater privation when the particular ship of wasteful consumption goes under.

What is most striking about Veblen's analysis is not, as is sometimes asserted, his reduction of all aesthetic judgments to assertions of position; nor is it even his sly introduction of moral disapproval under cover of sociological jargon. It is, rather, the fact that this homegrown theory of class has, in the century and more since its first appearance, been subjected to a relentless campaign of domestication. Every American generation since Veblen has demonstrated the deep truth of his central claims, even as it has imagined itself exempt from them.

Servile intellectuals are frequently deployed in the vanguard of this double movement. David Brooks's *Bobos in Paradise*, for example, declares that "the Thorstein Veblen era is over,"[5] even as it offers the glossy litany of bourgeois-bohemian desiderata I mentioned in an earlier essay—the house in Berkeley, Austin, or Madison with granite countertops in the kitchen and vintage sports cars in the garage; the

Ivy-League-takes-Wall-Street marriage announcements in the *New York Times*; the organic salad greens and choice heirloom tomatoes from the farmers' market. Brooks thinks that the social order has changed because the forms of consumption have shifted from Gilded Age luxury to postmodern liberal chic, from conspicuous to stealth wealth. But if his book proves anything, it is the still-chugging energy of the position system even as the author denies the existence of that system. Articulating the fiction of a post-Veblen era emerges as one of the key positional goods in the canon of bobo taste, just as conspicuous economy is a privilege in the present back-to-basics cultural moment. Now knitting your own socks, rather than sporting a Rolex watch, is the chosen manner of declaring class superiority—even as we go on denying that there is such a thing as class superiority.

Where does this weird negative energy come from? Are the political implications of class analysis simply too foreign to be admitted fully? Something must be at stake in these inverted dismissals, these artful missings of the point—the faux-intellectual stimulus package. Given the persistent inequality of American society, maybe obscuring the nature of social competition is a necessity for those working the margins at the top end.

———

Deyan Sudjic's recent book about the aesthetics of product design is an example of the Brooks gesture, but it presents an altogether trickier case. Sudjic, the director of London's Design Museum, represents the intellectual wing of the design world, a key constituency in the "creative class" that is supposedly the vanguard of economic recovery. Many of us are still not sure how that salvation works, exactly, but never mind. The book itself is an attractive, accessible, and sometimes clever series of meditations on why things appeal to us, and as such offers itself as an instant token of sophistication. Sudjic dwells on the making of objects, lingering on their appeal in order, he says, to parse the messages they send to us in order to elicit a loving response. And this is a lovely book, though its own appeal becomes just the sort of overlooked or apparently harmless phenomenon that bears some critical lingering.

In a familiar move, Sudjic begins with some theory—or perhaps "theory"—of design aesthetics. Just as Brooks invoked Veblen in order to set him aside, Sudjic summons the ghosts of Barthes, Baudrillard, and Berger—that is, John Berger and his classic investigation of how visual culture works, *Ways of Seeing* (1972). The last is a ghost not because Berger has fled the mortal plane—happily he has not—but because Sudjic's Berger is a pale shadow of the real critic who taught a generation how to look critically at art, advertising, and the contested space between them. The fanged social analysis coiled in Berger's book, which revealed the world of visual stimulation as shot through with cultural assumptions and political messages, is here dismissed as "an uncomfortable vantage point halfway between Karl Marx and Walter Benjamin." As a result, he does not understand the "complex blend of the knowing and the innocent" that attends our engagement with material things. "Objects are far from being as innocent as Berger suggested," Sudjic says, "and that is what makes them too interesting to ignore."[6]

Readers will search in vain for Berger's suggestion concerning the innocence of objects. What he actually says in *Ways of Seeing* is that we can only understand our relations to images if we accept both the pleasure they give and question the mechanisms of social manipulation that make us love objects in the first place, with their aura of branded specialness or celebrity approval, their stamps of good taste or authentic cool. That is why Berger's cleverly illustrated book moves from art history to its sharp take on advertising in the book's final section: they are both ruled by the same social forces. Glamour, Berger writes there, is the dominant quality of image-saturated social life. But glamour is not an essential feature of people or things; it is, instead, the quality of *reflecting the envy* of others. The fashion system is fuelled by this interpersonal glow, but so are more 'legitimate' aesthetic practices like art museums, where exclusive taste is ratified by institutional authority. As much as Veblen, Berger sees those practices driven by the energy of class distinction: the strange fact that "meaningful" encounters with works of high art remain unequally distributed despite any effort to increase access. (You can charge less than a NASCAR grandstand seat for an opera premiere and it won't much alter the demographic profile of either spectacle.)

Sudjic claims to be engaged in "understanding the world of desirable objects," (subtitle) and we might well expect a similarly sharp critical take, this time on product design. He says that Berger, Barthes, and Baudrillard give too much attention to psychology and social structure and too little credit to "the role of the designer," raising expectations of a social responsibility discussion, perhaps along the lines of Ken Garland's "First Things First" manifesto of 1964. Sudjic's design detour, however, is a rearguard move. As his book proceeds on its merry way, glossing everything from consumer durables to fashion and the art world, what emerges is a slick appreciation for desired objects that lacks any awareness of how the desire works.

———

Sudjic details with disarming frankness his superficial design-based decisions for a laptop purchase: he was first drawn to its white finish, then devastated when the power cord did not match the colour of the computer casing. He offers sharp analysis of the enduring nostalgic appeal of James Bond's favoured Walther PPK sidearm and the Nikon F series single reflex camera, especially if their black bodies are scuffed down to the gunmetal silver beneath the factory finish. The Moleskin notebook, the Bakelite rotary telephone, and the Braun pocket calculator all make appearances. There is also much to glean about the processes of innovation in design, in cars and lamps and chairs. The story of the Anglepoise desk lamp, for example, which any number of people take for granted every day, or of the affordable economy automobile—Volkswagen, Mini Cooper, Citroën 2CV—track the thinking behind these mini-masterpieces of industrial problem-solving. And Sudjic is appropriately withering about the "circus" the international art world has become, with its monster fairs in Miami and Basel, runaway bidding wars, and infestation by celebrity wealth.

Sudjic even seems to appreciate Veblen. In a middle chapter on "luxury," he invokes *The Theory of the Leisure Class* and details contemporary instances of invidious distinction in all walks of life—brakeless single-gear machines for hipster bike couriers, Swiss timepieces among bankers and gangsters—to which the reader can add his or her own stock: spit-cane fly rods for retro anglers or heavy Dupont fountain pens and handmade paper for letter-writing aesthetes. "There are those who have become obsessive about sunglasses in a way that comes close to high-functioning autism," he writes. "These are people who expect you to know that their specially made frames come from the same

Italian workshop that made the pair that Steve McQueen wears in *The Getaway* before they take you seriously."[7] Correctly, he sees that social distinction is not earned by quality workmanship or beauty but by the distance a thing confers—the gap created between insiders and outsiders, the hip and the lame. (Reviewer's invidious distinction: the illustration accompanying the shades-of-Steve-McQueen example is actually from *The Thomas Crown Affair*, not *The Getaway*.)

All of this is fine as far as it goes, but that is not very far. At the end of the chapter, Sudjic makes the following claims, which combine the obvious and the unsubstantiated: "Luxury in our times revolves more and more about the details that persuade consumers to spend money. But another definition of luxury—one that is closer to its original meaning—may prove increasingly pertinent. It sees luxury as the way to provide a sense of respite from the relentless tide of possessions that threatens to overwhelm us."[8] It is not at all clear what this means, and nothing in the remainder of the book illuminates it. Does Sudjic mean opting out of the luxury consumption spiral? Perhaps; but if so, we know all too well how that, too, can become a form of distinction, the ultimate in fake off-grid living. Does he mean setting less store by things themselves? Perhaps; but that position stands at odds with the bulk of his book, and presumably with the bulk of his life.

It is at about this point that the book's logic, never firm, begins to totter uncontrollably. The enjoinder at the beginning was to pay attention to objects, to confront our desire for them, but not in some presumptively reductive Marxist fashion. Now, albeit courtesy of Veblen rather than Marx, a systemic analysis is creeping back in. Luxury cravings are admitted, even deprecated to some degree. But they are not really analyzed in terms of a larger social context, let alone as a theory of class. The totter veers into a clear fall in the book's decidedly odd epilogue. Here Sudjic recalls a moment of social awareness whose real comic dimensions seem somehow lost on him unless we credit him with a degree of self-irony on the order of a Martin Amis narrator. "In Munich one Friday early in August 2008," he writes, "over lunch in a sleek restaurant that served traditional Bavarian cuisine in such a way as not to scare off those with suspicion of white sausages, it began to strike home to a group of curators, gathered to talk over the place of contemporary design in museums, that a decade of *fin-de-siècle* irrational exuberance was on the verge of imploding."[9]

Sudjic adds some detail to the image of those white sausages: the "fleeting consolations" offered by nearby shops with their "costly pens wrapped in chamois leather," the "carefully understated $1500 bag made by Hermès that one of my companions had under her seat," with its "subtly stitched leather handles and dusty pink canvas" in place of the previous year's more overt logo-based design. The scene thus vividly set, and even as Sudjic is idly contemplating his own sick wish to get one of these, the world changes. "As the coffee came, somebody looked at his Blackberry." Of course he did! And what did the Blackberry tell somebody? "The Dow it seemed had fallen by 400 points. The Federal Reserve and the governments of Britain, France and Germany were pumping billions of dollars into financial markets." It took a while to sink in—Sudjic's AmEx card was still up to paying the lunch bill in Munich, thank god—but gradually the magnitude of the economy's collapse became clear. And it put the designer in a reflective mood.

"While I was writing the first draft of this book—and beginning to sound like that fifteenth-century fanatic, Savonarola, calling for a bonfire of the vanities in Renaissance Florence—all this was some way off," he says, in the same passage. Looking back, it is as if the world has enacted its own bonfire, violently reacting against all the excess. But Sudjic gives himself too much credit. Although it's true that he mentions sumptuary laws in passing, and offers the occasional wry comment on wayward human appetite, he is no more a Savonarola than Virgin mega-mogul Richard Branson or opportunist-at-large Donald Trump. Far more than Berger, his vantage is an uncomfortable mixture of celebration and deprecation. And the note of repentance that comes on the final two pages of this work of high-end commodity fetishism is bizarre, if not simply hypocritical and self-serving. "Now, driven by our guilty carbon footprints, at our disgust at the activities of corrupt fund managers, and the absurdity of competitive yacht building," he says, "conspicuous consumption is going to take a back seat for a while." Tightening belts all round, designers and consumers alike will henceforth focus on craft and simplicity, maybe even spirituality.

Really? Or is this just the intellectual equivalent of fashion magazine features on "The New Austerity" or "Simple Chic," those walking contradictions of late capitalism? The overarching imperative of economic growth will not be denied, even (or especially) when times are bad.

Sudjic himself wonders if we are now in the same awkward position as people during the 1930s, who were told that it is "the patriotic duty of all of us to consume our way out of the Great Depression." Austerity is just the new luxury; craft the new high-end obsession. Worse, perhaps, is the ultimate tone of narcissistic self-flagellation: "I am still fascinated by the process of design," Sudjic says, a strangely qualified admission. "Yet it makes us susceptible to the same difficulties that we suffer in our relationship with food and alcohol, oscillating between binge and denial. The natural emotional relationship we look for with everyday things opens the way to a self-destructive narcotic addiction. The simple possession of a familiar well-crafted artefact is perverted to become a variety of substance abuse."[10]

Did it really take a global economic meltdown to force that basic insight on an apparently intelligent man? Addictive behaviour should be the beginning of a book on product design, not its conclusion; but that wouldn't allow for the seductive pleasures of the text, where objects are caressed and lingered over, their makers celebrated as geniuses of creativity and aesthetics.

———

Maybe this is all too subtle. Consumer products are just more or less useful things, after all, and their beauty or otherwise hardly of wider import. Who except product designers even cares how they get made? But that bluff sentiment is too hasty. The premise of this book does indeed reveal something important, namely the political dimensions of the design question—even if the book's execution fails to grasp the essential issue. That issue is the endless inventiveness of human desire when it comes to social competition.

Suppose for a moment that there are three clear stages of capitalism, defined minimally as the dominance of markets by money. The first, classical capitalism, defines the second half of the nineteenth century and the beginning of the twentieth, more or less the moment that Veblen analyzed. The engine at this stage of development is the straightforward production of goods and services. In order to clear the markets of these goods and services, the system works to cultivate desire. Accumulated capital—the most basic kind, primitive hoarding—is spent on conspicuous demonstrations of waste in the form of leisure. From the individual point of view, the central goal is integration of the self around the demonstration of good taste. Exemplary fiction of the age: Edith Wharton's *The Custom of the Country.*

The second stage, late capitalism, is what caught the Frankfurt School's gimlet eye in the middle of the last century. Now the engine of the system is the production not of goods and services but of consumption itself. That is, rather than merely cultivating longstanding desires in new aspirants, the mechanisms of economic growth must manufacture ever novel desires using the emergent feedback loops of advertising. Capital is reproduced, not merely accumulated; the shadowy shills of the culture industry want us to spend our way to wealth and happiness. Down on the ground, the individual experiences fractured multiple selves, or consumption identities, even while yearning for integration. Exemplary fiction: F. Scott Fitzgerald's *Tender is the Night.*

The third stage, postmodern capitalism for lack of a better label, is with us yet. We witness both cultivation and manufacture of desire, but above all the wild proliferation of it. The market engine is still producing consumption, but now it is consumption of the self *in the form of* the consumer. We're no longer interested in stuff, or even in the satisfaction that stuff promises; now we chase a certain idea of ourselves, as cool or fashionable or self-actualized. Thus the emergence of what we ought to call erotic capital, the most spectral and elusive form. I, with all my carefully constructed preferences for A&F shirts or Lululemon sweats, become the most desirable consumer product in the economy of taste. To paraphrase Slavoj Žižek, the superego is no longer a form of restraining conscience—*Don't do that!*—but instead expresses the paradoxical imperative of smarmy waiters everywhere: *Enjoy!* Consumption is both intimate and relentless: brand-conscious consumers cannibalize themselves, feeding on their jumble of layered identities. Exemplary fiction: David Foster Wallace's *Infinite Jest.*

The difficulty with analysis of the last stage is not just that political agency has been reduced to the dimensions of a webpage, though that is certainly true, but that the critical tools from earlier stages have become cultural properties within the economy. Hence the compulsion to assimilate the prickly insights of Veblen or Barthes rather than consider their perverse new relevance. Hence, too, the intellectual endgame demonstrated by *The Language of Things*. Offering a cheerful discourse of sophisticated consumption, the book becomes a beautiful object to be ingested as part of the meta-pleasures of design. One can safely predict that Sudjic's book will be prominently on sale in museum giftshops everywhere.

Now, it might be objected that this declension is no different from the routine academic consumption of Veblen, Adorno, Berger and the rest, which also seems to reduce criticism to commodity and insight to position. John Kenneth Galbraith, who had attempted his own critical social analysis in *The Affluent Society* (1958), noted that "No one has really read very much if he hasn't read *The Theory of the Leisure Class* at least once," adding that "[t]he book yields its meaning, and therewith its full enjoyment, only to those who too have leisure."[11] Veblen himself, in the last sections of the book, indicts the tenured ease of academic life as one of the clearest examples of conspicuous waste, and Bourdieu's great work on social distinction concludes its survey of taste as a class-based exercise with a keen sense of how intellectual and cultural capital underwrite each other.

So far from weakening a critical conclusion, these honest admissions that the theorist is not exempt from his own theory act to endorse the underlying logic. Yes, intellectual discourse, no less than shopping, is aimed at establishing position; but that does not render its conclusions meaningless any more than a designer handbag is rendered useless for carrying things because of its label. Sudjic's approach, by contrast, threatens to disappear into its own imagery. Focussing on the objects of desire rather than on the way objects function within a system, he has enacted, not examined, the whipsaw between attachment and revulsion that marks all ventures into Candyland.

The mild moralism on offer, meanwhile, is at once insufficient and self-defeating—insufficient since a much more robust disapproval would be needed to make a dent in the easy satisfactions of contemporary consumerism; and self-defeating because moralism never really works in this sphere anyway. Philosophers have for centuries tried to meet the perversities of human desire with elaborate projects of change or control, usually prefaced with eloquent expressions of disgust. Experience indicates that these projects fail, usually sooner rather than later, leaving the philosopher with few choices other than those drawn from the catalogue of misanthropy: reclusion, self-disgust, self-medication, suicide. In a rare case—witness the Unabomber—direct action may come to seem a viable option.

Critical thought must take care not to let judgments about particular desires undermine general analysis of desire. "In this arena nothing counts so heavily against a man as to be found attacking the values of the public at large and seeking to substitute his own," Galbraith warns. "[T]his has been the common error of those who have speculated on the sanctity of present economic goals—those who have sought to score against materialism and Philistinism. They have advanced their own view of what adds to human happiness. For this they could easily be accused of substituting for the crude economic goals of the people at large the more sensitive and refined but irrelevant goals of their own. The accusation is fatal."[12] Or, as Veblen more crisply has it, "Whatever form of expenditure the consumer chooses, or whatever end he seeks in making his choice, has utility to him by virtue of his preference."[13] (The personal preferences of the theorist are no exception: no one who reads Veblen or Galbraith can remain long in doubt about their respective dislikes for—among other things—dogs, horses, corsets, academic gowns, comic books, action movies, and the colours cerise and mauve.)

We don't get very far by deprecating specific longings. You can't change what people want short of dictatorial central authority, and maybe not even then; and we all know how anti-consumerism can become a form of empty self-congratulation on the order of Buy Nothing Day. Berger, like Stendhal before him, was more perspicuous. We are fetched by a beautiful thing, as we are by beauty in general, because of the "promise of happiness" it holds out. Sudjic's desirable things go on repeating that promise, day after day, but while the promise may be bogus, the seeking itself is not, and that's why it is never just about position—Veblen's aesthetic reductionism is too extreme. But that's also why we go on believing the promises even though we know they're empty, even when we realize that consumer goods reliably generate the *unhappiness* of restless aspiration. It's the language of the soul we should be parsing, not the language of things, our shared strandedness in the caverns of human desire. This project of psychic spelunking is as old as Plato and as fresh as last week's clearance sale.

There is of course no guarantee that self-examination, any more than strolling the mall, will prompt political change. For that we need things like luxury taxes, limits to cheap borrowing, and other structural curbs on competitive consumption. Nor will a consideration of our own place in the consumer economy necessarily lead to changes in individual value: this is theory, not therapy. Meanwhile, various inventive cultural escape hatches—hi-lo cultural slumming, the dandyism of camp, moving-target hyper-coolness—seem jejune if not flatly self-contradictory. There is nothing outside the system, and drives to escape are always just higher-order versions of distinction. You can't win, and you can't stop playing.

Here's some advice: stop worrying about it. The point of analyzing desire is neither victory nor escape; it is, instead, to indicate an alternative scale of value, where idleness and play—the everyday gift of cultural *détournement*—are cherished as the most divine, because least encumbered, dimensions of human life. If we could see that, maybe the closed promises of object-happiness would give way to the open invitation of thought itself.

Notes:

1   Thorstein Veblen, *The Theory of the Leisure Class: An Economic Study of Institutions* (Penguin Classics, 1998; orig. 1899), p. 64.

2   *Ibid.*, p. 64.

3   *Ibid.*, p. 32.

4   *Ibid.*, p. 119.

5   David Brooks, *Bobos in Paradise: The New Upper Class and How They Got There* (Simon & Schuster, 2000), p. 84.

6   Sudjic, *The Language of Things*, p. 11.

7   *Ibid.*, p. 88.

8   *Ibid.*, p. 114.

9   *Ibid.*, p. 191-2.

10 *Ibid.*, p. 194.

11 J. K. Galbraith, "Who Was Thorstein Veblen," in *The Essential Galbraith* (Mariner Books, 2001), p. 211.

12 Galbraith, *The Affluent Society* (Houghton Mifflin, 1958), p. 350.

13 Veblen, *The Theory of the Leisure Class*, p. 98.

13

Language Speaks Us:
Sophie's Tree and the Paradox of Self

I am sitting with a philosopher in the garden; he says again and again, "I know that that's a tree," pointing to a tree that is near us. Someone else arrives and hears this, and I tell him: "This fellow isn't insane. We're only doing philosophy."
—Ludwig Wittgenstein

I F YOU ARE READING THIS then the question "Why read?" *de facto* makes no sense—or at least it has been satisfactorily answered sufficient to the present occasion. Any member of the flashlight-under-the-covers family knows that if you have to ask *why* when it comes to reading, then you've missed the point, or maybe a whole bunch of points. You read because you can, whenever you can, whatever it is, against the rules, late at night, to the detriment of your eyes, eagerly and sadly and laughing out loud (and maybe LOLing). If you are not one of those people, then you are probably not reading this and words are at a loss. There may be ways to reach you, the non-reader, but this is not one of them.

You and I are one. These words, penned or in fact typed some time ago—a phrase I feel odd typing right now, throwing it into the optimistic future of your reading moment—these words bind us together, past, future and present, in a shared consciousness that both of us find somehow worthwhile. In one perfectly sound sense, the fact of reading answers the question of reading's purpose. *Why* becomes *that*.

From the other side, though, as Mikita Brottman points out in her book *The Solitary Vice: Against Reading* (2008), we have the equally paradoxical fact that reading seems to need constant promoting or boosterism. Radio networks broadcast competitions among novels to encourage more reading. Wealthy benefactors sponsor lucrative fiction prizes to encourage reading. Adolescent fad books such as the *Harry Potter* or *Twilight* series, or among adults the Stieg Larsson novels, are touted as good for reading, even if the books themselves are bad—the premise being, apparently, that fantasies, vampire tales and violent thrillers function as gateway drugs to the purer highs of Jane Austen or David Foster Wallace.

In back of all these efforts and justifications are the twinned beliefs that reading is good for you, something to be promoted like fitness or not smoking; and that this fact somehow cuts against our 'natural' tendencies *not* to read, just as eating french fries and smoking Camels is more 'natural' than not because both acts are surrenders to harmful temptation. The problem is not the moralism—life is full of moralism—but the self-contradiction. If reading is so great, fun or edifying or interesting, why does it need such aggressive promotion? If the gifts of the reading life are so manifest, why do they require defending? Paradox one meets paradox two: if *why* becomes *that* in the first, here *why* becomes *because we say so*. And that never convinced anyone, least of all the children who get it most.

Which means that anyone who considers the question a valid one—a live issue—is either not paying attention to their own literate commitments, which make the question self-defeating; or, more likely, asking some other, maybe related question or questions.

Such as: Are books worthwhile in their present form? Are they viable? Profitable? Are online or e-book styles of reading better, worse, or just different from the experience we associate with the four democratic centuries of print on paper? Will the codex, the block form of the book, with its bound pages and durable covers, survive? Will it continue, perhaps, only as an artistic medium, a pleasing atavistic object akin to a steampunk typewriter or hippie Victorian fashion? Is there anything inherently meaningful about folded and trimmed paper as the favoured hardware for running the software we call literacy? Does the notion of the 'inherently meaningful' even make sense any more? Did it ever?

The arguments over answering these questions are mostly futile, despite the volume of print (and 'print') they generate. In fact, the debates are so tediously predictable that there is now a drinking game keyed on repetition of familiar claims.[1] We might as well concede several of the main disputes right away. The experience of reading a physical book is probably superior in pure aesthetic terms, at least for those of us raised with such books, to reading a Kindle or iPad book. (Though spare a thought for those of us whose arms have gone to sleep while propping up a hardcover in bed, the book falling heavily across nose and mouth, threatening suffocation.) It is no more than fair that writers should get at least as much compensation from e-books as they do from hard copy books, if not more. Publishing's economic model, which for centuries has been a mixture of reckless trend-chasing (imitating last year's bestseller) and black magic (unwittingly creating next year's), is badly flawed and in need of an overhaul. But even if we grant all or part of this, we would get no closer to the heart of the matter about reading.

Why? Because the timespan necessary to settle this question is at once too long and too short. Too long, because the answers, such as they might be, lie outside the mortal span of anyone alive as I write these words; and too short, because the larger forces of human existence swirl in longer whorls than decades or even centuries. Even the debates have an air of history about them, if one pays attention to history amid the magazine throwdowns and Twitter-offs. Staying within the confines not just of Canada but of the University of Toronto's Department of English, one could note that in 1962 Marshall McLuhan published *The Gutenberg Galaxy*, arguing that moveable type changed the world by hypnotizing the eye to follow thousands of miles of printed words, while in 1967 Northrop Frye would respond with *The Modern Century*, castigating McLuhan's view as excessively deterministic and blind to the force of human will (also discussed in "What Are Intellectuals For?").

The debate is unresolvable because the terms are beyond settling. Not only do we not know the future of the book; we cannot know it. As Kant noticed as early as the preface to his *Critique of Pure Reason*, human consciousness is such that it must reflect on its own conditions of possibility. But it is likewise true that such reflection reveals, among other things, our inability to comprehend the nature of that consciousness. We can, at best, sketch the limits of what we can comprehend—itself a word rooted in grasping, encircling with the hand—and then speculate about what may, or must, lie beyond those limits.

Some debates are good at taking us to the limit, even if (especially if) they cannot be settled there. If the bare question "Why read?' can be settled by logic, or safely shuttled into paradox, that is not the case for the subsidiary question "Why *go on* reading?"—in particular, why go on reading the sort of thing we have been reading these last few centuries. To some extent this question holds regardless of the delivery vehicle, though the medium might just be part of the message. The issue worth confronting is this: are humans changing, whether gaining or losing or both but *changing*, as our reading habits change?

Writing is a kind of making, in the larger sense of *poesis*, even if it involves heavy lifting of only the conceptual or narrative sort. I want to say, selfishly, that one good reason to read is simply that someone else, somewhere else, has created the written thing, the *poesis* of print. A public act of creation has a claim on our attention, just as a plea from a stranger on the street has, and even if the claim turns out to be bogus, overstated, or irritating. Humans exist in a discursive world, a world of language. Creating new instances of discursive possibility, arrangements of the shared words that are unprecedented and unique, which maybe even make the words do unprecedented and unique things with consciousness, is hard work. Pay it the compliment of reading.

People write for all kinds of reasons, out of mixed and sometimes ignoble motives. Nobody sane writes for money, despite Dr. Johnson's judgment, so that makes all writers blockheads of one sort or another. Money may sometimes come, to be sure, but all writers, whether secretly or with great fanfare, seeking one or a million readers, write because they want someone to read what they have fashioned out of nothing but their own thoughts and the humble tools of ordinary language. Writing is, in this sense, at once the most hopeful and desperate act that a thinking human can consciously undertake. It appears to be an attempt by one consciousness to reach another by way of a curious magical inwardness, the mundane but actually mysterious experience of hearing the sound of another person's words inside your own head.

This *prima facie* case, and the imagery of interiority that I have just used to make it, contain several debatable premises. Of these I will isolate two that bear further urgent discussion. One is that human consciousness in fact depends on language. The other is that our current conception of that consciousness, in particular the idea of the individual self responsible to itself and others, will survive.

1. Tree
Maybe these things always happen in summer and involve children, those instinctive philosophers, but this scene is another encounter on the field of meaning during a summer retreat.

I was grilling burgers, hot dogs and corn for a Fourth of July celebration at an isolated house in New Hampshire. It was a large family gathering. Over by the weathered Adirondack chairs, the stars and stripes were snapping in the breezy blue sky. On the porch, people were drinking strong gin-and-tonics and criticizing various Republican politicians of evil repute. My niece Sophie, who is five, suddenly wanted to know: "Why is a tree called a 'tree'?"

Actually, she said it more like *treeeeee*, the way you do when you have repeated a common word over and over, to see how long before it starts to sound strange, even uncanny.

You can't take refuge in Saussurean structural linguistics with a five-year-old, still less take a stroll with her into Derrida's *mise-en-abyme*. There's actually not much you can say. We call it a tree because we do, we always have. Always? Because we do? We call it a tree because we don't call it a cat, and we need to be able to talk about both. We call it a tree because it works: when I say 'tree' other people know what I'm talking about. But how do they know? How do they know that you mean a tree? They must have known before you said it. How did they know?

It really is very tempting, as Wittgenstein knew, to adopt Augustine's mistaken view here, to say, well, we just went around and put labels on things. As if who 'we' are is obvious, or when 'we' are supposed to have done this. As if it's even obvious what a 'thing' is, let alone how the 'label' is supposed to stick to the 'thing'.

Sophie was right to worry. It's a mystery how words mean, how they wield sense and reference with such astonishing reliability—so that even their unreliability, in lies and metaphors and puns, is part of the reliability, part of the pleasure they bring. No wonder that children just a little younger than her are given to repeating words over and over in a different fashion, not seeking their uncanniness but savouring their ability to pick out distinguishable bits of the vast experience we call the world, pointing for confirmation: *Car! Car! Car!* What I actually asked was, "What else would you call it?" She liked that, because it was like permission to call it anything. *Bananapatch. Carburetor.* A poet's first taste of language's crazy freedom.[2]

Actually she already was a poet. Tasting the sound of a word to make it feel uncanny comes first, before the new move, the new transport of meaning from place to place that is metaphor. This is the essential aesthetic manoeuvre of all art, the discovery of pleasures buried deeply, but in plain sight. Language is everywhere, it has to be—a tree has to be called 'tree'—otherwise we would not be able to play in the various ways we do. Including serious play like building things, creating regimes, making ideas clash to improve our thoughts.

In the midst of these games, there is a governing puzzle, the search for what William James described as "the thought we call I." Wittgenstein (again) was rightly skeptical of the language of interiority that so often attends this puzzle. This Cartesian hangover, the habitual distinction between 'inside my head' and 'the outside world' is so common, in fact, that it has come to define the very idea of the person. I am the sum total of my consciousness, a temporally extended experiential stream that organizes itself around a 'centre of narrative gravity' which allows me to make sense of my existence.

This is a useful fiction, maybe even a necessary one, but a fiction nonetheless. And as a fiction, it hints at some possible untanglings, if not resolutions, of the paradoxes of reading, especially if that reading involves other fictions. What are they?

First, there is no such thing as a solitary vice of reading. Reading is always a social activity because it occurs in the poetic space of language. The self that we presume as the stable performer of this vice, the reading self, is in flux to a degree that no character in fiction could ever possibly represent. In fact, it is very likely that many, if not most, people enjoy characters in fiction precisely because they have fixed identities of the sort that we do not, indeed cannot, enjoy in life. The experience of that artificial fixity teaches, for better or worse, how to think about other people and, sometimes, ourselves.

'Character' is a notion we use in two apparently distinct but related senses: the naming of a fictional personage, and the reliable features of a living person, usually a moral agent. The two senses are really one. 'Character' is shorthand for the conventional presupposition of stable identity, a map of personhood that we can consult for direction. But we should always remember that, however useful, *the map is not the territory*. Character, identity, selfhood—all of these are abstractions. Reading fiction both reveals and conceals this troubling fact.

Second, there is no communion of consciousness in the act of reading, some elaborate mind-meld in which you become privy to my thoughts via the medium of language. The act of reading is, instead, a move in a larger game of language, perhaps distinct from other such moves in being inaudible but otherwise no more (or less) mysterious. Our shared suspension in language means, despite our usual ways of thinking, that writing and reading are not aspects of communication. Or rather, what is being communicated is not a message sent from one node to another, but a sense that the entire system or network exists. *Language speaks us*, Martin Heidegger said. Would Sophie understand that as a good answer to her question?

Third, there is therefore no point defending the book, or more precisely the novel, for its ability to foster interiority, or a keener sense of self. Everything that belongs to experience will tend to foster that, often despite our best philosophical efforts to the contrary. There is markedly more narcissism, understood as excessive regard for self, among the contemporary techno-autistics who indulge non-book linguistic interactions such as instant messaging and tweeting than among habitual readers of long-form prose. There is also, as recent studies have suggested, less empathy, understood as impartial concern for the non-friend other.[3]

Taken together, these three points highlight what I consider the underlying issue. Are we changing? Yes. Does it matter? Yes. But how? To put it more sharply, what are the (good) things that reading accomplishes that cannot be accomplished any other way?

2. Self

To say that I learned how to treat women by reading Raymond Chandler probably gives the wrong impression. But like so many other awkward young men, seeking a way to be in the world, I relished the cool disdain of Philip Marlowe's first-person narration, savouring the *weltschmerzlich* inner dialogue that I wished appropriate to my own paltry adventures. "On the dance floor half a dozen couples were throwing themselves around with the reckless abandon of a night-watchman with arthritis. Most of them were dancing cheek to cheek, if dancing is the right word. The men wore white tuxedos and the girls wore bright eyes, ruby lips, and tennis or golf muscles ... The music stopped, there was desultory clapping. The orchestra was deeply moved, and played another number."[4]

That cool appraising gaze, the confident outsider position. Marlowe sits and watches, sips his Gibson, amuses himself. He is self-contained, tough, always thinking. Always judging correctly. I first read those words when I was sixteen and have never forgotten the instant charge of appeal, far deeper than the swashbuckling fantasy and space-opera sci-fi that made up the bulk of my reading at that period. Here was a taste of grown-up individualism as intoxicating and addictive as the gin in Marlowe's drink.

Needless to say, I never engaged in private investigation or took down a hired hitman with smart blows of a tire iron to his wrists. I would go on to drink Gibsons, maybe too many of them, but I never went to bed with a platinum blonde lawyer's assistant or a red-haired mystery woman who might or might not have killed her husband. But there are surely dozens if not hundreds of mild-mannered men who wander their very ordinary worlds while entertaining, in dull moments, the inner voice of a Philip Marlowe. It is part of why we read. In later years, and in more apposite circumstances, I would find myself veering to the cynical rage of Kingsley Amis over the narcissistic boorishness of most people, the great bores who lurk in every corner of academic life. A lot of drinking goes on here too, so that at some moments, glass in hand, I might be entertaining a nearly simultaneous desire to baffle a colleague with a bit of insulting wordplay and to punch him in the nose with brass knuckles.

This is for me the beginning of what we can call the *humanist* defence of reading, in particular of reading fiction—though note that all reading may be construed in this wish-fulfillment manner. Whereas a child or adolescent may derive innocent pleasure from identifying with a sleuth or quest-bidden knight, we tend to believe that adult life demands graduation to more sophisticated engagements. But does it really? Do we not still take on the perspective of Portnoy, the reasons of Rabbit? Do we not, at another level, engage philosophy or history with an awareness, pleasing to self, that we are so occupied? "The image of ourselves reading the book, ourselves-as-intellectuals, can be just as strong as the fantasy that we are men or women of action," an A. N. Wilson narrator remarks. "All reading is therefore equally 'escapist' unless we purify ourselves from time to time by a recognition of the fact."[5] That this admonition, bound to be flattering to the reader, arises in the course of a novel just complicates matters even more.

We can generalize: a great swath of modern writing's history has been devoted to excavating the inner lives of individual human beings. At its best, this allows a twofold expansion on the part of the reader: he or she enriches the inner narrations which form the warp and woof of consciousness, the intertwined possibilities of self, even as the idea of the other is deepened and expanded. The novel, in this view, helps in the cultivation of both stable ego and of compassion or empathy. At its worst, though, the humanistic modern novel is a get-out-of-jail-free card for emotional terrorists. It elevates even the most banal and base-less feelings to a presumptive status of moral validity. The mere fact that someone felt something is now considered sufficient justification for what the feeling demands in action or decision. On the view, then, the novel is not an enabling device for coherent self-presentation but a generalized narcissistic invitation, the fictional equivalent of those ideo-logical self-esteem schools where all the children are above average.

The optimistic view of this tension is that, on the whole, the for-mer side wins. The endless search in conscious life for a stable personal identity is aided by fictions. I mentioned Chandler and Amis as forma-tive moments, but as with most readers greater and more lasting litera-ture is likewise part of my inner narration: Hamlet's indecision, Anna Karenina's betrayal, Emma's self-deception. Even if we grant that per-sonal identity is a fiction, it does seem a necessary one, not least in the matter of human responsibility. We can only call people to account, after all, including ourselves, if we can tie actions to individuals over time. It is not a valid defence to say, of a prior act, that one is no longer that same person as the one who committed it—even though this claim is both emotionally resonant (it really does feel that way) and philosophically sound (there is no metaphysical ligature binding Self@Time1 to Self@Time2). We reject this defence simply because we have to, on pain of contradiction—for there would be no 'we' if we allowed it.

As with the larger questions about reading, there are lurking pitfalls for sense, and for literature, here. Clear thought can tell us that a unified life is a chimera, an abstract construction, but readers seem to abandon clear thought when presented with words on a page. Biography, for example, is the most meretricious and false of literary forms, purport-ing to find narrative arc in a real lived life when such an arc can only ever be imposed, helicoptered in and dropped forcibly on the unruly terrain of experience. The best biographers acknowledge this, and some of them even write novels that offset their biographical 'non-fiction' with meditations on the violence and deception of narrative.[6] But if a biographer departs from the norm, he or she is liable to be punished by an angry readership.

My own writing experience here is minimally relevant. As a biographer of the pianist Glenn Gould, I decided to portray this deliberately fractured self, a person who lived his entire life through numerous personae, forever disappearing from view and reinventing himself, through a series of linked 'takes' on his music and ideas. It seemed to me only right that a 'life' of Gould should be an occasion for playing, as he did, with the very idea of a 'life'. One headline delivered its judgment succinctly: "Glenn Gould biography weighed down by philosophy." O, that burden of thought!

Readers likewise enjoy seeing the good rewarded and the wicked punished in novels, because it affirms the sense, rooted precisely in fear that the opposite is true, that justice ought to be done. Writers thwart this enjoyment at their peril. That books should be uplifting is the ruling dictum of most book clubs, I believe, and the general belief that a good book is either one about a good person (which often means a likeable character, 'one I can relate to') or the dramatic depiction of a bad person meeting his or her proper end, can be summed up as the Miss Prism Theory of Literature: "The good ended happily, and the bad unhappily," she asserts in *The Importance of Being Earnest*. "That is what Fiction means."[7]

3. Irony

Proponents of the Miss Prism Theory miss the irony of the formulation, which not only pokes fun at the aesthetic expectation but cheerfully concedes fiction's difference from reality on the main point. Nevertheless, it is a popular view and one that logically cannot be separated from the more respectable one that literature aids in the cultivation of self. Justice and selfhood are both fictions, as is the relation between them. Fiction, like language more generally, is not just a medium of these ideas, it is an entire field of meaning without which such ideas would not be open to entertainment. (Compare how paltry, and how largely unread, is the non-fictional discourse on justice and selfhood. I can tell you from personal experience that hardly anybody reads it.)

So the rather elementary aesthetic mistake about the point of fiction, namely that it should teach straightforward lessons about morals, actually reveals a deeper sense of fiction's status in our lives, and hence why reading matters. The tensions inherent in that status are only enhanced by the pressures of the moment. Do we really want more of the same selfhood-bolstering in our reading? Are we, with the energy of technological changes, moving into a new moment of human existence where the quest for selfhood, understood as the creation of stable personal identity, is over?

Here is Tom McCarthy, a young English novelist whose beautifully original second novel, *C*, a story of communications technology emerging in the first part of the twentieth century, was longlisted for the Booker Prize in 2010.[8] His first novel, *Remainder*, was an impossible-to-summarize meditation on selfhood, with a super-wealthy man attempting to recreate a single moment of contentment. "Where the liberal-humanist sensibility has always held the literary work to be a form of self-expression, a meticulous sculpting of the thoughts and feelings of an isolated individual who has mastered his or her poetic craft, a technologically savvy sensibility might see it completely differently: as a set of transmissions, filtered through subjects whom technology and the live word have ruptured, broken open, made receptive. I know which side I'm on: the more books I write, the more convinced I become that what we encounter in a novel is not selves, but networks."[9]

I am not convinced about the talk of 'networks' here; I think 'fields' gets it better, a term that implies no stable nodes at all; language is not a network of interconnected portals, it is a field or manifold space with instances of local coherence only. But the general point is valid, even if the polarity of our responses is not yet clear. In 1967, for example, it was very clear to Northrop Frye that this same movement of change was already afoot, but his version of the liberal-humanistic world view did not allow him to view the prospect with pleasure.

"The last stand of privacy has always been, traditionally, the inner mind," Frye wrote in *The Modern Century*. "It is quite possible however for communications media, especially the newer electronic ones, to break down the associative structures of the inner mind and replace them by the prefabricated structure of the media." The extension of the argument is then that loss of this inner mind makes a society prone to the worst kind of mob rule. This is not anarchy, or dictatorship, or police state. "It is rather the self-policing state, the society incapable of formulating an articulate criticism of itself and of developing the will to act in its light."[10]

It's impossible not to have sympathy with Frye's view here, especially if one has hopes of being one of those articulate critics. But too often this debate is cast in Manichean terms of anti-technology and pro-technology, Luddite humanists versus net-savvy wireheads.[11] And it is certainly the case that opportunistic cheerleaders of change for its own sake, usually older than the people for whom they claim to speak, will trumpet new realities, new loops of consciousness, new forms of intelligence in a manner evidently aimed at provoking objection, which can then be dismissed as fogeyish and square. Neither fact should blind us to the real heft in the question, which goes well beyond the question of reading as such. Allow me to conclude by making its political stakes explicit, in part as a message to Sophie, who may someday read these words or others like them.

4. Human

The great achievements of liberal humanism include the form of preference-driven democracy that now dominates, at least in part, throughout much of the developed world. The same humanism has demanded that non-trumpable rights claims should hold sway even where democracy does not. On this view, 1949's *Universal Declaration of Human Rights* is the most significant document of the twentieth century and indeed the culmination of four centuries of thought and struggle to pry power over daily life from the hands of dictators, bloodline sovereigns, and cabals. The presupposition here, whether in Locke's terms or Jefferson's, is that individuals exist and enjoy status prior to any state, and the state is therefore in the service of those individuals. A standard defence of literacy—the right to read, metaphorically speaking, since it is not usually enshrined as a right—would, on such a conception, emphasize that reading is itself democratic. Literacy, especially of the critical variety, is the software of citizenship, as essential to the liberal humanist state as the virtues of tolerance, respect, and discursive civility.[12]

An opposing view, sometimes called *anti-humanism*, works from different and, in some ways, more plausible presuppositions. What we call individuals are really 'dividuals,' constructions of subjectivity that emerge from lines of force in desire, media of communication, and the polis itself. There is a striking consonance between 'postmodern' versions of this view and the founding modernist himself, Thomas Hobbes. They are united in holding a position we should really call misanthropic humanism. The irony in the phrase—how can one be saddened by human foible while celebrating the value of the human— wedges open a gap in the self-congratulations typical of liberal humanism, its blithe confidence in the idea of the individual. 'Misanthropic humanist' is a *grenzbegriff*, or limit concept. It asks us to question the illusions of human existence even as it acknowledges that existence as the only source of meaning in the world. (For another version of this point, again see "What Are Intellectuals For?")

Hobbes is typically misconstrued as arguing in favour of personal selfishness and freedom from government interference, as if he were an American-style libertarian. In fact, Hobbes was a field theorist. His basic atomism demands that all things, including human beings, are conglomerations of matter in motion, animated by appetites and aversions. When these are sufficiently complex, we call them desires, and even virtues and vices. We construct an idea of self as a function of these desires and then try to meet as many of them as possible, consistent with the same being true of others; but this self is, always, a construct. Government, in the form of the sovereign, is necessary precisely because we cannot regulate these desires ourselves. Hobbes is not an advocate of dog-eat-dog markets, he's an advocate of big government.

The Leviathan and surrendered power are Hobbes's political conclusions from the inescapable awareness of the self as an emergent property of desires in conflict. Different responses to the same insight about constructed selfhood might well be infinite deferral of state authority, anarchism, or provisional engagements based on contingent value—the sorts of political commitments more typical of postmodern intellectuals. The worry that anti-humanism robs us of agency, meanwhile, is revealed as a garden path. We are no more incapable of acting on this view than on a deterministic account of the physical world. In fact, the recognition that action is predicated on the other, rather than the other way around, is what makes such a view superior to the sincerity, authenticity, and emotional resonance language typical of humanism.

I say the misanthropic-humanist presupposition may be more plausible because the view of self shared by anti-humanists old and new seems more and more accurate to the ways we and our technology are developing. Those changes are, after all, what brought us to the particular discursive space of this essay and this book. But anti-humanism should not be confused with transhumanism or posthumanism, those celebrations of human-machine hybridity that seek transcendence in technology. These aspirations to godlike status are by nature exclusive, whereas anti-humanism, though it does not fear technology, must be inclusive in its refusal of ego.[13] One is even tempted to call this simply 'genuine' or 'authentic' humanism, but the force of contrast with neo-liberal orthodoxies would thereby be lost, and anyway the language of genuineness and authenticity is itself part of what is rejected. What we seek here is a revelation of human limits as well as possibilities, with technology as a sort of Tiresias. The reading question is just a trace or indicator of this larger point, and though I seem to have come to it the long way around, it has in reality been the topic all along.

The standard defence of old-school reading is that it promotes inwardness and slowness, as opposed to the trivial extroversion and speed associated with contemporary culture, and thus helps cultivate the ironic and compassionate cast of mind we associate with liberal humanism. To this mind, the narcissism of today, together with its apparent empathy deficits, would be deplorable, a clear net loss. But what if this is a moment of evolutionary transition, from a humanist to an anti-humanist world? Now, the narcissism and excessive entitlement are revealed as symptoms of increasingly desperate 'meconnaissance', to use Lacan's formulation. These selves, in transition, are at once comprehensively networked and isolated in pursuit of self. Language is the medium, not of their self-discovery, as in the old model, but of their self-deferral. The underlying awareness, which can only grow, is that there is no self lying in wait, to be discovered and excavated by the many forms of reading. There is only the field, the manifold, in which different positions can be, for a moment, occupied. It's called a tree because that is what 'we' call 'it'.

The old view, rapidly fading, understood words and the discourse we created of them to be a sort of public space, an agora. It was as if we entered a civic square and, using the available accepted tools, made a contribution to something shared by all. Both reading and writing books were acts of citizenship, even if (especially if) they also brought pleasure. Though books can always be bought and sold, and though Mill would speak metaphorically of the marketplace of ideas, discourse itself can never be reduced to transactions in a market.

This view can no longer hold, but not because reading is over. Rather, the space of human interaction itself has changed, and with it the contours of those who are defined within its ambit. Human beings are always and already inside the field of discourse; this is not a matter of choice, even if reading this or that string of words remains something we choose. Discourse defines us, not the other way around. And so, maybe unexpectedly, the anti-humanist view accords more value to reading than the humanist one, which makes reading instrumental to other values. The anti-humanist understands, as the humanist never can, how necessary discourse remains to the very idea of selfhood—an idea that, though illusory, we need in order to exist. There is no self without reading, because without the discourse that reading underwrites—apt word!—there is no idea of self at all. There is no other way for desire to reshape itself, again and again, into the directed and retroactive forms we experience as subjectivity.

The insight is not new, even if the circumstances that lately force it upon us are. The resulting paradox of selfhood might well have been in the mind of the translator Samuel ibn Tibbon, twelfth-century scholar from Toledo, when he received a letter from his father that read, in part: "Make your books your companions, let your cases and shelves be your pleasure grounds and gardens. Bask in their paradise, gather their fruit, pluck their roses, take their spices and myrrh. If your soul be satiate and weary, change from garden to garden, from furrow to furrow, from prospect to prospect. Then will your desire renew itself and your soul be filled with delight."[14]

As a translator, ibn Tibbon would have known intimately how fluid and vast, how restless and indeterminate, the field of discourse remains—even as our own apparently infinite desires necessarily come to an end. It's called a tree because it has to be called something. And when you and I are gone, it will still be called a tree.

Notes:

1   It comes courtesy of *Bookavore* (July 2010). Some rules include: Every use of phrase 'real book' = one drink. Use of 'old-fashioned' also = one drink. Expert you've never heard of before predicting revenue percentages = one drink. Assertion that e-book prices are too high, and will lower soon = one drink. Assertion that e-book prices are too low, and will rise soon = one drink. Use of vague Amazon press release stats misleadingly = one drink.

2   Readers of a certain age may recognize that the poet here is comedian Steve Martin, who used to perform a sketch in which he advocated messing with children by teaching them the wrong words for things. The hapless child then raises his hand in class, needing the bathroom, and asks "May I mambo dogface to the bananapatch?"

3   Castigations of 'yunnies' (young urban narcissists) for their self-involvement are now common to the point of cliché. But an especially thoughtful assessment is offered by critic Alan Kirby in "The Death of Postmodernism and Beyond," *Philosophy Now* (2006; for those readers who have computers—ha!—see http://www.philosophynow.org/issue58/58kirby. htm). Kirby suggests that the current "age of autism" entails a shift from postmodern culture, which was suspicious of authority and especially of the idea of a single dominant reality, to "pseudo-modern" culture. Here 'reality' is just me and my personal experience of self. Pseudo-modern culture thus exhibits familiar pathologies: "[Technologized cluelessness is utterly contemporary: the pseudo-modernist communicates constantly with the other side of the planet, yet needs to be told to eat vegetables to be healthy, a fact self-evident in the Bronze Age. He or she can direct the course of national television programmes, but does not know how to make him- or herself something to eat—a characteristic fusion of the childish and the advanced, the powerful and the helpless."

4   Raymond Chandler, *Playback* (Pan Books, 1980; orig. 1958), p. 44.

5   A. N. Wilson, *Hearing Voices* (Sinclair-Stevenson, 1995), p. 120. This is the fourth in a sequence of five novels known as the Lampitt Chronicles, all narrated in the same first-person voice, that of actor and would-be biographer Julian Ramsay.

6   Wilson is one of these. He has written biographies of, among others, John Milton, Hilaire Belloc, and C. S. Lewis; his Lampitt novels, meanwhile, amount to an extended meditation on the impossibility of biography.

7   I owe this formulation of the issue to my friend, the novelist Russell Smith. When his novel *Girl Crazy* was published in 2010, even apparently intelligent critics tended to assess it according to recorded morals of the two main characters. Worse, they attributed attitudes contained in the narration—free indirect third-person, in which an ostensibly external narrator communicates ideas of the character being described—to the author. By a specious chain of reasoning, then, character's flaws = novel's flaws = author's flaws. Hey presto!

8   It's a nice coincidence, an amplitude of noise amidst the search for signal, that one of the main characters in *C*, the code-breaking sister of the main character, who suffers early sexual abuse and eventually commits suicide by poison, is called Sophie. For that matter, no doubt many readers will remember that the 1991 philosophical novel *Sophie's World*, by Norwegian writer Jostein Gaarder, almost unreadably tedious, was nevertheless a huge international bestseller—one of those books, like the *Harry Potter* or Stieg Larsson tomes, that everyone seemed to buy, if not read.

9 Tom McCarthy, "Technology and the novel, from Blake to Ballard," *The Guardian* (24 July 2010). McCarthy's general argument in this essay is that the greatest modernist novels are engagements with technological networks, not people. The implied but (mostly) unstated corollary is that popular fiction of our day is, instead, dominated by cheap and unexamined humanism. From an online post concerning his essay: "[A]fter all the Levinases and Célans and Kafkas and their tortured brilliance at thinking and writing their way around a traumatic century, to return to a regressive, kitsch version of nineteenth-century liberal-humanism is a form of revisionism. People like McEwan, who say we should just brush off 'the dead hand of modernism,' fill me with repulsion at every level."

10 Northrop Frye, *The Modern Century* (Oxford University Press, 1967), p. 38 and p. 45, respectively.

11 A clear example of this Manichean tendency can be seen in Stephen Marche, "The iPad and Twenty-First-Century Humanism," *Queen's Quarterly* 117:2 (Summer 2010), pp. 195-201. The author argues that text has become insubstantial (true if obvious) and then calls for a renewal of 'cosmopolitan humanism' in order "to weed out the nutjobs, to qualify, to humanize knowledge"(201)—hopeful but undemonstrated, and possibly false. The article does not investigate the nature of humanism; instead it concludes with familiar complaints that "the gerontocracy created in academia by tenure and the lack of mandatory retirement" means that "[humanities] departments can remain comfortably ensconced in their techno-phobia for decades"(201). This sort of rhetoric achieves nothing, maybe less than nothing.

12 I know, because I have offered versions of this defence myself, more than once.

13 There is perhaps no clearer expression of the (bad) transhuman ego, with its mixture of narcissism and transcendentalism, than this quotation from former advertising executive Alex Bogusky, who left a lucrative career to cultivate his own selfhood (from Danielle Sacks, "Alex Bogusky Tells All: He Left the World's Hottest Agency to Find His Soul," *Fast Company* (9 August 2010)): "I don't think we're good at being selfish. Most of humanity, we're total rookies at being selfish and being narcissists. Because if you're really good at narcissism, you get to the point where that rookie kind of selfish doesn't even exist. A really excellent narcissist would be a really powerful tool for saving the planet. If everyone was a perfect narcissist, there would be nothing to worry about because we'd automatically fix everything and our purchases would be so benign. It's not self-absorbed, it's just knowing what's good for self. Let's say that steaks, scotch, and lots of cigars are what you put in your body—that's a rookie-narcissistic move. That's where we're uneducated narcissists. But as we perfect our narcissism, it comes around where you're actually doing things that feel like sharing, that feel like connected behaviour." Wait, what?

14 Samuel ibn Tibbon (Yehuda Ben Tibbon), "On Books and Writing," Nahum N. Glatzer, trans., in Ilan Stavans, ed., *The Scroll and the Cross: 1,000 Years of Jewish-Hispanic Literature* (Routledge, 2003), p. 51.

14

The Trick of It:
Poetry and the Plane of Immanence

A DOZEN YEARS AGO, in a review of the Gilles Deleuze collection *Negotiations,* a survey of his occasional interviews and late essays, I wrote this paragraph:

"When the French philosopher Gilles Deleuze died last November, throwing himself from his apartment window, he joined a long line of Parisian thinkers for whom defenestration, or some other act of self-inflicted violence, is a *de rigeur* sign of intellectual seriousness, a final argumentative flourish. The writer Andrew Hussey, reporting on the trend in an essay called '*Au Revoir*, Cruel World', anticipated the demise of Deleuze by some months. The 1994 suicides of philosopher Sarah Kofman, writer Roger Stéphane and situationist theoretician Guy Debord, Hussey noted, proved that for the post-1968 generation of radical intellectuals '*not* to seek death by one's own hand would be disgraceful, implying some kind of academic fraud'. In France, Hussey added, the falling bodies and gunshots are simply considered 'inevitable casualties of the postmodern condition'."

What I did not mention then was that Deleuze, a heavy smoker, was suffering from lung cancer at the time of his 1995 suicide. One of his lungs had been removed. After a tracheotomy, he found it difficult first to talk, and then to breathe, complaining that he was "chained like a dog" to his oxygen machine. Simple tasks, tragically including writing by hand, had become intolerably painful.

But there is more than one kind of death, and more than one kind of meaning in death. Death by one's own hand need not signal despair, still less a concern about authenticity. Death is, to use a Deleuzian word, a *machine*: a structure of shared normativity, shaped by but also shaping our desires and fears; an apparatus of power. Creative opposition to machines means not escaping them—there is no escape from this one, certainly—but instead negotiating the "lines of flight" that open up when we find our deeper ontological possibilities. The arc of Deleuze's own final nomadic act is, in its wry fashion, a kind of philosophical joke. Serious play.

In a fax sent to *Le Monde* upon the news of the suicide, Jean-François Lyotard, a close friend, wrote that Deleuze was "too tough to experience disappointments and resentments … He laughed, he is laughing, he is here. It's your sadness, idiot, he'd say."

Idiot!

—

Writing, too, is a machine, as Deleuze well knew. It is perhaps the most dominant one of the last two millennia, the one in which, as he said, "[t]he all-embracing but narrow opposition of signifier and signified is permeated by the imperialism of the Signifier." You cannot avoid the power of signification in writing—if you are writing at all, the words will *be there*, trying to mean things, because that is what words do. That is what writing is, and even as I write this the power of the big-S Signifier is not so much reinforced—it is too entrenched to allow of reinforcing—as revealed, once more, in its power.

No one who takes pen in hand or hangs poised over a keyboard can escape this imperialism. Our very freedom—the infinite possibilities of twenty-six letters plus spaces, comma, full stops, and the rest—is our bondage, the prison of infinite meaning. We can, and do, sometimes playfully, sometimes wickedly, subvert the domination, turn it inside out and link the inversions together, like a chain made out of Möbius strips. We can run the narrative in reverse, hide the meaning in a play of voices, compress and layer the meanings like the overlaid impressions of a palimpsest. But we can never outrun the longest shadow of all, the one cast by our own wish to communicate.

Deleuze often spoke and wrote using geometrical tropes—the most famous of these of course being the main image and title of his monumental 1980 work, co-authored with the psychoanalyst Félix Guattari, *A Thousand Plateaus*. The creative nomadism advocated there, the project of ceaselessly fleeing the power-grip of machines, was itself also a philosophical play on words. It alludes to one of Deleuze's favourite philosophers, Benedict de Spinoza. Spinoza's elaborate metaphysical system, set out in geometric fashion as a series of axioms and proofs in his own magnum opus, the *Ethics* of 1677, depends upon the monad, or stable chunk of substance. Monads reflect and interconnect with each other, governed by a divine structure, and our sense of self as well as our responsibilities in action are ordered likewise—hence the ethical dimension of a work that seems to bear no kinship to any feature of the usual ethical discourse.

If a *monad* sits and connects, *takes up its place* in a transcendent grid of being, a *nomad* is forever on the move, enacting its being, its living, as a series of movements. Even 'series' and 'movement' are not quite right, however, since there is no sequence of discrete actions or moves that aggregate to make up a life. Nor is there even a unifying sense of self, or personal identity, that underwrites the experience of continuity over time. There is instead, Deleuze argued, the *plane of immanence*.

The phrase has a kooky ring, and always reminds me a bit of an exhibit from the Museum of Jurassic Technology—itself a form of serious play, where fictional human practices and weird quasi-science are displayed deadpan, destabilizing the authoritative mien of museums everywhere. One of the central displays gives an account of Geoffrey Sonnabend's theory of *obliscence*: the idea that memory is an illusion, since the natural outcome of any experience is forgetting, not remembering. As Sonnabend put it in the Introduction to his book *Obliscence: Theories of Forgetting and the Problem of Matter* (1946): "We, amnesiacs all, condemned to live in an eternally fleeting present, have created the most elaborate of human constructions, memory, to buffer ourselves against the intolerable knowledge of the irreversible passage of time and the irretrievability of its moments and events." In Sonnabend's resulting model, the Cone of Obliscence is forever being penetrated—bisected—by Planes of Experience, which hit the Cone at varying but precise angles. Once through the cone, an experience is gone forever and any "memory" of its occurrence is little more than an illusion.

That is all gently mocking palaver, of course, whereas Deleuze's plane of immanence is not.[1] But the two ideas share more than a geometrical expression. They also agree that memory is an untenable platform for selfhood. In his defence of immanence, Deleuze also sought to break its traditional binary relation with transcendence, a conceptual dyad that reduces these two expansive ideas to a mere threshold between outer and inner, or at best the limit-line. Not that such thresholds are without their own deep interest; but that is part of the problem, since philosophical attention remains focussed on the line as a condition of possibility (as in Kant), or perhaps on getting 'across' the line to the transcendent realm (as in Plato). Deleuze instead sought an immanence unrelated to transcendence, a pure inwardness. "It is only when immanence is no longer immanence to anything other than itself that we can speak of a plane of immanence," he wrote near the end of his life.

The plane image is well-chosen. In Euclidean geometry, a plane has extension in two dimensions only but extends infinitely in the notional space created by the two. It is infinitely expansive even while having literally no thickness at all. Where most theorists of immanence tend to employ images of enclosure or shrinkage, a kind of self-collected interiority, Deleuze reverses this move, all too susceptible to the larger machine of binary opposition, and conceives immanence as flowing ever outward, in all directions and without division, indeed as being, we might say, *always already infinitely outflowed*.

Deleuze would go on to defend his own version of an ethics entailed by a metaphysics. Immanence, he says, highlights a life that is sufficient unto itself, but not self-enclosed. "We will say of pure immanence that it is *a life*, and nothing else," he wrote. "A life is the immanence of immanence, absolute immanence: it is complete power, complete bliss." On this view, subject and object are not prior to immanence, but instead both derivative of its singularity, "the events and singularities that are merely actualized," as he put it.

"Academics' lives are seldom interesting," Deleuze told an interviewer, fighting off speculation about his eccentricities. But he could and perhaps should have gone further. People's lives are seldom interesting, because they are merely records of these actualized events and singularities we call ourselves and events in the world. What is interesting is what makes these specific things possible, the plane of "complete power, complete bliss" from which they spring.

It can be no surprise that this late work of a great thinker was derided as mystical or, worse, mad. But if it is mystical, it is mystical the way

Wittgenstein's *Tractatus* is; if it is mad, it is mad after the fashion of Lao Tzu or Bataille. Only plumbing the depths of thought can reveal thought's own basic predicament, namely, the impossibility of thought thinking systemically about itself. If writing is the big Signifier machine, then thought is the Skynet system running all the basic system software. How does a mainframe consider the conditions of its own possibility without using those same conditions in the attempt? Where does a mind stand in order to think about the fact that it needs to stand somewhere?

In terms of these hard questions, Kant's transcendental idealism is just as mired as Plato's transcendental realism in the self-enfolding contradictions that define the philosophical tradition, at least in the West. Deleuze, a dedicated historian of ideas as well as an original thinker, detects the tones of mystery and weirdness that run beneath the official story of that tradition, with its long decline into analytic precision for its own sake—a kind of bad philosophical joke, the sort where it's on us. Idiots!

Which brings me, finally, to poetry—though one might say that poetry was the subject all along.

Philosophers are notoriously hostile to the idea that they bear any resemblance to poets. So much so, in fact, that the comparison can be used as a weapon of deprecation. In one of the key texts of the analytic decline mentioned above, A. J. Ayer's *Language, Truth, and Logic* (1936), the sentences of metaphysicians are mocked as being merely poetic— uttering nonsense, to use Ayer's favourite word, literally meaningless locutions that masquerade as meaningful in the costume of declarative sentences. The kicker is that, unlike poets, metaphysicians don't know that they are spouting *nonsense*. They think they're saying meaningful things! It follows that, in Ayer's books, the only thing worse than a poet is a poet who doesn't know he is one, and somehow imagines that he is making sense.

This is slanderous to poets and metaphysicians alike, but not for just the obvious reasons. Like many philosophers, Ayer's book confuses the narrow notion of truth with the expansive notion of meaning. Even the dominant sign-making machine of writing cannot govern the realm of meaning entirely. Meaning sprawls and expands, folds and collapses. The mystic's silence is one kind of response to this. So is the special form of language we know as poetry.

An effective poem is a life as much as any human consciousness, a pure immanence whose presence is detected, if only partially, by its own merely actualized events and singularities. The mere words are not the poem, any more than my mere actions are my life. Consider Archibald MacLeish's beautiful "Ars Poetica," worth quoting in full:

> A poem should be palpable and mute
> As a globed fruit
>
> Dumb
> As old medallions to the thumb
>
> Silent as the sleeve-worn stone
> Of casement ledges where the moss has grown—
>
> A poem should be wordless
> As the flight of birds
>
> A poem should be motionless in time
> As the moon climbs
>
> Leaving, as the moon releases
> Twig by twig the night-entangled trees,
>
> Leaving, as the moon behind the winter leaves,
> Memory by memory the mind—
>
> A poem should be motionless in time
> As the moon climbs
>
> A poem should be equal to:
> Not true
>
> For all the history of grief
> An empty doorway and a maple leaf

For love
The leaning grasses and two lights above the sea—

A poem should not mean
But be

Notice immediately a couple of things about this poem. First, it flatly self-contradicts: as with all *ars poetica* statements, it is a normative manifesto, an argument. There are six instances of the word *should* peppering its lines! Thus its meaning is clear and definitive; it has a thesis. But that thesis—that a poem should not mean—is overturned by the performance, indeed the very being, of the poem making the claim.

And yet, at the same time, that thesis is also brilliantly realized, not denied, in the series of deft concrete images: of things and experiences that move us, or (we might better say) make us suddenly still. A poem should be like that, "palpable and mute." Mute? But if a poem does anything, it speaks. I mean, there it is, sitting on the page (or coming from the speaker's mouth). It's as *un-mute* as almost anything we can imagine. And so it goes, idea and expression at eternal war with themselves within the special paradoxical immanence of this poem about poems, this thought about thoughts.

Logically speaking, the contradiction can be resolved with a move to deepen the meaning of *meaning*. That is, poems are evaluated incorrectly if meaning is construed narrowly as *propositional content or truth conditions*. They have neither, and we make a mistake if we seek them in poetry, reducing the living power and bliss to distilled summaries or morals. We make an even worse mistake if, failing to find propositional content or truth value, we denigrate poetry in contrast to philosophy—Ayer's move. If, on the other hand, the notion of meaning is expanded, we can speak of the meaning of a poem, not just its being or its music. Of course that meaning will remain elusive, layered, fugitive: that is part of its appeal. Nomad, not monad.

As Deleuze would have said, there is always a *negotiation* in poetry, between the poem and the reader but, more profoundly, between the immanent essence of the poem and its expression. Fixity in language, however imperfect or partial, is the vehicle of the poem's existence. It means to be; but it must be to mean.

In a series of lectures delivered as part of his duties as Oxford Professor of Poetry—before that venerable post was sullied by the Ruth Padel-Derek Walcott scandal—Paul Muldoon considered the idea of the *end of the poem*. (The lectures were published in a book of that name in 2006.) Muldoon defended his use of "this somewhat booming, perhaps even slightly bumptious phrase" by noting its layers of meaning. The booming or bumptious quality of the phrase belongs, perhaps, to either or both of the two most obvious meanings: poetry coming to an end, the demise of a cultural practice not much noticed by anybody; and, conversely, poetry having a point, the purpose or *telos* of poetry as a form of engagement. And yet it is the simplest meaning of the phrase that reveals the most: What does it mean for a poem to end, to come to its conclusion?

In poetics, *enjambment* is the technical term for the effect achieved by line breaks within a sentence, the pressure built back on the previous line by dropping down. The word comes from the same root that gives us *jamb*, that limb or leg that holds up the gate or door, and traces back ultimately to the Latin *gamba*, for hoof or leg. We are familiar with the feet in poetry, the beat-structures of *iamb, dactyl, trochee, spondee* and *anapest*; now we see also the legs of poetry, if only in their breaking. (But don't be fooled by appearances: iamb does not come from the same Latin; instead it descends from the lampooning style of the Greek satirists who first favoured its short-long rhythm of stresses.)

The sentence and the line are two grids of meaning, two frames or machines. The skillful breaks of enjambment wrest unexpected meaning from their simultaneous ripping and collision. Here's an example from Damian Rogers, a poem called "Dream of the Last Shaker" from her 2009 collection, *Paper Radio*:

We stream into the meetinghouse
through two doors

like twin cords
in the same braid.

The Trick of It 235

I love the men,
all of them

lined up like
God's long finger.

The sun attends everything
equally: the wood, the bend

of her white muslin sleeve,
the outstretched arm of the apocalypse.

Take hold of my shoulder.
Shake me awake.

Here there are particularly nice breaks at 'cords', 'them', and 'bend'. The only line in any poem that is not subject to this reverse-pressure effect is the last one, which itself bears the whole weight of the lines above. The oneiric command to be shaken awake, with its echo of the Shakers' rapt vision-trances and ominous sense of impossibility—if the dreamer is the last Shaker who will be the shaker who shakes her into wakefulness—is the kind of last line that makes the end of poem bear all the meanings of end at once.

It is hard to say whether coming to an end or making a beginning offer the more difficult prospect. What is clear is that, at their best, philosophy and poetry are engaged in the same kind of beginnings and endings, working on the same plane, the plane of immanence.

As a way of ending, then, an anecdote about beginnings. Not long ago I gave a version of the same lecture to two different audiences. The lecture was based on my book *Opening Gambits* (2008), which plays with art and philosophy by suggesting that they are both forms of play. The first audience, mainly academic philosophers at Cornell University, reacted with almost universal hostility. The suggestion that they were engaged in a form of play made them, as one admitted, "indignant." The second audience, at the Art Gallery of Ontario, was considerably more creative. Among other things, one member of the audience pointed out to me that my image of art and philosophy working as *gambits*—moves in a game, ways to begin play or attack, tactics of getting started—was more interesting than I knew.

Gambit, it turns out, is not cognate with other playful words like gamble and gambol; instead it descends to us from Italian and so ultimately from Latin. And it means, as in wrestling, to open with a move that uses the *gamba*, or leg, to trip your opponent. Thus the cross effected by the leg creates an opening for further moves; it is the leg as lever, the trip-trick. Enjambment, you might say.

It's your meaning, idiot!

Mine too.

Notes:

1   The layered fictions of the Museum of Jurassic Technology are examined with subtlety and humour by Lawrence Wechsler in his book *Mr. Wilson's Cabinet of Wonder: Pronged Ants, Horned Humans, Mice on Toast, and Other Marvels of Jurassic Technology* (Vintage, 1996).

15

As It Were:

On the Metaphysics (or Ethics) of Fiction

I N THE WESTERN TRADITION of inquiry, the subfield of metaphysics, with its questions about the nature of substance and existence, is considered 'first philosophy'. Before we can say anything else, we must establish what is real. Everything follows from that. As a philosopher who has been bewitched by fiction since childhood, and whose own books show alarming (to some) elements of narrative, I want to ask: What are the metaphysics of fiction? What is real here, and what follows from it?

"Art is a lie that makes us realize the truth," Picasso said, to the general satisfaction of everyone. A wondrous paradox! The untruth of the invented form, otherwise known as the mystery of art, reveals the truth better than the bare factuality of the documented one. This puts everyone in their proper place. The creators are elevated above the reporters, and higher truths of emotion and wisdom now trump lower ones of mere accuracy. The sentiment even has classical sanction. In Book X of Plato's *Republic*, Socrates lays down as a general principle that myths, or invented stories that communicate general conclusions, have more to teach us than simple history, which can do no more than recount what happened in particular.

Before we accept this claim, though, we should remember that Plato was no friend to poets and that the myth Socrates is about to recount in Book X—the metempsychotic journey of Er, who has to be reincarnated multiple times before he can unshackle his immortal soul from his desire-ridden body—is part of a larger program of political control. This is a myth to tame a population, an afterlife fable that has inspired everything from Christian eschatology to the dark-future visions of *1984* and *Logan's Run*. The myth shall set you free!

Except it won't. Socrates and Picasso were both mistaken, and maybe dangerously so, because their lies are justified as noble from a special point of view with only elite access—the transcendental Forms, modernist aesthetics. In reality there is no paradox here, wondrous or otherwise. Art is not a lie; it is a fiction, and that is a very different thing. In fact, to call art a lie is itself a lie—when, at least, it is not simply a self-serving confusion. A lie, if it is anything, is a deliberate untruth presented as though it were a truth. Lies may not always be advanced with deliberate intention to deceive, but that intention is certainly captured by the most common use of the word 'lie'. Someone lies if and only if they speak or write what they know to be false *even as* they also know, or anyway believe, that the hearer or reader does not know that.

So what is fiction if it is not a lie? I think we must conclude that it is, like the language of work but in a importantly distinct manner, a species of *bullshit*.

Why? Well, as we saw in the "Wage Slavery" essay, no matter how comprehensive or extreme, all falsity or lying remains a function, albeit a negative one, of regard for the truth. That is, something cannot be false unless it is also possible for it to be true, and one cannot lie except as a departure from telling the truth. Bullshit, by contrast, is neither true nor false—in the philosophical jargon, it has no *truth-value*. To quote Frankfurt once more, the bullshitter "does not reject the authority of the truth, as the liar does, and oppose himself to it. He pays no attention to it at all. By virtue of this, bullshit is the greater enemy of the truth than lies are."

Fiction is likewise composed of a set of sentences that are neither true nor false; a novel has no truth-value, nor does it purport to. This latter fact, especially, makes it clear that fiction is an example of what one philosopher has described as "non-serious illocutionary utterance"—which is to say that it is composed of meaningful sentences which, however, are not meant in the normal sense of meaning.[1] Thus fiction is a matter of *pretending*, or if one prefers the peculiar language of my tribe, a matter of "non-deceptive pseudoperformance." This basic fact about fiction—that it is composed of sentences that only act *as if* they stated that which is the case—has led some people, including a few of my more literal-minded colleagues, to abandon it. For some people, life is too short to read sentences that have no truth-value, that do not even purport to be true.

Such a position may sound crazy, and it probably is a little. I'm happy to say that the closest I have ever come to this pathology was a moment in a university library during graduate school when I was asked by a friend what I was reading. I replied, with great embarrass-ment as at the admission of a guilty secret, or being caught masturbat-ing, that it was "just a novel." And even though I regard the essay as the highest literary form there is, a locus of intellectual and emotional power, and think Wittgenstein's *Philosophical Investigations* perhaps the most accomplished work of human imagination of the past hundred years, the novel's deep appeal is woven through my everyday life.

Of course, the boundary between fiction and non-fiction is much discussed and disputed, especially in the recent era of 'fictionalized memoir' and 'creative non-fiction', but actually the distinction is straightforward. Search as we might, we can find nothing in the words themselves, no formal qualities of the prose, that reliably distinguishes fiction from non-fiction. Both may employ any of narrative, discursive argument, dialogue, metaphor, and flights of imagination with impu-nity. Therefore, it must be the case that the distinction is a matter of intention and presentation. Fiction is as fiction does; placing the words 'a novel' underneath a title declares an intention, even if sometimes a sly one. That is, if an author wishes to blur the distinction by setting up ironies between said and meant, well, we can take that under advise-ment. But if the blurring is sneaky or disguised, we may end up feeling abused, even outraged.

So much is obvious. But what about the background charge that the bullshitter is an enemy of the truth? The Plato-Picasso line is that the artist was a servant of the truth, or at least of some kind of truth, not an enemy at all. How can we untangle this skein of judgmental confusion?

We begin with further analysis of the varieties of bullshit, or more precisely, of bullshitters. In a well-turned review of Harry Frankfurt's book *On Bullshit*, Jonathan Lear—a psychoanalyst as well as a philos-opher—made a telling point about the larger ambit of communica-tion: Frankfurt had apparently ignored the special case of the *bullshit artist*.[2] The bullshit artist, in contrast to the bullshitter *simpliciter*, is not just shooting a line for the hell of it. He or she (but usually he) is attempting to create a kind of complicity between himself and us. Lear writes: "The bullshit artist in effect says, 'This is bullshit, but you will accept it anyway. You may accept it as bullshit, but you will honour it anyway.' In this respect, the bullshit artist is a knight of decadence.

Frankfurt ignores this example; indeed, his analysis of bullshit rules it out as impossible. And in this way he fails to confront the most interesting—and influential—style of bullshit in our time."

This, Lear notes, is really a demonstration of power, and so it raises ethical and political problems that are not in play with ordinary bullshit. Lear's example of a paradigmatic bullshit artist is former U. S. president Bill Clinton, a judgment that retains validity even as that statesman enters a distinguished period of less rampant influence.

Despite their differences, both Frankfurt and Lear discuss these questions under a general rubric of suspicion. This is an occupational hazard for philosophers, since we like to imagine we have some sort of duty to the truth, or at least a responsibility for clearing up conceptual confusions. But suppose that a really accomplished bullshit artist is not an enemy but an edgy kind of friend. Not to the truth, but to something else that we find compelling enough to take up the book: the resonant, the moving, the revelatory. The fiction writer is the bullshit artist extraordinaire, the perfection of the bullshit artist.

No mere knight but a monarch of decadence, the writer of fiction establishes complicity between the author and the reader, and does so in one of the most intimate ways we know: the whispering inner voice of a human consciousness engaged in the act of silent reading. We accept this, may even accept it as bullshit (what else is the willing suspension of disbelief?); but the main difference is that we accept it with great and willing pleasure.

The question then becomes: what sort of pleasure is this, and how can we possibly justify it in light of our basic commitments, often ethical and political, to telling the truth?

—

It is a commonplace among philosophers that there is nothing meaningful to be said about the future actions of fictional characters, or even about possible actions not taken. Such talk forms a special class of what we like to call nonsense, meaningless utterance, or defective speech. Yes, there are different classes of nonsense. Don't worry: philosophers invoke this charge of nonsense against themselves more than anyone else. As mentioned earlier, A. J. Ayer notoriously said that most metaphysicians were poets *manqués*, spouting fine-sounding gibberish as if it were truth.[3] At least the plain old poet is not, allowing a few Keatsian exceptions, self-deceived on that score!

So: "The present king of France is bald" is defective because the definite description names an empty set, and no meaningful attributions can be made of it. There is sense to the sentence, but no reference. (The present king of France is not *not-bald* either.) This is different from saying "Colourless green ideas sleep furiously," another standard example of nonsense. Here, there is both direct contradiction (ideas that are green *and* colourless) and bizarre attribution (ideas that have colour in the first place; sleep that is furious). Both classes of nonsense are distinct from this claim: "Mr. Darcy wrote a great work of political economy soon after his marriage." That, too, is nonsense even though there are no logical contradictions in it and, moreover, 'Mr. Darcy' names a character who enjoys a sort of existence and hence can support genuine reference. Such characters may even have their own wikipedia entries, when lots of 'real' people do not, and enjoy a degree of immortality— their existence called into the consciousness of another—denied most mere mortals.

But things get very confusing when we can say, meaningfully, that Mr. Darcy married the former Elizabeth Bennett, or that there is no Mrs. Sherlock Holmes but there is a Mrs. John Watson, married to that affable veteran of the second Anglo-Afghan War. These latter claims are contained by the 'as if' contract between writer and reader, and so count as notional facts within the fictional frame. There may be real facts in the frame too: Regency habits of dress, historical events like naval battles, actual London streets and Bath establishments. Authors can make mistakes about these. They cannot make mistakes about characters they have invented, though they can of course strain credulity (too-rapid shifts in action, incoherent motivation) or introduce internal errors (hair that is brown in chapter one turns red in later ones). These gaffes may generate a breach of contract: I throw the book across the room.

All that granted, rare is the reader who confines his or her thoughts about a novel just to the 'facts' contained within it. We think and talk about fictional characters all the time as if they had real possibilities. We bemoan Dorothea's bad choices in *Middlemarch* or celebrate Pip's complicated good fortune in *Great Expectations*; we wonder what would have become of Huck Finn or Jay Gatsby if things had gone a bit differently; we allow our impatience to rise at Holden Caulfield and indulge our fear at the fearsome sociopathology of Anton Chigurh. Indeed, our emotional attachment to these characters constitutes one of the most important ways that fiction matters to us. A given character becomes part of our consciousness, not just for the duration of the reading experience, but often for a lifetime.

The subjunctive mood of many of these sentences about fiction's own conditional sentences ('would have happened') clearly answers an emotional mood in us that lacks a precise name but might as well be labelled the subjunctive imagination. We derive great pleasure not only from the implied comprehensive contingency of all fiction ("If all this were true ... though of course it isn't"), but also from the micro-contingencies opened up by relating to characters as if they were real people, with both past actions and future choices—which by definition they do not have.

Fine, and nobody is going to take that pleasure—call it the pleasure of costless gossip—away from us pretense-lovers without a fight. But consider two rival versions of what is going on here, both hinging on the argument that fiction, in particular the naturalistic novel, performs an ideological function. We can call the two versions, respectively, the ideology of bourgeois opiate and the ideology of culture-critique. Suspicion and belief. Take the second position first.

On this view, which has been associated with, for example, Roland Barthes and Martha Nussbaum and more recently with James Wood, the importance of the novel is that is enacts imaginative possibilities that are otherwise absent from social discourse. Thus, the fictionality of the novel and its characters are an advantage, not a drawback, precisely because the open-endedness of questions about them—what is married life going to be like for Emma and Mr. Knightley? would Emma Bovary have been happier if she had married a different man?—prompt investigations, maybe ethical, maybe political, that cannot be pursued by other means. The novel is a lever of normative insight about life and its demands *in virtue of* its being neither true nor false. The novel alone can challenge existing patterns of desire and standards of behaviour in a manner that cultivates emotional engagement and exercises ethical imagination.

On the other side lies the countervailing theory, perhaps most vividly argued by Theodor Adorno and Fredric Jameson, but finding its recent voice with David Shields, that the novel is a drug of conformity, an easily digestible wafer of communion with the current arrangement. On this view, fiction at best palliates its readers and at worst makes them actively complicit with a given social order. By breaking market forces and structural inequalities down into enticing morsels of narrative, even superficially critical fictions play the role of court jester to the dominant culture: they amuse and titillate, but do not challenge, power. The naturalistic novel is at one with the mass culture of production and consumption, dominated by sentiment and spectacle. David Foster Wallace defined popular culture as "the symbolic representation of what people already believe." Here, the naturalistic novel becomes just a tony adjunct to the larger institutions of the popular market and, worse, the generalized narcissism of web-based social media. They are all facilitators of the great modern fetish of selfhood, the wonderfulness of me.

Most readers of novels, especially so-called 'literary' ones, would be dismayed and annoyed to find themselves lumped together with the audiences flocking to the latest 3-D big-screen cartoon or the dopes who dote on their Pinterest selections, but it is consistent with the tenets of this view that such feelings of distinction are themselves ideological markers. The sense of edification one may indulge in reading 'quality' fiction rather than watching television or going to the movies is nothing more than a cultural-capital dividend, something we consume alongside the novel itself, like a cocaine bump taken with your cocktail.

It is perhaps a mark of respect for the sting in this insight that some people label it 'nihilistic', as Michiko Kakutani of the *New York Times* did when discussing Shields's 2009 book, *Reality Hunger*. It is not nihilistic, in my view, but it generates its own set of problems. What, after all, is the 'reality' we hunger for, in Shields's version, and how is it immune from ideological infection? We know that much of the outrage mentioned earlier, aroused when fiction masquerades as fact, is rooted in twisted Oprahnic desires for 'authentic' experiences and 'real' suffering. Dashed by the deception of James Frey, say, these ideological bits of cultural detritus emerge in anger, with braying calls for the blood of author and publisher alike. Adorno, the musicologist turned philosopher, placed his faith in innovative classical music, not realizing how smoothly Schoenberg and even John Cage could be assimilated to a highly capitalized and bourgeois version of the concert situation. Neither Adorno nor Shields seems attuned, in fact, to the late-capitalist hybrid known, after David Brooks's analysis as discussed earlier in "All Show" and "Ways of Not Seeing," as the bourgeois-bohemian: the bobo, who for better or worse dominates far too much cultural discourse and practice.

All true. But, on the other side, can anyone be sanguine about the idea of fiction as exerting some special ethical traction? This position seems to demand both too much and too little from the form. Let us put the matter, again, in the terms suggested by Archibald MacLeish's often-quoted line that "a poem should not mean / But be"—itself a paradoxical statement, perhaps an intentionally so, since this meaning-ful message of non-meaning is delivered via a poem.

The fiction-as-morality position calls for *too much* because it asks fiction to mean rather than be, reducing it to moralistic vehicle; at the same time, it calls for *too little* because, well, it asks fiction to mean rather than be, when being in the relevant sense is a higher task alto-gether than merely meaning. Worse, and without reeling headlong into Adorno territory, it seems doubtful that one can hold this view without raising some ethical questions of another sort, questions concerning the ethics of doing ethics with fiction. To see what I mean, consider this little story—that is, a narrative with a possible moral.

—

For some years I taught a small university course called "Ethics and the Creative Imagination." The idea was to use literature, in my case mostly twentieth-century novels and a few films, as the primary texts for what was in reality a seminar on ethics. So I set some obvious works, such as *A Clockwork Orange* and *The Fountainhead*, not so much for their literary merit (whatever that might mean, as Adorno would say!) but because they illustrated easily discernible, and debatable, moral issues. Other works, such as *Lucky Jim* and *A Complicated Kindness*, extended a loose theme of individuals struggling, sometimes comically, between sets of moral obligations. I always ended with Louis Begley's *The Man Who Was Late*, his best work and an underappreciated minor masterpiece. There was a good deal of parent-child conflict in the books, which the students could relate to; there was also a good deal of suicide, which I did not consciously plan, but there you go.

I enjoyed this seminar tremendously at first, even though it was an extra commitment and the students, high achievers all, were very demanding. It seemed exactly right to spend three hours a week discussing a book we had all read and wondering about Iris Murdoch's distinction between the nice and the good, or whether Philip Marlowe was a cynic or a knight of virtue. Did Lily Bart, that beautiful fool, take too much sleeping draught deliberately? Was Dr. Sloper, that narcissistic egotist, too harsh in cutting himself off from daughter Catherine? How exactly, apart from being dead, was Ben, the Holocaust survivor so successful at self-creation and living the American dream, 'late'?

As time went on, however, doubts began to nag at me. Was this a proper use of literature, to make it a vehicle of value? Was it not, perhaps, to instrumentalize fiction in just the way that Plato used his myths and lies? Well, maybe not *just* the way, since I had no transcendental program of social control on the table, but still, was it not in some important sense unethical to deploy fiction as ethics? A little of this, even in a seminar room, and pretty soon you're veering into that disreputable book-club territory where a book is no longer judged according to whether or not it is any good, but whether you 'like' or 'can relate to' the characters— indeed, where its being any good or not becomes *a function* of that 'liking' or 'relating to'. The conjunction in the titular phrase 'ethics and the creative imagination' started to mock me with its vagueness. What did that 'and' signify? More importantly, what justified it? Should it be, could it be, replaced by another word or phrase: 'of', or 'as', or even (maybe best) 'as if'? What would happen then?

Possibly I was losing my mind, but only in the sense that philosophers habitually do. In that madness, it seemed to me, the metaphysical questions of fiction reveal themselves as ethical questions all along. Let us go further and say, with Emmanuel Levinas, that ethics, not metaphysics, is first philosophy. Answering the call of the other is a philosophically prior task to answering the call of being. Or, more precisely, we can only ever answer the latter call in the form of the former. The Other is who calls us; the Other asks us for recognition and care. Thus philosophy, so often translated as the *love of wisdom*, receives its proper translation as the *wisdom of love*. Love means openness to the call of difference; and wisdom— not happiness, not consolation—is what the openness may eventually bring us. That wisdom might then include some version of Wittgenstein's claim in the *Tractatus* (§6.421) that "ethics and aesthetics are one and the same." What could this pregnant insight mean when it comes to fiction?

It is pretty obvious why we enjoy the inventions of narrative and imagery, the subjunctive contracts of *as if* and *as it were*. These contracts are undertaken in the gift economy that runs beneath, or maybe above, the transactional economy at large. Fictions are not possible worlds in the technical sense of the term used by modal realism, the philosophical position which holds that all possible worlds are real. Fictions exist in this actual world, after all, and we must account for their ontology here, not elsewhere. If there are other possible worlds, certainly some if not most of them also contain fictions. But the fictions of any world depict *aspects of possibility*, and no matter how naturalistic or otherwise—the differences negotiated by subcontracts against time travel, in favour of levitation, and so on—they allow us to lose ourselves in something that is not actual. I think that getting lost is in fact the chief druggy pleasure of fiction, the immediate contact-high of suspension from reality. We experience the frisson of tension between our rational beliefs (the fictional world is not real, the roller coaster is safe) and what psychologists have come to call our *aliefs*, those primitive cognitions typically provoked by threat or risk: Emma Bovary is going to die! I am going to fly off the summit of this speeding metal contraption![4]

On this view, we do not in fact suspend disbelief when we experience the pleasures of fictional narrative; instead, we simultaneously set belief off to one side, indulge alief, and cover over the whole process by performing it without hesitation or forethought. Add the larger cognate pleasures of big themes, eye for detail or image, narrative coherence, and perhaps the meta-pleasures of narrative twists or reversals, postmodern tricks of line-blurring, authors-as-characters and so on—it's a heady tonic of complicated imaginative excitement, all conducted with appropriate safety mechanisms.

Meanwhile, the organic structure of most narrative tames the contingencies of life into linear coherence. The end of a narrative retroactively confers meaning on what came before, making sense of events in a way that is painfully absent from lived experience. Counter-narratives—inversions, multiple perspectives, fractures in the timeline—only call attention to the dominance of linearity in the act of deviating from it. Sometimes unwilling prisoners of contingency in life, we are willing prisoners of meaning in narrative fictions. Roland Barthes's celebrated "five codes" of narrative are just different aspects of this happy self-imprisonment, where the text gives pleasure by offering resistance. In his 1970 study of Balzac's fiction, *S/Z*, Barthes distinguishes the codes this way: (1) the hermeneutic code, where the fiction's meaning is withheld, subject to interpretation; (2) the proairetic code, where what happens later is structured by what happens first; (3) the semantic code, where elements in the story signify certain ideas; (4) the symbolic code, where larger meanings are structured in the story as a whole; and (5) the cultural code, which enfolds and sometimes critiques elements of shared knowledge or taken-for-granted belief. Perhaps most important, from the reader's perspective, is the proairetic code. This code dictates—as Chekhov famously put it—that if a gun appears onstage in act one, it must be used by act three.[5]

That *must*, the implied aesthetic-ethical force of Chekhov's gun, can stand for the whole issue. Such a necessary combination of the contingent and the necessary—fiction's basic premise cluster, its presupposition payload—is absent when it comes to created personae, such as the avatars of *Second Life* or the game-characters we play in videogames such as *Halo* or *Grand Theft Auto*. Here we may identify with a character but we can never empathize with one; we can experience excitement, but not compassion. Whether or not these forms of leisure are art is not to my present purpose, but one thing is clear: there is no possibility of tragedy in such pastimes, because there is no structure of inevitability. Only narrative can deliver the peculiar emotional engagement Aristotle described as catharsis, the experience of fear and pity aroused when Oedipus drives events to his own doom. There is no doom in *Doom*.

The attractions of fiction are thus centrally aesthetic, in the root sense: arousing a set of *feelings*, by which I mean to include emotional, psychological, intellectual, and moral reactions. Contrary to the ideology of suspicion, the presumption of the contract is that none of these feelings are possible, or anyway *as* possible, outside the contractual space of as-if. The temporary loss, or bracketing, of reality is essential to the phenomenological task of revealing consciousness. In this sense, every great work of fiction is also an *ars poetica*, a fictional manifesto about the possibility of fiction. (Note for completists and anyone who skipped the previous essay: the MacLeish poem mentioned earlier is called just that.)

But, contrary to the ideology of belief, fiction is not the servant of some cognitive payload, or 'message'. A novel is like the Scandinavian legend about life, related in the Venerable Bede's history of the Anglo-Saxons and recalled by the central character in Turgenev's *Rudin*. Our mortal span is likened to the flight of a bird entering a feast hall at one end and exiting at the other. The flight represents the experience of living, our fleeting span of consciousness with voids before and after. No life has a simple moral—or, if it does, it likely falls into the category of the unlived life not worth examining. Likewise no great fiction has a simple moral, though it may have many serious things to communicate using its non-serious discourse. Taking seriously the ethics of doing ethics with fiction shows us that using fiction as ethical tutelage is dubious—not because literature has no ethical heft but rather because reading that heft as argument by other means instrumentalizes, and hence violates, fiction itself. If fiction were reducible to propositions, that would obviate fiction. Fiction speaks something, but it is not something as simple as the truth, ethical or otherwise.

At this point, we could have recourse to other notions of 'truth': psychological acuity, emotional subtlety, cultural deftness. But why not use those notions instead? After all, they're more precise and do not confuse the issue in the Platonic/Picassan manner. Nor are fancier theories of truth much more helpful. I might favour Heidegger's claim that the work of art opens a clearing of Being, the truth of *aletheia*; but saying so doesn't much help in understanding why *Underworld* is a great novel and *Cosmopolis* is not.

We do better to adopt a different approach. It has the benefit of resolving some of the apparent paradoxes of fiction, such as the fact that meaningful words are used in a meaningless manner, even as it takes seriously the provocation that beauty, in all forms, offers a promise of happiness, but never happiness itself. What if we were to distinguish the normative in general from the ethical in particular, noting that fiction can prompt direction-altering reactions or expansions of compassion without ever having to issue, or embody, any particular directive. Then I believe we would be able to endorse—subjunctively, but in keeping with our peculiar pretended contracts—something like the wisdom found in Rilke's meditation on the statuary remant known as the archaic torso of Apollo, namely, that the 'moral' of all great art is simply this: *You must change your life.*

Archaic Torso of Apollo

We do not know his unheard of head,
in which the seeing of his eyes ripened. But
his trunk still glows like a thousand candles,
in which his looking, only turned down slightly,

continues to shine. Otherwise the thrust of the
breast wouldn't blind you, and from the light twist
of the loins a smile wouldn't flow into
that center where the generative power thrived.

Otherwise this stone would stand half disfigured
under the transparent fall of the shoulders,
and wouldn't shimmer like the skin of a wild animal;

it wouldn't be breaking out, like a star, on
all its sides: for there is no place on this stone,
that does not see you. You must change your life.

Notes:

1 J. L. Austin, *How To Do Things With Words* (Harvard University Press, 1975).

2 Harry G. Frankfurt, *On Bullshit* (Princeton University Press, 2005); as I noted before, this little book was a revision and reissue of a much earlier paper by Frankfurt. Jonathan Lear's review of the book appeared in *The New Republic* (25 March 2005) under the laconic title "Whatever." It is available at http://www.tnr.com/article/whatever

3 See the Preface to A. J. Ayer, *Language, Truth, and Logic* (Dover, 1952; orig. 1936).

4 For the basic argument here, see Tamar Szabo Gendler, "Alief and Belief," *Journal of Philosophy* (2008) 634-63.

5 There are multiple versions, and sources, for this claim. In 1889, 24-year-old Ilia Gurliand noted these words down from Chekhov's conversation: "If in Act I you have a pistol hanging on the wall, then it must fire in the last act." Related in Donald Rayfield, *Anton Chekhov: A Life* (Henry Holt & Co., 1997).

16
Self-Slaughter, Poetry, and the Interfaith Blurb Universe

A lot of suicides in that group. Funny suicides, but still.
—*Simpson's* character Krusty the Klown, on his fellow comedians

THE NEWS CAME, very late in 2009, that the poet Rachel Wetzsteon had killed herself. On Christmas Eve. She had been depressed, her mother told the *New York Times* two days later. Perhaps over the recent breakup of a romance. Perhaps not.

Rachel Wetzsteon was a fine poet, a graceful master of form and irony. Dark themes, elegant deployment. Funny in a sombre way. Rooted in real places, the streets and parks of Manhattan which she loved. You can tell, reading her work, that she is a walker: not a *flâneur*, an aesthetic taster of experiences, but also not a jaywalker, the aggressive New York antithesis. Just a walker, brisk but meditative. She walks and walks, walks and thinks, walks and shapes words, rolls them around. Her poems dart insight at you using deft little jabs of imagery underneath the rolling rhythm of their structure. Good poems, celebrated and rewarded. Good reviews, and prizes, and invitations to teach, to anthologize.

It was not enough. How often is it not enough? Oh, often enough. Too often.

I didn't really know Rachel—she dated a friend of mine from graduate school back in the 1980s—but the news rocked me anyway. They say a strong predictor of suicide is knowing a suicide, and though I feel no particular existential danger—philosophy's Socratic definition as *learning how to die* tends, maybe paradoxically, to keep the act at bay—the number of these keeps growing for me. I dug out my copy of Rachel's first collection, *The Other Stars*, and ordered the two later collections I didn't have. These orders were then mysteriously cancelled two days later, I can only imagine because the booksellers were planning to hike prices in the wake of her death. An English used bookseller was less savage: he sold me Rachel's *Home and Away* priced as before. I'm glad to have it.

I was reading Nicholson Baker's novel *The Anthologist* at about this time.[1] The novel is about a fairly successful but minor poet, one of those poets that other poets know, who is trying to write the introduction to an anthology of great poetry he has collected. The task is proving insuperable, and the poet's life is therefore, after the manner of these things, falling apart. His girlfriend, a cheerful crafter of beaded ornaments and jewelry, leaves him. A lover of four-beat line and rhyme as against the, to him, un-English cult of iambic pentameter, free verse, and willy-nilly enjambment, he is stuck defending a position that means Dr. Seuss might just be a greater poet than Billy Collins, "[c]harming, chirping crack whore that he is."

"Anthology knowledge isn't real knowledge," he tells himself, and us. "You have to read the unchosen poems to understand the chosen ones. And you have to be willing to be sad ... Poetry is a controlled refinement of sobbing." The rhythms of poetry are the rhythms of air and mouth, the sucking in and puffing out. Children, he says, cry in regular metre: "Ih-hih-hih-hih, ih-hih-hih-hih." Maybe that can account for all the suicides, the poetic ones and the funny ones, and all the ones in between. Can it?

No. Because there is no accounting. And anyway, poetry should be the cure, not the disease. "All these poets, when they begin to feel that they are descending into one of their personal canyons of despair, use rhyme to help themselves tightrope over it. Rhyming is the avoidance of mental pain by addicting yourself to what will happen next." Well, maybe. But even if that is so, self-medication—addiction—doesn't feel like a reliable solution. And what about poems that don't rhyme? And what about when you can't get the poem, or the anything, to come at all?

Baker's book belongs in the same small category of great works about procrastination, in which Geoff Dyer's *Out of Sheer Rage* (unfinished book about D. H. Lawrence) stands alongside John Edgar Wideman's *Fanon* (unfinished study of Franz Fanon) and Thomas Bernhard's *The Loser* (unfinished essay about Glenn Gould).[2] In fact, Bernhard is the acknowledged master of the genre, since his steady fictional output— he does not procrastinate himself—also includes *Concrete* (unfinished monograph about Felix Mendelssohn) and *The Lime Works* (unfinished treatise on the sense of hearing). *The Anthologist* is also a very funny depiction of the routine indignities of small-time literary life, in the tradition of Anthony Powell's *O, How the Wheel Becomes It!*, the Richard Tull sections of Martin Amis's *The Information*, and good portions of Russell Smith's fiction, especially the stories in *Young Men*. You know what I mean: the sad little back-of-the-store readings, refreshed only by book-club cookies and apple juice; the paltry 'honoraria', a Latin word defined as the fee too insultingly small to be called a fee, for fear of arousing ill feeling; the pervasive emotional cocktail of envy mixed with shame at indulging the envy; and so on.

Baker's narrator is called Paul Chowder. At one point in his slow decline he writes, on the back of a paperback collection of Mary Oliver's poems, a list of the people he's jealous of: James Fenton, Sinéad O'Connor, Lorenz Hart, Jon Stewart, Billy Collins (not really a crack whore). Sinéad O'Connor, really? Others he sets beyond all jealousy: Mary Oliver, W. S. Merwin, Howard Moss, Elizabeth Bishop. Bishop—not a suicide, but the lover of one   is in some ways the book's guiding spirit, and her great, much anthologized poem "The Fish" is discussed at some length. I reproduced this poem in its entirety as the epigraph to my book *Catch and Release*, which is, as I have written elsewhere, a book about fishing in something of the way that, of course at a far-beyond-any-possible-jealousy level, *A la recherche du temps perdu* is a book about pastry.

Chowder's take on "The Fish" (heh) is this: "The fish doesn't want to be described. That's what gives the poem its pull. The fish resists description because it just wants to be back in the water, and not to be seen, but she's insisting on looking at it and coming up with one simile after another. All these wonderful similes take time, and meanwhile the fish is starting to suffocate." But the caught fish then transforms in the poet's hands, and the piled similes generate a payoff that neither angler nor fish could have expected. The held fish becomes poetry, the five pieces of broken-off fishing line in its noble mouth traces of the written lines that have attempted to describe this one real thing, this creature. And with that, there arrives an awareness of the combined triumph and tragedy of this everyday moment. Here are the penultimate lines of Bishop's poem:

I stared and stared
and victory filled up
the little rented boat,
from the pool of bilge
where oil had spread a rainbow
around the rusted engine
to the bailer rusted orange,
the sun-cracked thwarts,
the oarlocks on their strings,
the gunnels—until everything
was rainbow, rainbow, rainbow!

But there is—there has to be— one more thing to say, and to do. The last line of the poem is: "And I let the fish go."

Now he can breathe again. And so can we. Because we always have to let go, because every attempt is always only partial, the sometimes painful suspension of poetry released. "A line in the water is hope extended," Paul Quinnett said of angling. A line on the page is the same. But hope is not optimism. Hope is beyond all expectation, beyond all rational interest. It is, as Jacques Derrida argues, "the affirmation foreign to all dialectics," that which remains unresolved when all arguments have been run through.

—

Paul Chowder's insistence on rhyme and metre may not be to everyone's taste. The position feels conservative, somehow politically as well as aesthetically. It put me in mind immediately of the poetry contests run out of the back pages of *Private Eye* (or was it *The Spectator*?) that insisted all entries had to be real poems, that is, they had to rhyme and scan. He is also down on enjambment, as mentioned, though it seems to me that enjambment, as much as rhyme though in its altogether different fashion, is an addiction to what happens next, based on what happened before. Or so I have previously argued.

Notwithstanding that, in the novel enjambment is defined this way: "the syntax pokes at you and says hustle it, pumpkin, keep walking, don't rest. So naturally, because you're stepping out onto nothingness, you fall.

You tumble forward, gaaaah, and you end up all discombobulated at the beginning of the next line, with a banana peel on your head and some coffee grounds in your shirt pocket." Though, to be fair, he admits to loving "many poems that enjamb all over themselves."

Chowder writes his introduction, and he endures the sadness of the anthology. He might even get his girlfriend back, but I don't want to spoil it for you. He does not join the ranks of the departed, the victims of "self-slaughter," as Hamlet bluntly labels it. Good for him.

Walker Percy—not a suicide, though both his father and grandfather were—understood the urge to self-slaughter better than most. In *The Moviegoer* we come across a different brand of suicide avoider, though he bears some resemblance to Paul Chowder. Binx Bolling is a connoisseur of suicide, like his creator the son of one. Binx's salvation functions by way of a sort of workaday Louisiana version of Kierkegaardian paradox: suicide is ruled out precisely because it is an option. Only if it were impossible would it be pursued. "They all think I'm going to commit suicide," Binx reflects. "What a joke. The truth is the exact opposite: suicide is the only thing that keeps me alive. When all else fails, all I have to do is consider suicide and in two seconds I'm cheerful as a nitwit. But if I could not kill myself—ah then, I would. I can do without Nembutal or murder mysteries but not without suicide."

In another work, *Lost in the Cosmos: The Last Self-Help Book*[3], Percy elaborates the distinction between a *non-suicide* and an *ex-suicide*, the latter being that person who has considered and passed over the option of self-slaughter, while the former is everyone else. "The non-suicide is a little travelling suck of care, sucking care with him from the past and being sucked toward care in the future. His breath is high in his chest," Percy writes. "The ex-suicide opens his front door, sits down on the step, and laughs. Since he has the option of being dead, he has nothing to lose by being alive. It is good to be alive. He goes to work because he doesn't have to."[4]

Some critics have claimed that Percy's position carries echoes of Camus as well, and the stark assertion in *The Rebel* that suicide is the "one truly serious philosophical problem." Camus means that all the other questions of philosophy, and of life—what can we know? what should we do?—are mere games, premised on a judgment that life is worth living. In fact, though, the resonances are entirely different. Percy is not making a judgment about life's value; rather, it is an awareness of the absurdity of the condition of life that makes him move on from the prospect of ending life. Judgments that one's life is lacking in value or meaning are, in fact, precisely the sort of thing that may lead to thoughts of suicide. Camus was right about that aspect of the question. But there is an implication here that he does not mention, namely that most people (and even some suicides) are not in the business of making judgments about whether life is worth living. Judgment doesn't come into it. They just live. Or they don't. The emphasis on judgment, and on individual choice, is a fatal philosophical error.

The essence of suicide seems to lie in the power we have, the sense of choice. So choosing to end my life can feel like a right, something it is open to me to exercise; and therefore, like other rights, something immune from other people's moral judgments. But ending a life without sufficient reason is never justified, even if it is your own life. Why should any life be treated with less respect than another, especially on the basis of the idea that it is yours? That is why we will try to stop you. I will try to stop you. And we may fail, but that will not justify what you have done. Please remember above all that we are here, and we want you here with us. We value your life even in those moments when you don't, when you can't.

In *The Anthologist* Paul Chowder coins a sly phrase for the literary world, the ladder of creation and (sometimes) success on which he is perched along with so many other hopefuls. He calls this world the "interfaith blurb universe." It's funny because it's true: the circulating economy of endorsements, the back-cover quotations passed around like the gift tokens of a perfervid cargo cult worshipping the twinned but antagonistic gods of sales and critical repute.

Life is an interfaith blurb universe. Sometimes the blurbs are birthday cards or evenings together or the things lovers whisper to each other in the dark. Sometimes the blurb is the just the fact of being here, to see you, the reciprocity of perspectives. The fact of it, that we are all here together. That we are all here alone.

I have another sort-of friend, another poet from New York; Jennifer Michael Hecht is her name. She's written books about happiness and doubt, and she fashions lovely poems about these and other things. She was a close friend of Rachel Wetzsteon. Like me, she has known more than one suicide. Not long after Rachel's death, and thinking too of the 2007 suicide of another poet-friend from graduate school days, Sarah Hannah, Jennifer wrote what has been called "a secular injunction against suicide."[5] Though the arguments she makes are similar to the doctrines of some Christian sects, especially the Roman Catholic injunction against despair, the sin 'against the Holy Spirit', the text is not religious. But I wouldn't call it secular exactly, if that somehow means that its message particular to non-believers. It is just heartfelt and straightforward, a sane plea that, though life can be almost unbearable, it is after all bearable. These are the last lines: "Don't kill yourself. Suffer here with us instead. We need you with us, we have not forgotten you, you are our hero. Stay."

It is too late for me, or anyone, to tell Rachel Wetzsteon that she is my hero, a poet and a person whose loss makes the world just that much less bright, less interesting, less everything. But I can say it to you.

Stay, hero.

Be addicted to what happens next.

Stay.

Notes:

1   Nicholson Baker, *The Anthologist: A Novel* (Simon & Schuster, 2009); all subsequent quotations are from this edition.

2   Jessica Winter had a nice essay on "Procrastination Literature" in *Slate* in 2008 (http://www.slate.com/id/2191252/).

3   Alas, it was not.

4   In this sense, the *ex-suicide* is akin to, if not quite identical with, the *idler*.

5   Jennifer Michael Hecht, "Stay," *The Boston Globe* (7 February 2010); adapted from "On Suidice," *The Best American Poetry* (11 January 2010). The former version is available at http://www.boston.com/bostonglobe/ideas/articles/2010/02/07/stay/

17

The (In)dividual, Beyond the Uncanny Valley

The negative prefix un- *is the indicator of repression.*
—Sigmund Freud, "The Uncanny" (1919)

A CURIOSITY OFTEN REMARKED is that Freud's landmark essay on the uncanny, published in a war-shadowed 1919, is itself a piece of uncanny writing. With elements of literary criticism, autobiography, aesthetics, etymology, psychology, and fictional survey, it is *sui generis* in Freud's otherwise admirably lucid body of work.[1] This labyrinthine essay about labyrinths begins with an odd confession, namely that its author wrote it because he felt "impelled" to enter the dark cave of aesthetic theory, something a psychologist ought not do. Later, the same author—or is it?—notes how he has "yielded to a temptation" in crafting his strange account of literary strangeness. In between there are disjointed bits of analysis, looping intratextual returns, two choice episodes from Freud's personal life, and a lot of chasing after word origins and characters from E. T. A. Hoffmann. Hélène Cixous has said that the text reads "less like an essay than like a strange theoretical novel," but I would venture that it reads more like the morning-after account of a dream.

The personal episodes are suggestive, one of them shunted to a footnote as if in embarrassment. Freud notes how he once found himself in the red light district of an unfamiliar town. He knew this because the women he saw were heavily made up and standing in the shadows. Alarmed, he attempted to leave the area—only to find himself, again and again, returning to the self-same spot despite his efforts to flee. The other experience, perhaps more common, involved catching sight of a disagreeable elderly man attempting to enter his railway carriage—only to realize with a start that the 'man' was in fact his own reflection in the looking glass of the train's washing compartment. These examples are actually the most vivid in the essay, and not only because they are personal rather than literary. Freud's uncanny analysis of the uncanny reveals that psychoanalysis itself is the uncanny. In an important (and doubled) sense, Freud can't help himself.

The etymology is not idle, meanwhile. The German word translated as 'uncanny' is *unheimlich*, which tangles and complicates its relation to intimacy, familiarity, and strangeness. *Heimat* means home, and *geheim* means homely—but it also means secret, as in the *Geheime Staatspolizei*, or Gestapo, who were founded in the decades after Freud's fortunate flight from Austria. What is familiar can become, in a totality of intimacy, what is held close and apart from the public. Freud notes with approval Schelling's insight about the doubling of meanings in sameness and difference, so that a homely thing can be a secret thing, and then drops the repressive *un-* on unsuspecting home and gets the uncanny: the familiar made strange, or the strange encountered under the sign of the familiar.[2] The English *uncanny* is likewise not the contrary of *canny*, a word rooted in Old English and Old Norse verbs for *know* and meaning shrewd or sly. Instead the uncanny is, somehow, a doubled negation, the known and unknown at once.

Thus we find uncanny "something that was long familiar to the psyche and was estranged from it only through being repressed." Indeed, these psychic familiars prove to be of the usual sort, as if Freud found in the uncanny just the homely mechanisms his psychoanalytic mind expected to encounter: compulsions, especially towards repetition; animism, where objects are invested with meaning or even consciousness; spurious relations of causality; death wishes; and overall, what he calls "the omnipotence of thoughts," as when my barely accepted desire for someone to disappear then coincides with their actual death. At a higher level of particularity, the uncanny tosses up the Freudian version of the usual suspects: death, castration fear, scary female genitals, and *döppelgangers*.

"[T]he uncanny element we know from experience arises either when repressed childhood complexes are revived by some impression," he sums up, "or when primitive beliefs that have been *surmounted* appear to be once again confirmed." We repress the idea that things are alive, or that thoughts can cause death, or that an alien entity confronts me in the mirror. We entertain conscious knowledge that no actual force makes our steps turn back again and again to the same dreaded spot. But the feeling of uncanniness remains and returns, a trace or memory of these ideas which we formerly entertained. The uncanny always functions by a looping effect, and its array of dou-bleness tropes—reflections, golems, androids, clones, dolls, zombies, and cadavers—can be conceived as ambulatory agents of its structural doubling, its basic psychic entrelacement. Doubles are always signs of attempted return, efforts to stitch up identity through gesture or will. "Anything that can remind us of this inner compulsion to repeat is per-ceived as uncanny," Freud notes, not bothering to say that this is simply the human condition.

Döppelgangers are of particular interest here because they animate the psychic conflict coiled in the heart of the Freudian theory. He notes how Plato introduced the theme in his own psychology of the tripartite soul, but he does not (strangely!) provide an example. We can repair that rift. In *Republic* Book IV, Socrates reminds his young friends of Leontius, who, coming up the Piraeus one day, happened to catch sight of a pile of fresh corpses. He found the spectacle sickening and yet, as with today's rubbernecking motorists or celebrity-magazine subscrib-ers, could not tear his eyes away. In a burst of anger, he condemns those very eyes, looks again, and rants, "Very well, you evil things, have full measure of the gorgeous sight!"

The corpses here are not uncanny, but Leontius's self-inflicted dis-embodiment is. His real conflict—between desire and reason, between base urge and better feeling—generate a third kind of cognitive state, anger. (Plato will argue that this third state is actually a third compo-nent of his psyche.) But the anger is self-directed, a sign of pathology or disharmony in his soul. Metaphorically he tears out his own eyes, by disowning them, and thus refuses responsibility for his own desire, and indeed his own site of conflict, the soul itself. We want to say: in this moment, Leontius is not himself, he is not whole.

Wholeness endlessly eludes us, which is why the *döppelgangers*—the double-goers who remind us of our failed singularity—are so alarming.

But what of the uncanny in the aesthetic realm? That, after all, was Freud's (repressed) site of analytic desire, what got him started.

Hugh Haughton has suggested that, all protestations to the contrary, Freud is always and from the earliest moments engaged in a kind of aesthetic theory. "Included in Freud's hermeneutic dream of the dream," he notes, "is the wish that psychoanalysis should cast light upon the riddle of art." Freud is the hermeneut par excellence, a buccaneering *hermenaut* in fact, who sets sail on restless seas to find a key to all the riddles that our febrile imaginations are capable of setting upon ourselves. He is the magician at the maze's centre, the sage capable of rendering intelligible all that first appears unintelligible.

And yet, here we observe another structural doubling that will not be resolved or untangled, the one between life and art, with all its tangled threads and bleeding edges. *Mimesis* sets up the original twinning of thing and mirror, offering a deceptive re-presentation of our world of experience—this is why Plato deplored it. *Mimesis* reaches its uncanny perfection, and creepy cul-de-sac, in *trompe l'oeil*. Pliny the Elder relates the story of a painting competition in which the artist Zeuxis deceived half-starved birds into thinking his painted grapes were real, and Shaftesbury tells a story of a painting showing a slain rabbit so lifelike it drove the artist's hungry dog to tear it to pieces. The impecunious apprentices of Giotto's studio bent over to pick up dropped coins—only to find them painted on the floor. Even art that surrenders the ambition to fool us is suspended in this shadow-space between reality and its depiction.

Freud tries to account for this basic *döppelganger* effect of art by noting that the experiential and the aesthetic uncanny are distinct, because imagination is exempt from the reality principle. Full flights of imagination may serve the original (later repressed) wishes, but they do not induce that feeling of familiar strangeness, strange familiarity. Thus fairy tales themselves do not seem uncanny, but modern fictions that echo or invoke such tales will be. But, further, fiction in general is constrained by the medium of prose, which cannot replicate experience. "The apparently paradoxical upshot of this," Freud ventures, "is *that many things that would be uncanny if they occurred in real life are not uncanny in literature, and that in literature there are many opportunities to achieve uncanny effects that are absent in real life.*"

I have been considering this claim in connection with a medium Freud could not have experienced in 1919, cinema. I plan to offer a senior aesthetics class with the theme of the uncanny in film. Because of its immersive qualities, and the peculiar conjunction of sound-and-light projection to summon spaces and human physiognomy, film is an ideal medium for uncanny possibilities. It opens its own kind of shadow-space between the everydayness of waking life and the solitary brain-drive of reading literature. It is the most oneiric of aesthetic mediums.

But this quickly became a problem. I assembled a list of films with uncanny elements, beginning with (to me) obvious contenders: *Pan's Labyrinth* (2006), *Minority Report* (2002), *Eyes Wide Shut* (1999), *Blue Velvet* (1986), *Body Double* (1984), *Videodrome* (1983), *The Shining* (1980), *Alien* (1979), *The Tenant* (1976), *Don't Look Now* (1973), *High Plains Drifter* (1973), *La Jetée* (1962), *Mr. Sardonicus* (1961), *Last Year at Marienbad* (1961), *Vertigo* (1958), *Orpheus* (1950), *Spellbound* (1945), *Cat People* (1942), *The Testament of Dr. Mabuse* (1933), *Nosferatu* (1922), and *The Cabinet of Dr. Caligari* (1920). There was also the special case of the Groucho-Harpo mirror-double skit, a Freudian nightmare rendered as physical comedy, which alone makes *Duck Soup* (1933) qualify for any such list.

Worried that I was missing others that were equally obvious only not to me—that everyday uncanny category—I called on a group of friends expert in cultural navigation to provide more. Which they did in great numbers, including the Robert Dreyfuss-Bill Murray black comedy *What About Bob?* (1991), the Lee Marvin action-thriller *Point Blank* (1967), Humphrey Bogart's navy-and-courtroom drama *The Caine Mutiny* (1954), and Fred MacMurray as film noir villain in *Double Indemnity* (1944). It was hard, just by looking, to discern the uncanny elements of these films. Come to think of it, though, Fred MacMurray is the villain in *The Caine Mutiny* too. Maybe Fred MacMurray himself is uncanny? In any case, the category seemed to be expanding beyond all reasonable proportion such that, perhaps, any film *at all* could be viewed under the sign of the uncanny. That film itself is an uncanny medium.

Because it was wikileaks season, with those secret diplomatic cables exposed for all the world to see, a great debate about transparency and statehood was then raging. And I recalled this bit of insight from Hans

Magnus Enzensberger, in "Toward a Theory of Treason" (1964): "One can therefore draw two opposite conclusions: either that everything is a state secret or that state secrets no longer exist. In a certain sense both sentences mean the same thing; the first changes into the second, but with the following result: the betrayal of such secrets is prosecuted ever more ruthlessly the more eagerly statesmen proclaim them. The absurdity of this situation is apparent; but the very delusionary character of the taboo prevents its dissolution."[3]

That is precise psychoanalysis of the uncanny in politics. But consider also the analogue to cinema. Every film is an uncanny film; or there is no such thing as an uncanny film. In a certain sense, both sentences mean the same thing. Cinema's pervasive uncanniness means that no single film or films can be picked out as uncanny. This truth is not obviously political, but it carries a perpetual reminder of the *geheimshaft*—the familiar secrecy—that attends all human affairs, and which can turn *unheimlich* at any moment, under the sign—the negative prefix *un*——of repression.

—

A film that nobody suggested as part of my list is Russ Meyer's B-list sexploitation flick, *Beyond the Valley of the Dolls* (1970), which lives on for many people as the site of a Roger Ebert writing credit he wished to erase, or forget. But this "schlock melodrama," as Wikipedia accurately calls it, exerts another interest. "Originally intended as a sequel to the 1967 film *Valley of the Dolls*—'dolls' being a slang term for depressant pills or 'downers'—*Beyond the Valley of the Dolls* was instead revised as a parody of the commercially successful but critically reviled original." (You have to love Wikipedia's austere insertion of scare quotes around 'downers', as if this were some obscure and faintly disreputable term gleaned from 'the street'.)

Note the salient fact: *BVD* is deployed not as a sequel but as a *döppelganger* of its prequel, an irresistible gesture of return in the form of parody—this parodic movement itself being a turn on Marx's famous dictum that history repeats itself, first as tragedy and then as farce. Ebert would later claim, in comments written for *Film Comment* (1980), that the film is meant to be "a satire of Hollywood conventions, genres, situations, dialogue, characters and success formulas, heavily overlaid with such shocking violence that some critics didn't know whether the movie 'knew' it was a comedy." That is, a film might not know whether or not it is itself a comedy, and critics viewing the film might then not know whether or not this was so. Uncanny!

Ebert said more in the same vein, in what amounts to an effective definition of cinematic uncanniness under the signs of repetition, return, and repression: "I think of it as an essay on our generic expectations. It's an anthology of stock situations, characters, dialogue, clichés and stereotypes, set to music and manipulated to work as exposition and satire at the same time; it's cause and effect, a wind-up machine to generate emotions, pure movie without message."

Meyer was less psychoanalytical but no less revealing. His intention, according to an interview, was for the film to "simultaneously be a satire, a serious melodrama, a rock musical, a comedy, a violent exploitation picture, a skin flick and a moralistic exposé (so soon after the Sharon Tate murders) of what the opening crawl called 'the oft-times nightmarish world of Show Business'." In short, *BVD* is meant to be part of the great tradition of self-reflexive Hollywood films that expose the ethical and aesthetic bankruptcy of Hollywood, joining *Sunset Boulevard* (1950), *The Bad and the Beautiful* (1952), *Stunt Man* (1980), and *The Player* (1992).

Well, maybe. But the passing reference to Sharon Tate is more to the point. Tate, the wife of director Roman Polanski, had starred in the original *Valley of the Dolls*, earning a somewhat surprising Golden Globe nomination for her efforts. Two years later, in August of 1969, the pregnant Tate was brutally murdered, along with four others, by Charles Manson and his 'family'. The clear suggestion from Meyer is that the sudden violence that marks the end of *BVD*, not included in the original script, was inspired by the murders. The film started production less than four months after the murders. Creepy, for sure, if not quite uncanny.

There is another valley to traverse before we leave this dark territory—at least until our next return, when our unconscious steps bring us circling back like it or not. Like it *and* not.

Nerds everywhere know that the uncanny valley is the cognitive dip observable in our reactions to certain kinds of *döppelgangers* as plotted along a vector of human likeness. An obvious non-human robot, such as a mechanical arm, bears zero resemblance to us and therefore excites no reaction. As robots begin to appear more human, in the form of androids, our initial reaction is typically positive. They're cute! Following the example of an episode of *30 Rock*, where a character asks to be taught the uncanny valley "in *Star Wars*," we can note the genial appeal of C-3PO. But as the likeness grows, our positive reaction peaks and then begins to fall. An android too much like a human becomes creepy—as, indeed, a human too much like a robot might do. Zombies, corpses, and Michael Jackson are all *creepy* because their familiarity is both too close and too far. Then, of course, as likeness begins to approach simple identity—which we naively assume as possible—our reaction climbs positive again. A human is just a human.

The resulting dip is the uncanny valley, and it is impressive how consistently this curve of reactions can be observed in us humans. In fact, without this consistency, Freud's idea of the uncanny would have no purchase. But now consider what might happen on the other side of this valley—beyond the uncanny valley where dolls don't mean 'downers', they just mean dolls. Is there another valley waiting?

Some people think so. In a diagram that is itself a kind of mirror—an uncanny doubling—we see plotted a second, posthuman uncanny valley. Now we move from the familiarity of the standard human figure to growing creepiness of transhumanism. But, as with the left-hand side of the curve, a sense of acceptance asserts itself as we move into the so-called 'near posthuman', where recognizably human figures are smoothly incorporated into technologies and extensions of media. Then, at the far right side, the fully or radically posthuman figure excites no special reaction, any more than the industrial robot who is its mirror twin on the far left.

The guiding insight here is, of course, that our implication into posthuman conditions is already well under way, and the second valley is a sign of resistance and repression, not true alienation. We may react to technological incursions and assimilations *as if* they were alien, but by definition all technology that we encounter on this earth is human. When we speak of posthuman or transhuman, we are really just picking out aspects of the human and setting them in place in our consciousness. Thus, while the word *cyborg* conjures for most people something from the *Terminator* franchise, in fact, as Donna Haraway noted so many years ago, *we are all cyborgs now*.[4] You have a Bluetooth phone jacked into your ear, perhaps, or a machine that regulates heart rate in your chest cavity. You carry a device that extends your lines of communication and knowledge well beyond the paltry limits of embodiment. Even a cane or a pair of eyeglasses is an example of the smooth integration of non-carbon-based elements of the material world into our common experience of *extended mind*. So, for that matter, is a note left on the fridge, or a piece of performed music captured in the recording studio and then encoded in wax, vinyl, magnetic tape, laser-etched disc, or binary code.

The emergence of faster versions of posthuman and transhuman carry their own special implications, however. In part the uncanniness we feel before the near posthuman is a matter of speed's dislocation effect. Too fast, too furious! But our reactions, as so often, only serve to reveal fear; and fear serves to reveal desire.

As we have seen, the uncanny is always rooted in problems of identity. The doubles we see in mirrors, the fractures and displacements of the familiar into the unfamiliar, are traces of anxiety about selfhood. How is it possible to be a unified person? What sort of narrative structure would be sufficient to the task of binding and making coherent the time-bound fragments of experience, the past, future, and present selves of life, the riven and edge-tattered chunks of consciousness we call waking life?[5] Even as we try to impose coherence on these tales of self, the effort itself makes the creation come apart in our hands: we are revealed to be, as Gilles Deleuze put, *dividuals* rather than individuals, fragments rendered up for consumption and deployment.[6] And then, just to add danger to mere failure, haunted and haunting counter-narratives intervene, and we are forced into the dreamscapes and weirdlands that disrupt and distort all our efforts to make sense. The uncanny is an irruption of what we prefer to deny, namely that identity is no walk in the park—or rather, that the park in which we walk is, no matter how we pretend otherwise, also a graveyard.

It can be no surprise that our bodies offer special opportunities for this haunting. The facts of embodiment and its extension are so central to human experience as to constitute its main field of interest. Thus do mimicked or reanimated or living-dead bodies hold forth such uncanny vibes. The uncanny is a reminder that—despite injunctions from self-help gurus, consumer advocates, and democratic politicians everywhere—it is not possible to be *comfortable in your own skin*. In fact, the injunctions themselves have a creepy tinge! As if one could be commanded, or could will, a degree of comfort within the integument, the fragile cellular threshold between me and the world!

Film is a special site of the uncanny not just because of its immersiveness and dream-like qualities. The celluloid projection of the cellular, the mimetic capture of human physiognomy, is at its essence. (This is one reason the films of Michael Haneke, which work to shift focus from the face to other elements of the body, are so effortlessly uncanny.) The humans we encounter in films are always doubles of their 'real-life' counterparts, the human actors who portray them, but they are also monstrous and luminous technological clones of any and all human figures. The mediated human encountered in film—a medium that unfolds in time—is ever an uncanny-near-posthuman other, confronting us with ourselves extended beyond comfortable limits. The often-remarked experience of the cinema as womb-like, the dark comfort of the viewing experience alone in the company of unfamiliar others, is the clinching doubleness that reveals our intimacy and distance, the cozy alienation of the movie theatre.

To be sure, insofar as people can now experience cinema without the cinematic experience, extending their own transhuman dividualism by viewing movies on portable computers in broad daylight, this special experience is losing cultural and philosophical traction. It remains to be seen what sort of post- or transhuman future is in store for us under these emerging conditions. There are those, such as Giorgio Agamben, who believe we will recover simple embodiment—what he calls the 'whatever' body, the human body as *quodlibet*, without definition—out of the collapse of advertising, pornography and other routine estrangement-machines of the human body, "which escort the commodity to the grave like hired mourners."[7] Others, including those already claiming transhuman status, hope for smoother and more complete future fusions of carbon, steel and silicon, perfected and happy cyborg-selves who have passed beyond alienation and embraced the Skynet future or the New Flesh regime.

Both types are optimists, and there is certainly a place for them in our evolving discourses about the self. But watching movies should, above all, remind us of what happens to optimists. You know why *What About Bob?* is uncanny? Because Bob, the multiphobic patient who haunts his egotistical psychiatrist's vacation, will not go away. He's always there, needing attention and demanding acknowledgment. Worse, he insinuates himself to such an extent in the doctor's life that his own family comes to see Bob as a better version of the doctor: more sensitive, more attentive, more fun. He is the perfected doctor-double, in fact, whom not even violence can eliminate from the scene. "You think he's gone?" Dreyfuss shouts in his role as the psychiatrist driven to distraction and, eventually, to attempted murder. "He's not gone. That's the whole point! He's never gone!"

That's the whole point.

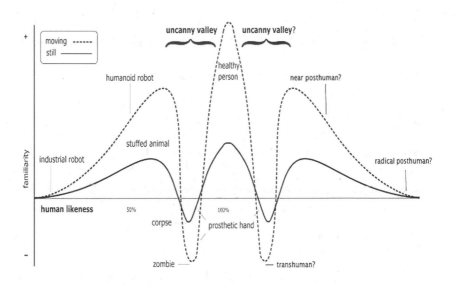

The Double Uncanny Valley

Notes:

1   Sigmund Freud, *The Uncanny* (David McClintock, trans., Penguin Books, 2003); all further quotations are from this translation and edition.

2   The Oxford English Dictionary, in its general entry on *un-*, notes laconically that "[t]his prefix has limitless applications in English." German too. The *OED* goes on to say that two general functions are served by *un-*: it may denote absence (e.g., *unconscious*) or it may indicate contrariness (e.g., *unlock*). (Yes, these Freudian examples are chosen deliberately.) Both *unheimlich* and *uncanny* defy this general prescription, though they are perhaps to be classed as special kinds of absence.

3   Included in Hans Magnus Enzensberger, *Politics and Crime* (Seabury Press, 1974).

4   Donna Haraway, "A Cyborg Manifesto: Science, Technology, and Socialist-Feminism in the Late Twentieth Century," *Socialist Review* 15: 2 (1985); also included in her collection *Simians, Cyborgs, and Women: The Reinvention of Nature* (Routledge, 1991), pp. 149-81.

5   The philosopher Daniel Dennett has identified selfhood as we experience it not with any essence or core but as a 'centre of narrative gravity'. Like the centre of gravity in a physical body, this has no fixed position and is, instead, the result of summing vectors, in this case of time and experience. But the suggestion, though tempting, is far too optimistic about the prospect of achieving and maintaining such selfhood. See Daniel C. Dennett, *Consciousness Explained* (Little, Brown & Co., 1991). See also "Language Speaks Us," in this collection.

6   See Gilles Deleuze, "Postscript on the Societies of Control," *October* 59 (Winter 1992), pp. 3-7; reprinted in *Negotiations* (Martin Joughlin, trans.; Columbia University Press, 1995). As noted earlier (in "Wage Slavery"), Deleuze distinguishes three modes of social structure: sovereign states (pre-modern); discipline societies (modern); and control societies (post-modern). Whereas a discipline society molds citizens into subjects through various carceral institutions—schools, armies, prisons, clinics—a control society can be radically decentred and apparently liberated.

7   See Agamben, *The Coming Community* (Michael Hardt, trans.; University of Minnesota Press, 1993), p. 49: "Thus the glorious body of advertising has become the mask behind which the fragile, slight human body continues its precarious existence, and the geometrical splendor of 'the girls' [in stocking ads] covers over the long lines of the naked, anonymous bodies led to their death in the *Lagers*, or the thousands of corpses mangled in the daily slaughter on the highways … To appropriate the historical transformations of human nature that capitalism wants to limit to the spectacle, to link together image and body in a space where they can no longer be separated, and thus to forge the whatever body, whose *physis* is resemblance—this is the good that humanity must learn how to wrest from commodities in their decline. Advertising and pornography, which escort the commodity to the grave like hired mourners, are the unknowing midwives of this new body of humanity." Awesome.

Acknowledgments

THE ESSAYS IN THIS COLLECTION were published in a variety of venues, a fact that is likely reflected in the range of tones and inflections in the writing, from the popular (chs. 1 and 2, say) to the more scholarly (chs. 6 and 9) and literary (chs. 14-17). I hope they cohere as the expression, in diverse locations and styles, of a series of preoccupations, obsessions, and arguments that have lately been the chorus of unruly voices in my head, the sound-texture to this particular human consciousness and imagination that I call my self.

I thank in particular Jennifer Szalai, Ben Metcalf and Gemma Sieff at *Harper's Magazine*, John Macfarlane, Jeremy Keehn and Jared Bland at *The Walrus*, Karen Mulhallen at *Descant*, and Boris Castel at *Queen's Quarterly* for their always welcome invitations to contribute. The highest compliment an editor can pay a writer is the call or email asking to publish a second, or third, piece of writing. Here are the details for all the essays, with thanks to the editors who believed in these ideas and their specific expression by the '(in)dividual' called by the name on this book's cover.

The opening section of the Introduction is drawn from "The Shout Doctrine," which first appeared in *The Walrus* (April 2010); "All Show: Justice and the City" was first published in *The Walrus* (January/February 2008) under the title "Justice Denied" and in David Macfarlane, ed., *Toronto: A City Becoming* (Key Porter, 2008); "The American Gigantic" also appeared first in *The Walrus* (January 2006). "Masters of Chancery" started as a commission from the *Literary Review of Canada* (April 2008) and was later adapted as the (more complete) keynote essay in Mark Kingwell and Patrick Turmel, eds., *Rites of Way: The Politics and Poetics of Public Space* (Wilfrid Laurier, 2009).

"Retouching the Void" was first published in *Harper's* (March 2012) and was later revised and translated into French for *Nouveau Projet* (Fall 2012); "The Tomist" also appeared first in *Harper's* (August

2011). "Throwing Dice" was an invited essay for the philosophy journal *PhaenEx* (Summer 2012); "Intellectuals and Democracy" was a commission from *Academic Matters* (May 2011) and was later revised for *Independent School Magazine* (Spring 2012); "What Are Intellectuals For?" was first published in *Queen's Quarterly* (Spring 2011).

"'Fuck You' and Other Salutations"—what might be considered the core essay of this collection—was an invited submission to Deborah S. Mower and Wade L. Robinson, eds., *Civility in Education and Politics* (Routledge, 2012); this essay reprises and expands on the core arguments from "The Shout Doctrine." "The Philosopher President Sets Forth" was first published in *The Walrus* (April 2009) as "All in the Game." An early version of "Wage Slavery, Bullshit, and the Good Infinite" was published in *Queen's Quarterly* (Summer 2010) and then adapted as the introduction to Joshua Glenn and Mark Kingwell, *The Wage Slave's Glossary* (Biblioasis, 2011); it was excerpted in *Harper's* under the title "The Language of Work" (July 2011) and later appeared in German translation in *Philosophie Magazin* as "Die Arbeitslüge" (February/March 2012).

"Ways of Not Seeing" was initially published in *Harper's* (November 2009); "Language Speaks Us" first appeared in *Descant* (Summer 2011); and "As It Were" was commissioned for Jared Bland, ed., *Finding the Words* (McClelland & Stewart, 2011). "The Trick of It" was first published in *Descant* (Fall 2009), as were "Self-Slaughter, Poetry, and the Interfaith Blurb Universe" (Spring 2010) and "The (In)dividual" (Spring 2011, with the title "Beyond the Uncanny Valley of the Dolls"). Some parts of the Introduction also first appeared in *Descant* (Winter 2012, as "The End of *The End of Democracy*").

The most recent of these essays were composed, and all of them were revised and collected, during my time as a faculty fellow at the Jackman Humanities Institute at the University of Toronto. I thank the Institute for the freedom thus provided, and the fellows for a year-long conversation on the theme of "location/dislocation." I hope further work will emerge from that stimulating exchange of ideas. Wendy Byrnes and Tracy Pryce, meanwhile, contributed invaluable editorial and research assistance.

My thanks, finally, to Dan Wells and Tara Murphy at Biblioasis. Their colophon says it all: we are tilting at windmills. But what else? The rest is fucking silence.